THE OHIO RIVER SERIES

Rita Kohn and William Lynwood Montell
Series Editors

Flatheads
& Spooneys

Fishing for a Living
in the Ohio River Valley

Jens Lund

THE UNIVERSITY PRESS OF KENTUCKY

Editorial and Sales Offices: The University Press of Kentucky
663 South Limestone Street, Lexington, Kentucky 40508-4008

Library of Congress Cataloging-in-Publication Data

Lund, Jens, 1946-
    Flatheads and spooneys : fishing for a living in the Ohio River
Valley / Jens Lund.
        p.   cm. — (Ohio River Valley series)
    Includes bibliographical references (p.   ) and index.
    ISBN 0-8131-1927-8 (acid-free recycled paper)
    1. Fishing—Ohio River Valley—Folklore. 2. Fishing communities—
Ohio River Valley—History. 3. Ohio River Valley—History.
4. Ohio River Valley—Social life and customs. I. Title.
II. Series.
GR107.F53   1995
398′.0977—dc20   95-23982

One would like to know more of that race of fishers . . . who openly professed the trade of fisherman, and even fed their townsmen creditably, not skulking through the meadows to a rainy afternoon sport. Dim visions we still get of miraculous draughts of fishes and heaps uncountable by the riverside.

—Henry David Thoreau

Contents

Series Foreword

The Ohio River Valley Series, conceived and published by the University Press of Kentucky, is an ongoing series of books that examine and illuminate the Ohio River and its tributaries, the lands drained by these streams, and the people who made this fertile and desirable area their place of residence, of refuge, of commerce and industry, of cultural development, and, ultimately, of engagement with American democracy. In doing this, it builds upon an earlier project, "Always a River: The Ohio River and the American Experience," which was sponsored by the National Endowment for the Humanities and the humanities councils of the states of Illinois, Indiana, Kentucky, Ohio, Pennsylvania, and West Virginia, with a mix of private and public organizations.

The Always a River project directed widespread public attention to the place of the Ohio River in the context of the larger American story. The Ohio River Valley Series expands on this significant role of the river in the growth of the American nation in volumes that present the varied history and folklife of the region. Each title's story is told through men and women acting within their particular place and time. Each reveals the rich resources for the history of the Ohio River and of the nation afforded by records, papers, and oral stories preserved by families and institutions. Each traces the impact the river and the land have had on individuals and cultures and, conversely, the changes these individuals and cultures have wrought on the valley in the passage of years.

As a force of nature and as a waterway into the American heartland, the Ohio (and its tributaries) has touched us individually and collectively. This series celebrates the story of that river and its valley through multiple voices and visions.

Flatheads and Spooneys represents the first major study of the commercial fishery of the lower Ohio River Valley and of the men and women and the indigenous culture that is defined by their life and work as fisherfolk. It is thus of interest both as an account of a colorful, little-known way of life and as a fund of historical and cultural information.

Beginning in the early 1800s, numerous occupants of the Ohio River Valley made a living by fishing, shell-gathering, and trapping in and along the waters of the main stem and its tributary streams. Those persons presently involved in fishing activities are the inheritors and practitioners of a complex body of traditional skills and verbal folklore associated with river life. Among the skills described in this volume are the making and use of hoopnets, jumperlines, fish traps, and mussel brails. Also described are the types of boats used in fishing and musselling and the different kinds of fish and mussels that are taken. The men and women who fish commercially are conscious of an occupational and social identity that represents a meaningful alliance with nature and the river. Additionally, many of them have close ties with a nomadic houseboat subculture that flourished on the Ohio from the early nineteenth century to the 1950s.

Flatheads and Spooneys by Jens Lund focuses largely on the Lower Ohio River Valley since at the present time commercial fishing is confined to that area, but it is undoubtedly an accurate portrayal of the occupational activities of fisherfolk that formerly could be found in the entire Ohio River Valley country. Lund's recording of the verbal lore of the river people, his articulation of their sense of identity, and his historical and descriptive information provides a vivid picture of an interesting way of life created and perpetuated by the fisherfolk of the river.

Rita Kohn
William Lynwood Montell
Series Editors

Preface

My forebears and I are from the fishing village of Aså, Denmark. One of the fondest memories of my childhood is of a herring fishing trip on the Kattegat on a neighbor's purse-seiner. Although my family members were farmers and skilled tradesmen, we were taught to admire our fishermen neighbors for their independence and resourcefulness.

There is something paradoxical about the idea of inland commercial fishing. This may be one reason I was attracted to this subject as a research topic. My first personal encounter with Ohio Valley fisherfolk was an interview with the Durham family of Old Shawneetown. After that interview, I was hooked, and I began to seek out other river folk. I made the acquaintance of Orval Loven, a Wabash River fisherman in Grayville, Illinois. Orval took me under his wing and allowed me to accompany him on a number of fishing trips. Here I really began to learn about the ways of river fish, and of river fishermen and their gear. My research eventually led to a dissertation titled "Fishing As a Folk Occupation in the Lower Ohio Valley" (Indiana University, 1983). Much of the research data in this book comes from that dissertation, with substantial follow-up during the 1980s and early 1990s.

In the mid-1980s, I had the privilege of working with Dillon Bustin producing the documentary film "The Pearl Fisher," about the Wabash Valley pearl and mother-of-pearl industry, focusing on the lives and work of musseller Barney Bass Sr. of Vincennes, Indiana, and of other people in southwest Indiana involved in that trade. Much of the material on musselling in this book comes from that project. The film, which was a project of the Hoosier Folklore Society and the Indiana Committee for the Humanities, can be rented or purchased from Documentary Educational Resources, 101 Morse St., Watertown, MA 02172.

This book is dedicated to the river people of the lower Ohio Valley and elsewhere—fishermen, marketers, cooks, boatbuilders, netmakers, mussellers, pearl and shell dealers, and their family members—who patiently took the time to answer my questions and share their knowledge. Thanks go to all of them, including any I may have overlooked in compiling this list: Joe Amore of Nylon Net Company, Memphis, Tennessee; Loren Angleton of Cave-in-Rock, Illinois; Barney Bass Sr. of Vincennes, Indiana; Marge Bass of Vincennes, Indiana; Steven Brown of Nylon Net Company, Memphis, Tennessee; Anne Marie Burch of Jewel Craft, Vincennes, Indiana; the late Emil Bushey of Smithland, Kentucky; Ira Gene Bushey of Smithland, Kentucky; Ralph Carver of Woodland, Kentucky; the late Willie J. Carver of Old Leavenworth, Indiana; Louis Castile of Memphis Net and Twine Company, Memphis, Tennessee; the late Roland Causey of Solitude, Indiana; Sarah M. Clark of Van Buren, Missouri; Nelson Cohen of M.D. Cohen Company, Terre Haute, Indiana; Jack Coker of Saline Landing, Illinois; Harold Courtney of Markland, Indiana; the late Bill Cox of Golconda, Illinois; Bob Cox of Golconda, Illinois; Turk Curtis of Cairo, Illinois; Jack Dickey of the Village Board, Village of Ridgway, Illinois; Jim Dixon of Cave-in-Rock, Illinois; Charlotte "Pinky" Durham of Old Shawneetown, Illinois; the late Clifford Durham of Old Shawneetown, Illinois; Howard Durham of Old Shawneetown, Illinois; Jack Emory of Carmi, Illinois; the late Carl Eswine of Shawneetown, Illinois; John Farmer of Grayville, Illinois; Louisa Green of Olmsted, Illinois; Don Harrington of Russellville, Illinois; Viola Harrington of Russellville, Illinois; Tommy Horton of Unionville, Kentucky; the late Harlan Hubbard of Payne Hollow, Kentucky; Roy Jackson of Paducah, Kentucky; the late Bob Kelly Sr. of Lawrenceville, Illinois; Fred Killius of Olmsted, Illinois; Curtis Lang of Metropolis, Illinois; Vergil Leibenguth of Caseyville, Kentucky; Orval Loven of Grayville, Illinois; Dennis Lueke of Maunie, Illinois; Fred Lueke of Maunie, Illinois; Melvin Mann of Tatumsville, Kentucky; Ed McClain of Alton, Indiana; William McCorkle of Memphis Net and Twine Company, Memphis, Tennessee; the late Paul McDaniels of Apco Company, Metropolis, Illinois; Floyd Miller of Princeton, Indiana; Owen Miller of Rosiclaire, Illinois; Laurel Millis of Golconda, Illinois; Donald "Dutch" Moore of Cave-in-Rock, Illinois; Stanley Murphy of Metropolis, Illinois; Bill Nichols of Horseshoe Lake, Madison County, Illinois; Joe "Bunk" Owens of Metropolis, Illinois; the late Granville "Granny" Palmer of Vincennes, Indiana; Jim Parish of Hazleton, Indiana; Charlie Patton of Cave-in-Rock, Illinois; Harold "Pat" Patton of Cave-in-Rock, Illinois; Rudy Phillips of Shawneetown, Illinois; Walter Ramsey of Rosiclaire, Illinois; Jim Reeves of Cairo Point, Illinois; Bonnie Sharp of Smithland, Kentucky; Earl Sharp of Smithland,

Kentucky; Herbert Sharp of Smithland, Kentucky; the late Leo Simon of Simon's Jewelers, Vincennes, Indiana; Marge Simon of Simon's Jewelers, Vincennes, Indiana; Ralph Simon of Simon's Jewelers, Vincennes, Indiana; Tommy Sherer of Tolu, Kentucky; the late Jim "Stoney" Stone of Crayne, Kentucky; Eugene B. "Happy" Thomas of Paducah, Kentucky; the late Bill Tinsley of Tolu, Kentucky; Jane Tislow of Vincennes, Indiana; the late Tom Tislow of Vincennes, Indiana; Matthew Vaughn of Cairo Point, Illinois; Roy Lee Walls of Urbandale, Illinois; the late Harold Weaver of Antioch Harbor, Tennessee; the late Theodore Weatherford of Point Township, Indiana; Billie White of Princeton, Indiana; Bill Williams of Ragland, Kentucky; George Williams of Cave-in-Rock, Illinois; and Mary Williams of Cave-in-Rock, Illinois.

Many others also contributed to this project. Part of the research was made possible by an Ozark Studies Grant from the Regional Studies Center of Arkansas College, Batesville, Arkansas. Other financial support came from Barbara R. Lund, my parents, Irving and Lisbeth Lund, and Peter and Ellie Revill. Logistic support came from Barbara R. Lund, Jerry and Mary Nurenberg, Peter Ortoleva, the late David Roberson, Cave-in-Rock Fish Market, Cave-in-Rock State Park, the Folklife Center of the Ohio Valley, the Indiana University Oral History Research Center, the Office of the Dean of the School of Fine Arts of Eastern Illinois University, and Southern Illinois University Community Development Department.

Access to rare old photos of river life came from Sarah M. Clark, Bill Cox, Bob Cox, Bob Kelly Sr., Curtis Lang, Chris McHenry of Aurora, Indiana, Bill Nichols, and Harold "Pat" Patton. Richard Day of the Vincennes University Library guided me through the historical archives of the Wabash River pearl industry. Harry Winters of Cave-in-Rock lent me home-recorded cassettes of stories, jokes, poems, and songs that Harold Weaver had mailed to him after leaving the Ohio River. Don Hubbs of the Tennessee Fish and Wildlife Service in Camden, Tennessee helped me with biological classifications of mollusks. Tom Rankin acquainted me with the work of Maggie Lee Sayre.

M. Dillon Bustin, Dr. Janet Crofton Gilmore, Dr. Robert G. Gunderson, Dr. W. Lynwood Montell, Dr. Warren E. Roberts, and Dr. William H. Wiggins, Jr. made editorial contributions. Philip Roberts did the musical transcriptions. The staff of The Evergreen State College, Photo Production Services, did the photographic printing. Graphic artist Gerry Rasmussen did the drawings and the maps.

Jack Rice created the music graphics. My daughter, Sara L. Lund, supplied companionship and encouragement while accompanying me on many of the field trips.

Thanks especially to my wife, Sharon K.P. Rasmussen, for persistent editing and encouragement, and to her and the other members of my family for their patience during the completion of this book.

All photos were taken by me, except where otherwise indicated. I thank the Indiana Humanities Council for assistance with photographic expenses.

Introduction

▶◗ Roy Lee Walls's twenty-foot fiberglass boat leaves the
Corps of Engineers dock at Mound City, Illinois, at about 6:30
A.M. The former Coast Guard rescue boat carries nets, cheese net
bait, anchors, and a homemade grappling hook. Walls heads
across the river from Illinois to Kentucky. The Ohio River is
more than a mile wide here, less than ten miles from its confluence with the Mississippi. Near Henderson's Landing, in
sight of the Conrail bridge, Walls looks for broken willow
stems. One of them lines up with a protruding treetop farther
inland, and he begins to cast his hook. After three tries, he snags
an underwater anchor line, brings it up, and starts to haul it in.
A hoop breaks the surface. He grabs it by hand and eventually
hauls an entire hoop net aboard, full of debris. A thunderstorm
the night before has swelled the river. In the net are six small
catfish of the best market size. Not a large haul, but surprising,
in light of the storm.

He reaches into the net and retrieves the bait bag. Most of the
cheese is gone. He replenishes it and places it in the far end of
one of the nets he has brought from shore. He then hauls in the
anchor of the net he has just emptied, stows the dirty net in the
bow, and throws the anchor of the new net in the water. He
grabs an oar and maneuvers the boat upstream a few yards,
then carefully feeds out the hoop net, one section at a time, so
that the river's current opens it like an accordion. Walls's eyes
scan the riverbank. The treetop is now to the right of the broken
limb, and there is a rock at the river's edge.

Roy Lee Walls is glad that the rain has come, even though it
brings fewer fish. The current seems to have washed away the
sand fleas (aquatic isopods) that often abound in this part of the
river. Their bites irritate, and once they build up on a net, fish
will not enter.

This morning, Walls runs fourteen nets, replacing ten of them
that are filled with debris and need cleaning. He lands a total of
about forty marketable catfish, ten carp, and eleven so-called

Roy Lee Walls lifting
a hoop net in the
Ohio River, near
Cairo, Illinois, 1978.

white perch (actually freshwater drum). He throws back six
white perch, which he feels were not of marketable size. Also in
one of the nets is a white crappie, a game fish that he returns to
the river, as it would be illegal to keep it. It is a relatively good
haul, considering the storm the night before. The freshing of the
river by the storm can produce an excellent haul the next day,
when the nets are no longer debris-clogged. Walls comments
on the most opportune time to set a hoop net: "One of the best
times to set a net is after a storm. Seems like it stirs up their
appetite, or maybe just they can better smell the bait in the
cleaner water. But they don't want to go into the nets when
they're full of junk."

Roy Lee Walls never marks a net with a float, because
there are too many thieves. Instead, he "fishes blind," lining
up onshore landmarks (called "marking the bank") to find
the approximate place where he set the net the day before. He
explains: "Some say these willows all looks alike, but I don't
think so. There's a difference in them. I'm more used to them
than anyone else. Yeah, I got different kinds of willows, you

know about where. I know where they're supposed to be. See that little willow in it, that's got a bark on it, and a dead top? Boy, there's lot of dead tops up and down here, but not like that one."

Walls believes that one must learn fishing blind in one's youth. He has recently been trying to teach a new fisherman the technique, without much success. This he attributes to the fact that the man is already in his thirties.

After a storm or a water release from a dam, the net may move a considerable distance downstream, so he does lose an occasional net. On this day, he accidentally snags one that he has lost a few months before. It is full of mud and debris and contains no fish, but it is otherwise in good condition. He recognizes it as his own from the colors of twine in the anchor line.

By 10 A.M., Walls is back at the dock in Mound City. He moors the boat at the dock and loads the fish, the motor, and the two gas tanks into his pickup and heads for his market on State Highway 37 in Urbandale, Illinois, just north of Cairo. ◂●◂

This account of a hoop net fishing trip, or run, exemplifies commercial fishing as pursued on large open waters in the lower Ohio Valley. There are other fisherman who use other fishing methods, using various hooks and lines, wooden fish traps, or such specialized equipment as the mussel brail or the crowfoot dredge. All of these fishermen of the lower Ohio Valley are part of a historical continuum of small-scale commercial and subsistence fishing tracing back to the earliest days of non-Indian settlement of the American Midwest and upper South.

The Ohio River is 981 miles long from its source at the junction of the Allegheny and Monongahela in Pittsburgh, Pennsylvania, to its junction with the Mississippi at Cairo, Illinois. Its major lower tributaries are the Cumberland, 720 miles; the Tennessee, 652 miles; and the Wabash, 512 miles. The Ohio River basin covers almost 204,000 square miles and is home to more than thirty million people and such major cities as Pittsburgh, Columbus, Cincinnati, Indianapolis, Louisville, Lexington, Evansville, Knoxville, and Nashville. Thirty miles above its mouth, at its confluence with the Cumberland and Tennessee, the Ohio becomes more than a mile wide. The Ohio Valley and its major tributary basins are part of the greater

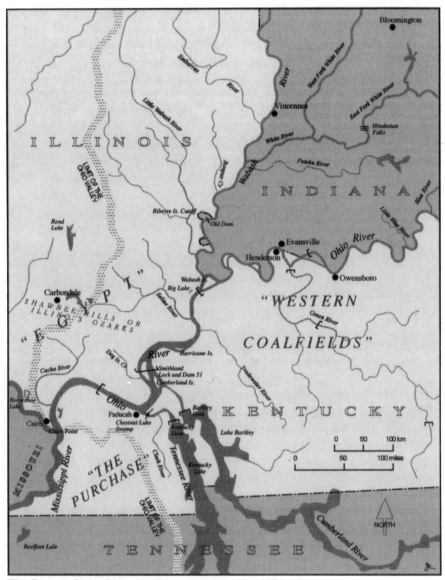

The Lower Ohio River Valley – Geographical Features

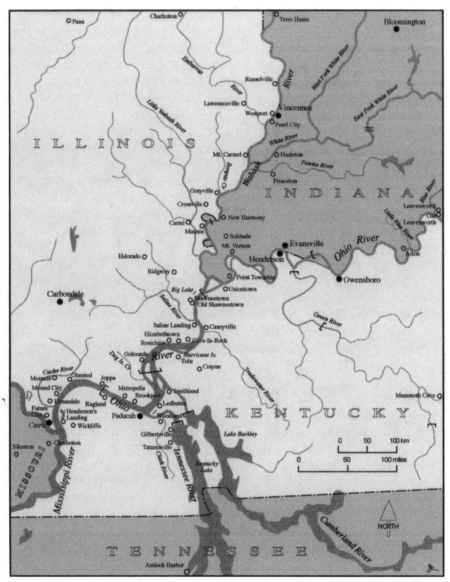

The Lower Ohio River Valley – Communities of Field Research

Mississippi-Missouri River basin, one of the largest river systems in the world.

Practically all of the Ohio River is impounded by giant navigation dams, so it is mostly wide and still. The Cumberland and Tennessee include large reservoirs, such as Lake Barkley and Kentucky Lake. The Wabash River is the second longest free-flowing river in the lower forty-eight states.

Today the Ohio is an industrial river, lined with manufacturing centers and traversed by a fleet of great diesel towboats and barge trains. A profile of the Ohio shows it as a staircase of pools behind the dams, the purpose of which is to keep the minimum channel depth at nine feet for barge traffic. Despite this change, there is still a remarkable variety of life in the river, not the least of which consists of fish. Some species once common, such as shovelnose sturgeon, spoonbill (paddlefish), black bass, and crappie, are now rare; and others, such as giant alligator gar, blue sucker, lake sturgeon, and striped bass, have vanished from the system. Still others tenaciously persist. Carp, a voracious exotic introduced from Germany in the 1880s, thrives throughout the Ohio River Valley. Catfish and buffalo largely support what is left of a once thriving commercial fishery that began with the establishment of towns along the river in the early 1800s.

Pioneer zoologist Constantine Samuel Rafinesque described commercial fishing in the Ohio Valley during the 1810s. His observations were based in part on interviews with commercial river fishermen: "Fishes are very abundant in the Ohio, and are sometimes taken by the thousands with seines; some of them are salted . . . In Pittsburgh, Cincinnati, Louisville, &c., fish always meets a good market, and sells often higher than meat . . . The most usual manners of catching fish in the Ohio are, with seines or harpoons at night and in shallow water, with boats carrying a light, or with the hooks and lines, and even the baskets."

In the early nineteenth century, many people pursued small-scale commercial fishing on the rivers of the Midwest. At the end of the century, the growth of cities and immigrant populations made it a major industry for a few decades, until overfishing and environmental degradation pushed it back to the economic margins. By then, a community of houseboat-dwelling river nomads had made river fishing and related activities into traditional family occupations.

When commercial fishing thrived on inland rivers, roughly from the 1870s through the 1940s, there were also many fishermen—perhaps even the majority—who were sedentary. They tended to dominate that branch of the industry that shipped fish to urban centers. The nomadic folks' fishing economy was marginal and depended on local sales. Perhaps because of the nomadic families' traditional ties to the river and willingness to endure economic uncertainty, they and their descendants stayed on the river pursuing fishing, musselling, trapping, and other seasonal occupations longer than those accustomed to a more certain livelihood. This seems to have been the case in the lower Ohio Valley, if not elsewhere in the greater Mississippi River basin.

Although river folk are no longer nomadic, they are still fishing. Some still carry with them the oral culture of the houseboat folk, derived from southern frontier culture adapted to river life and sustaining both material culture and jokes, ballads, tales, and songs.

Commercial fishing in the lower Ohio Valley endures because of the availability of fish and gear, the legality of fishing, and the demand for fish. But it is doubtful that these factors alone could have sustained the fisherman's way of life to this day. Instead, motivations less tangible and more difficult to measure seem both to unify the above factors and to function as the underlying reasons these activities endure. Despite regular entry into and departure from licensed commercial fishing by many individuals, there is a core of traditional river families who respond to river life in the way that other people might identify with their religion, ethnic group, race, or their home town or state.

The primary expressions of river folk identity are in their traditional and distinctive gear techniques. Also sustaining that identity are a shared "love of the river," which includes the joy derived from the beauty of the river and its surroundings, and pride in the ability to subsist on the river's wild resources and to master such skills as finding, catching, and dressing fish, preparing and handling gear, and building boats.

In this book, the term *river folk* refers to those individuals who are part of a traditional culture that identifies its home, life, and work with the river. *Fisherfolk* refers to most of the same individuals, but only those who make all or much of their living directly from fishing. Although the majority of the commercial fisherfolk in the Ohio Valley are men, there are also a few women who fish and more who prepare gear. However, regardless of gender, all refer to themselves and other local people who fish commercially as *fishermen*. For that reason, the term *fisherman* here indicates any person, male or female, who fishes commercially in the Ohio Valley. The term *fisher* will be used when referring to a person who fishes for sport and when referring to the general occupation of commercial fishing throughout the world.

In order to write about the culture of those river folk who practice small-scale commercial fishing, I conducted field research in the late 1970s and early 1980s and follow-ups in 1989 and 1992–1993 along the lower Ohio River and nearby portions of its tributaries. Most of my research took place on the Ohio proper, from below Evansville to Cairo, and on the Wabash below Terre Haute, Indiana. A few research forays also extended farther up the Ohio and into tributary streams, parts of northern Kentucky Lake in Kentucky and Tennessee, and into Memphis netmaking shops and east Arkansas catfish farms. The people I visited during the course of my research and described in this book share a common accumulation of cultural expression, or "folklife," derived from their lives on the river and from their regular dependence on its natural resources.

Interspersed in the chapters are vignettes rewritten from my field notes. I included them because they portray typical and important river fishing activities and because they give a human dimension to the knowledge, tools, and techniques of the lower Ohio Valley's river fishermen, fish marketers, and fish cooks.

Lower Ohio Valley river people have a complex affective bond with the river, to which they refer when they say, "The river gets in your blood." In the words of Roy Lee Walls: "It's just something that you don't believe in giving up. You think you will, but you will not. It's just that there's a lot of sport in it, I guess. Something about it like a magnet. It'll draw you back, regardless of how far away from it you get.

ONE

A History of Fishing and the River Folk

The lower Ohio Valley was once the home of major urban concentrations of Native Americans, collectively known as the Mound Builders. The remains of their settlements are the great mounds, such as those at Angel Mounds near Evansville, Indiana. The last of these civilizations had already collapsed by the time the first white explorers arrived in the 1690s.

The Mound Builders were avid fishers, a fact revealed by remains found in their middens. They also harvested freshwater mollusks on a large scale, using them both for food and for their beautiful mother-of-pearl, an important trade item. Later arriving Indians seem to have preferred hunting. Little is known of fishing methods of the Mound Builders or later Indians. Fishermen still occasionally find peanut-shaped stones grooved around the middle, which they call net sinkers, believed to have been fashioned by the Mound Builders to weigh down the lower end of a seine or set net. Their use in this manner is by no means certain. Hernando De Soto's 1540s expedition described urban Indians on the lower Mississippi dragging the river with seines. Perhaps their northern neighbors did the same.

French fur traders, priests, and soldiers started coming into the area around 1700. It became British territory after the French and Indian War and was ceded to the United States in 1783. Settlement in earnest began down the Ohio from Pittsburgh in the 1790s.

In the early days, whites in the valley regarded fish as an important resource. American military expeditions relied heavily on fish for food. One early Ohio River soldier-fisherman was George Washington, in 1770. He was familiar with river fishing from the Potomac, where he operated a fishery at Mount Vernon. Missionaries, including French priests and Moravians; explorers like John Filson and St. John de Crèvecoeur; and soldiers like Hessian surgeon Johann Schöpf and U.S. Army Captain Daniel Bradley all fished to feed themselves and their companions and later wrote about it. American Colonel John May, in 1788, wrote of families commercial fishing in the Pittsburgh area and of his expedition buying food from them.

The exploration and settlement of the Ohio River generated a veritable library of travel literature, some by naturalists, others by professional writers. There were also many guidebooks for the traveler. Zadok Cramer's yearbook, *The Navigator* (1801–1820s), was the best known of these. Cramer described fishermen using "seines, baskets, pots, trotlines, and hooks" at Pittsburgh (1805) and fish markets in Pittsburgh (1805), Wheeling (1811), and Steubenville (1814).

The abundance of fish caught by commercial fishermen was noted as early as 1805 by the *Frankfort* (Ky.) *Palladium,* which described the mouth of the Three Forks as the best fishing place on the Ohio River: "In a small crib, they can get five hundred pounds of fish in a day and may get by seine, five to seven hundred barrels per annum."

F.A. Michaux's 1805 journal detailed musselling for mother-of-pearl, "employed to make sleeve buttons," on the Allegheny, Monongahela, and Ohio Rivers. In 1819, Englishman John Woods recounted his experience on the Ohio:

> Aug. 22nd: (anchored near Richmond and Susann, Ohio, not far from Cincinnati, on Ky. shore)
>
> After we got to bed, 2 men & a boy came close to us & began to fish by torchlight, striking the fish with a gig or grig like a dung prong, with barbed points. I believe they had also some hooks & lines over the side of their canoe, & went on shore and made a fire to dry themselves, then spreading some small boughs under a tree, they laid down till day-light.

> Aug. 23d: At dawn the fishers offered us some cat-fish, of between 30 & 40 lb. each for 25¢ a piece, but as we had a store of provisions, we did not purchase any. They then started for Cincinnati with their fish.

The high price fresh fish could bring on the frontier is reflected in Thomas Hulmes's 1819 observation in Maysville, Kentucky: "Saw a catfish in the market, just caught out of the river with a hook and line, four feet long and eighty pounds in weight, offered for sale for two dollars."

The first fish and game conservation laws were passed in the old Northwest Territory during the 1810s, and in 1818, overfishing problems led the General Assembly of Kentucky to outlaw weirs that blocked streams in their entirety and to forbid fish-poisoning.

Before the 1830s, the chief fishing gear used in the Ohio Valley were brush dragnets and seines made from local natural materials. Other common gear included spears, trotlines, hooks and lines, and weirs. In the 1830s, twine seines were introduced. Also during that decade, settlers constructed numerous mill ponds, and fishermen rented the privilege of seining below the dams as fish attempted to swim upstream during spawning runs.

Naturalist Jared P. Kirtland, writing in the 1840s and 1850s in the *Boston Journal of Natural History* and the *Family Visitor,* described many species of Ohio Valley fish, their capture by seine, hook and line, and spear, and their sale by local fishermen. He may have been the first Ohio Valley writer to describe commercial spoonbill fishing (on Ohio's Licking River), and he blamed the depletion of fish in smaller tributaries on overfishing.

Before the 1840s, nets were not commercially manufactured in the United States, and the fishermen made nets themselves out of hemp or linen twine. In 1844, cotton twine and nets became available, and the first machine-knit nets came out in 1858. Not until late in the century did midwestern river fishermen begin to use manufactured nets. By then nets were being manufactured in Chicago and St. Louis. The availability of manufactured nets facilitated the large fisheries that later supplied midwestern cities with fish. Gill nets, brought to Lake Erie from Europe in 1850, were introduced into the Ohio Valley later in that decade.

Some river cities had their own specialized fisheries. The Falls of the Ohio at Louisville, for instance, attracted numerous spearfishers early in the century. After the building of the lock and dam there, water flowing over the Louisville Dam became the focus of a blue sucker fishery based on jigging (snagging by dragging naked hooks through shoals of fish). Still later in the century, the Wabash River at Terre Haute, Indiana, was the site of a specialized yellow bass fishery. By the 1860s, both Illinois and Indiana were regulating commercial fishing in their waters.

Although fish were widely available in the early years of settlement, fishing did not become an important industry in most of the Ohio Valley until after the settlement of midwestern cities. Large numbers of Germans, many of them Catholic or Jewish, and Irish came to Cincinnati, Evansville, Louisville, Paducah, and St. Louis.

Other German Catholics (as well as Protestants) established farms in rural areas of western Kentucky and southern Illinois, Indiana, and Ohio. Catholics needed fish for fast days. Jewish settlers were eager consumers of freshwater fish, as fish were exempt from the strictures of kosher preparation. Observant Jews, however, had to forgo scaleless catfish and spoonbill. After the Civil War, many African Americans moved to midwestern cities. They also had a taste for fish, which was often the only fresh protein they had regularly enjoyed during slavery.

The newcomers' demand for fish spurred a great increase in fishing on the rivers, the Great Lakes, and the artificial lakes in central Ohio that had been built to supply the inland canal system. These reservoirs (Buckeye Lake, Grand Lake Saint Marys, Indian Lake, and Lake Laromie) were the chief source of fish in Ohio during the 1870s, exceeding Lake Erie and the Ohio River and its tributaries. They may also have been the first sites in the Ohio Valley to see the use of hoop nets, probably for cold water capture of catfish.

Hoop or fyke nets are the mainstay of inland river fishing today, as they were a hundred years ago. They are an ancient invention, probably originating in Scandinavia or the Baltic countries. Dutch fishermen probably brought them to the East Coast during colonial days. In the same period, French settlers brought them into the Saint Lawrence River. They were used in the eastern Great Lakes at least as early as the 1850s. Their first use in the whole Mississippi River basin is not cited until 1868, when an illustration and description of hoop net fishermen in the Mississippi River near Memphis appeared in *Frank Leslie's Illustrated Newspaper*.

Government biologist S.P. Bartlett described a buffalo fishery that supplied the nineteenth-century urban midwestern fish demand for years: "For a great many years previous, on both the Illinois and Mississippi Rivers, it had been the practice of fishermen and farmers in the area, when the buffalo-fish `rolled' [made spawning runs], to take them by shooting, spearing, or with pitchforks, and, packed in sugar hogsheads, they were shipped by river to St. Louis and other markets."

The increase in demand for fish led to more regulation of the fisheries. In Kentucky, an 1876 bulletin publicizing the new Commonwealth Fish Law noted "constant and indiscriminate use of set nets, gill nets, traps, and other contrivances," adding that the inhabitants of Louisville alone paid "a quarter of a million dollars annually" for retail fish, only 5 percent of which came from Kentucky waters, and that the new law was "the first step towards obtaining an abundance of cheap and wholesome food."

The building of more navigational dams and clearing of more agricultural land made inland rivers muddier and more sluggish toward the end of the nineteenth century. Around 1880 the true carp of Europe was introduced to the Ohio Valley. It flourished in muddy midwestern rivers, doing better than native species. This resulted in an abundant supply of fish easily caught by commercial methods. Carp, never popular with most Americans, was a favorite of Jewish immigrants and some African Americans.

Expansion of railroads in the 1870s and the invention of artificial ice during the 1890s spurred commercial fishing by facilitating marketing far from the fishing grounds. The first refrigerated railroad carload of fish was shipped from the Midwest to New York in 1896. These developments increased inland commercial fishing at the end of the nineteenth century.

Statistics of river fisheries first appeared in the late 1890s. Because of inconsistencies in reporting, one cannot arrive at consistent figures for numbers of fishermen by state or river, type and distribution of gear and craft, and landings, as a whole or by species. As late as 1971, government biologist Louella E. Cable listed reasons that statistics for inland fisheries are "virtually useless": "Statistics for the Mississippi River Basin record amounts far below true values. Fish and other aquatic products are landed at thousands of places on the shores of lakes and streams, making recordkeeping difficult. Not all commercial catches reach the limited markets where landings are recorded. Some commercial fishermen sell catches in their local communities. Others sell part of their catches locally and ship the rest."

One can note some general trends for about a four-decade period. Figures were published, years after the respective studies and seemingly arbitrarily, for 1894, 1899, 1905, 1908, 1922, and 1931. During the 1890s, two species now classified as game, largemouth bass and pike, were among the leading commercial fish, and thousand-pound seine hauls of pike were recorded in Illinois. Numbers of fishermen and boats were greatest in the 1920s. Houseboats engaged in commercial fishing were reported as most numerous in the 1890s. Hoop nets were most numerous in the 1890s, but a decline in numbers may indicate an increase in efficiency, especially as some boats were motorized and baited nets were introduced.

Musselling was not widespread until the 1900s. None was reported before 1899, and then only on the Illinois and upper Mississippi Rivers. Trotlines (most of which were probably what today are called jumperlines) fluctuated greatly in number, but later declines may indicate an increase in efficiency or length of lines or a decrease in reporting. Commercial species that later became game species, such as black bass, crappie, largemouth bass, pike, sauger, walleye, and white bass, declined precipitously. Carp landings increased phenomenally. Catfish landings fluctuated wildly. Turtle fishing died out for a while early in this century, and musselling peaked by 1908. All fish species in the whole period sold below ten cents per pound.

The statistical reports contain interesting narrative details. Hugh M. Smith, in 1894, commented on the traditional nickname for Illinois, "the Sucker State," attributed to the abundance of suckers (including buffalo) in its waters and to their use by that state's pioneers. In his 1899 report, C.H. Townsend described the shipping of live carp to New York and the gaffing and hand-grabbing of turtles. He also explained the mussel brail and its use, noting that it was invented in 1897. In 1899, waste cheese, actually stale rinds trimmed from large cheeses in cheese factories, began to be used for net bait. This practice began on the Lake Pepin impoundment of the upper Mississippi and quickly spread throughout the rivers. Before that, hoop nets were set unbaited, a far less efficient practice.

At the turn of the century, many commercial fishermen seined privately-owned oxbow lakes in the bottomlands. At some lakes, landowners hired fishermen. Others fished themselves. Some fishermen rented fishing privileges from landowners.

Much of the literature on midwestern fishing from the 1890s through the 1920s concerned musselling, which was booming at the time, concentrating on the upper Mississippi, northern Illinois, and Arkansas, where mussellers were most active. Before the establishment of the button industry in the 1890s, most musselling consisted of speculative searches for valuable freshwater pearls.

When a particularly precious pearl was found, nomadic pearl fishers would descend on the area, camp out for months or even years and tear up every freshwater mollusk for miles around. This was the era of great "pearl rushes," such as the "Arkansas Klondike," which attracted ten thousand people to the White River of Arkansas from the 1890s through the 1910s. "Pearlers" included local farmers, unemployed nomadic young men (both black and white), and commercial fishermen, who used the meats for bait. Gemologist

George Frederick Kunz described pearlers in 1898 as "a lively, free-and-easy set of people, working hard all day, subsisting a good deal on fish caught in the river, and dancing at night to the banjo around campfires that line the banks."

After several valuable pearls were found in the lower Wabash around 1900, a pearl rush brought thousands of mussellers to the Vincennes, Indiana, area. German pearl buyer Frank Koeckeritz set up business in Vincennes in 1900. He described the local mussellers as two classes: "One, consisting of the clam fishers, who for the market value of the clam shells, gather these to sell to the numerous button manufacturers, only perchance, while cleaning the shells while removing the clam, finding a pearl occasionally. The others, called Pearlers, men in a little better financial condition, who gather the shells for pearls, mainly."

The mainstay of musselling was the button mill. German buttonmaker J.F. Boepple established the first button blank factory in the United States on the Mississippi at Muscatine, Iowa, in 1889. The industry took off from there, and button mills appeared in many lower Ohio Valley communities. Pearl buyer Koeckeritz, who had ties with the Muscatine button industry, established the Vincennes Pearl Button Company, with several plants along the lower Wabash. One of them was, for a time, the largest button blank mill in the United States.

During the 1920s and 1930s, many commercial fishermen motorized their boats, thus increasing their efficiency and number of landings. Quick freezing became available during the 1920s, making it possible to ship fish greater distances. On the other hand, pollution and overfishing caused declines. Most river communities in the lower valley had several floating markets. As the depression took hold, more people took to the river, dropping prices for fish but also increasing dependence on this inexpensive food resource. Travel writer Ward Dorrance visited a floating fish market in Old Shawneetown, Illinois, during the 1930s and supplied this literary description: "Men naked to the waist, reptilian with tattooings that expand and contract with their movements, are receiving fish from small boats that approach in line from the river side. There is the grunt of the hoist and the quick fall of the fish to the floor—gaping, gooey, and thick of shoulder. `Cats' are affixed to hooks and skinned, the honey and ivory flesh emerging as if in an anatomical drawing. `Buffalo' are beheaded and emptied: heaps of sliced bodies lie waiting for the ice. There is on all sides an uninhibited carnivorousness, a thrusting and wading in gut and scale and blood; an unquestioning acceptance of what the Lord provides."

In the 1930s and 1940s, the Tennessee Valley Authority dammed the Tennessee River, producing large reservoirs. From the start, the TVA saw these artificial lakes, particularly Kentucky Lake, as potentially rich fishing grounds. Biologists noted major increases in commercial fishing in Tennessee River impoundments. The snagging of spoonbill became very lucrative, since there was a demand for its caviarlike roe as World War II shut off supplies of real caviar from abroad. The biologists were dismayed to find a major increase in the ratio of "rough" or "scale" fish (buffalo, carp, suckers, and white perch) to game fish, and they advised the agency to encourage an increase in the commercial catch of rough fish. Rough fish were then still very much in demand in Illinois. There, in the winter, a motorized under-ice seining fishery landed thousands of tons of carp.

Nylon twine and netting first became available after World War II. Nylon substantially increased the efficiency of lines and nets and substantially decreased gear maintenance. A nylon net, properly cared for, does not rot but lasts until it is lost or irreparably abraded. Nonetheless, river fishermen only gradually converted to the new material, and as late as the early 1950s, some still used cotton gear. The physical properties of nylon made gill and trammel nets far more efficient, causing an increase in their use after the war and their subsequent outlawing in many areas.

Three other major innovations also increased efficiency. First, inexpensive and dependable outboard engines became widely available in the late 1940s. Second, the aluminum boat became common in the 1960s. And third, on the TVA impoundments, fishermen adapted the snagline, a row of dangling, closely spaced, unbaited hooks derived from the Eurasian sturgeon fisheries and used here to catch spoonbill. These innovations increased the independence and efficiency of the individual fisherman. The late Harold Weaver, longtime Ohio River fisherman at Cave-in-Rock, Illinois, remembered the introduction of the snagline to the lower Ohio from Kentucky Lake during the 1940s, by two Jewish fish and caviar merchants named Copland and Hill.

After World War II, practically all valley fishing was done by lone fishermen. Seining declined, as the cost of hiring additional hands could not compete with individual fishermen running lines of set nylon nets in outboard-motor-fitted boats.

Until 1993, the Commonwealth of Kentucky legally controlled the entire Ohio River along Kentucky's boundaries. Legal status of Ohio River fishermen living in Illinois improved markedly after an incident in Pope County in 1946. Bill Cox of Golconda, Illinois, was tarring and repairing eighty-four hoop nets on the Illinois shore when he was apprehended by two Illinois conservation officers. Cox was licensed by Kentucky to fish the Ohio. The officers confiscated his nets and burned them because he was not licensed in Illinois. Golconda attorney John Palmer argued the case all the way to the Illinois State Supreme Court. The judgment, rendered in 1949, found the officers at fault and established that an Illinois fisherman fishing the Ohio need not comply with Illinois law, if complying with Kentucky law. The case made Cox and Palmer heroes among Illinois's Ohio River fishermen.

According to a 1958–59 study by the interstate Ohio River Valley Water Sanitation Commission (ORSANCO), fishing had, by then, died out on the Ohio upriver from Carrollton, Kentucky, largely because of pollution. The midsection, between Carrollton and Owensboro, was still fished regularly, but the lower Ohio had then, as now, the most active fisheries. Also, as now, many lower valley restaurants specialized in locally caught fish.

The year 1960 saw a reopening of musselling on the Wabash and White Rivers, where it had been outlawed during most of the 1950s. Luckily the reopening coinciding with increased demand for freshwater mother-of-pearl by Japan's revitalized cultured-pearl industry. High prices for good quality shell led many fishermen and others to take up musselling as a part-time seasonal pursuit. But by the late 1970s and 1980s, musselling had largely died out in the lower Ohio Valley, because the Japanese preferred to buy mother-of-pearl from the upper Tennessee and other southern rivers, where it was supposedly of a higher quality. By the late 1980s, this supply no longer met the demand, and many lower valley fishermen were back on the rivers with their musselling boats and crowfoot brails.

Pollution, regulation favoring the sportsfisher over the commercial fisherman, general decline in numbers of fish, and unfair marketing practices led to several attempts to organize midwestern and southern river fishermen, from the 1940s through the 1970s. In the late 1970s, Bill Nichols, a fisherman and net-shop operator from Horseshoe Lake near East St. Louis established an Illinois Fisherman's Association and managed to recruit some members from the Wabash and other Ohio Valley rivers, as well as from the Illinois and the Mississippi. Although the organization was short-lived, Nichols was able to use the organization to lobby the Illinois legislature for more consideration of the commercial fisherman's plight.

For the three states in our study area—Kentucky, Indiana, and Illinois—as a whole, the number of fishermen has declined sharply and the proportion of part-timers has increased. But the ratio of units of gear to the weight of fish landed continues to decrease, indicating greater efficiency. Gill and trammel nets are illegal in Illinois and Indiana, but legal in Kentucky and in the entire Ohio River proper. Indiana has seen the greatest decrease in numbers of fishermen. Landings declined continuously from the late 1940s until 1975, when they began to increase again. During the early 1980s they declined again but then increased again, at least in fish landed per fisherman. Dry years in the early 1990s caused another major decline of fish that drove many out of the industry. Since 1993, by agreement among Illinois, Indiana, Kentucky, and Ohio, an "Ohio River License," available from all four states' authorities, has supplanted Kentucky's exclusive right to license fishing in the Ohio River.

Pollution seems to have been at its worst in the late 1960s. Enforcement of new environmental protection laws has probably helped. Rough or scale fish landings have shown the greatest decrease, as demand for buffalo, carp, and white perch has disappeared in many places. On the other hand, demand for catfish and spoonbill (sold as "boneless cat") has increased, partly owing to the greater availability of farm-raised catfish from Alabama, Arkansas, and Mississippi. The successful promotion of farm-raised catfish has raised all catfish to between two and three dollars per pound, an unheard of price in previous years. This has more than offset the rise in cost of bait, fuel, and gear.

Most fishermen and biologists agree that the building of the high-lift dam system by the Corps of Engineers from 1959 to 1979 created a less favorable environment for most species of fish by transforming the Ohio River into a chain of more or less stagnant pools. The old wicket dams aerated the water they passed over the top. The high-lift dams pass water underneath. Effect on fishing was simply not considered when these structures were designed and built.

From the early decades of the nineteenth century to the middle of the twentieth, thousands of Americans lived nomadic lives on homemade houseboats, sometimes floating from one landing to the next one downstream on a regular basis, other times mooring for years at the same landing but avoiding both house and ground rent.

The transient houseboat-dwelling population originated in the early nineteenth century and persisted as late as the mid-1950s when regulations pertaining to waste disposal, craft safety, and tie-up began to be enforced. The larger barge trains used in later years produced wakes so strong as to make houseboat life uncomfortable, unsafe, and impractical, and by then the competition of industrial and construction wage-labor was too great for formerly self-sufficient houseboat folk to ignore. Houseboaters were most numerous during the Great Depression.

Houseboat folk were engaged in many different livelihoods, and most of them regularly changed activities, depending on what resources and opportunities were available. Many were fishing families, but there were probably more sedentary fishing families living on the river's banks than there were nomadic fishermen. Despite this, many of the surviving commercial fishermen in today's lower Ohio Valley grew up in houseboat families. The negative stereotype of the "river rat" (an epithet often applied to houseboat folk by land-dwellers) was equivalent to "poor white trash," but most houseboat folk were industrious and self-reliant, though poor. Several former houseboaters have said, however, that certain urban concentrations of moored houseboats, such as one on Pigeon Creek in Evansville and one near Cairo, had reputations for crime and violence.

In the nineteenth and early twentieth centuries, much was written about the great rivers of the Midwest, particularly the Ohio. The authors were often fascinated by the lives of nomadic river folk and paid a great deal of attention to these people. Reuben Gold Thwaites, writing in the 1890s, noted that land-dwellers considered them larcenous, but he called them "a race of picturesque philosophers" and "followers of the apostle's calling." He noted their colorful speech, their occupation as fishermen, and their folktales, which, "told with an honest-like open-faced sobriety, would do credit to a Munchausen." He also noted their complaints of pollution's harmful effects upon their livelihoods. In 1906, Clifton Johnson described them thus: "Of all the dwellers in the valley of the great river, those who live in the houseboats have, by far, the most picturesque environment. You find them everywhere, from St. Paul to New Orleans, and not only on the main river, but on all the larger tributaries. There are many thousands of these water-gypsies, in all."

Johnson described the diversity of their architecture, the circumstances of poverty or disaster that periodically swelled their ranks, and their varied occupations, including driftwood-gathering, peddling, stovewood-sawing, preaching, shake-splitting, and, of course, fishing, and he found Cairo to be a concentration of them. Most writers were relatively kind in their description of the houseboat folk, but a few emphasized the negative "river rat" stereotype. The United States Commission on Fish and Fisheries also took notice of these people and their craft, registering 153 houseboats as engaged in commercial fishing in Illinois, Indiana, and Kentucky in 1894, 220 in 1899, but only 84 in 1922. By then most were tied up in Kentucky.

The most detailed and reliable account of houseboat life in the Ohio Valley is Ernest Theodore Hiller's study, based on fieldwork on the Ohio River and the Illinois River-Mississippi River confluence. Hiller estimated that in 1935 there were fifty thousand houseboat folk in the entire greater Mississippi-Ohio basin. He found them poor but industrious and described their "river self-help occupations," the same as those listed above, with the addition of musselling. quilting, woodcarving, and chair bottoming. They often planted squatter gardens on bottomland near where they were tied up. Most of Hiller's informants traced their origins to the South, and he noted the similarity of their lives to lives on the southern frontier: "The free squatting and floating privileges and the pursuits of the self-help opportunities supplied by the stream are survivals of the frontier traditions, rather than unique adjustments induced by the depression. . . . The people of the river environs are seen to have a like background of skills and occupational attitudes which, since pioneer days, have enabled and predisposed them to use the opportunities supplied by the river." Some nomadic fishermen specialized in the fabrication of fishing gear for use by other river people.

Hiller found that many houseboat folk had once been tenant farmers forced off the land by hard times. Their larcenous reputation he attributed to the traditional habit of foraging for available resources, such as game or timber, stray chickens, or standing green corn. Although Hiller was not explicit about it, his research, others' articles, and my own interviews suggest that almost all houseboat folk in the Midwest were white. There were, however, African-American houseboaters in the South.

The most prolific author on the subject of houseboat folk was local-color fiction and travel writer Ben Lucien Burman. He gathered material for his books while traveling as a tramp along the Ohio and Mississippi Rivers, toting a mandolin, on which he played folk melodies to allay fears that he was a revenue agent. During the early 1930s, many houseboaters practiced moonshining, a pursuit that Burman heartily defended. Burman's interest in folk culture led him to describe such activities as basket making, boatbuilding, fishing, hunting, trapping, root and herb gathering, and willow furniture making. He also described varieties of religious worship among houseboat folk and emphasized the people's close familial and clan ties.

In the late 1940s, Kentucky artist and author Harlan Hubbard and his wife, Anna, floated down the Ohio and Mississippi Rivers from Cincinnati to New Orleans in a homemade houseboat. Their journey, which took nearly three years, was chronicled in Hubbard's book *Shantyboat: A River Way of Life*, published in 1953. Hubbard described his nomadic fishing neighbors and their way of life in considerable detail. *Shantyboat* captured the public imagination and inspired children's writer Lois Lenski to research and write *Houseboat Girl*, about the life of a real houseboating and commercial fishing family from Metropolis, Illinois.

Another excellent source of information on houseboat life is the collection of photographs made by former houseboater Maggie Lee Sayre from 1939 through 1965. Sayre, who was born on the river near Paducah, Kentucky, and now lives in Parsons, Tennessee, photographed hundreds of scenes of houseboat life. She spent a total of fifty-one years as a houseboat dweller. She fished and made and repaired gear. Part of that time, she operated her own fishing boat and ran her own lines and nets, all the while chronicling her family's life with her camera. In *Houseboat Girl*, Lois Lenski also noted that women and girls fished alongside men.

By the end of the 1950s, houseboat folk had practically disappeared from most rivers, except for a few cutoffs and sloughs, mostly in the Deep South. Some of the houseboat folk who settled on land continued to work the river as seasonal fishermen, trappers, mussellers, and salvagers. Most of the fishing families in the lower Ohio Valley in the last few decades have been of houseboater origin.

Mentions of Ohio Valley fishermen in recent literature have emphasized nostalgia and retrospect, sometimes claiming to have found "the last" fisherman or riverman. Although fishing is by no means the industry that it once was, there are still commercial fishermen on the rivers of the lower Ohio Valley. Many are part-time, a few are full-time, but most still maintain a way of life based on the traditions of the rivers and their resources.

TWO
The River's Resources

Fisherfolk classifications of fish do not always agree with those of biologists and sportsfishers. Official common names recognized by the American Fisheries Society are often very different from local common names. (For corresponding local, official common, and scientific names of Ohio Valley commercial species, see Appendix 1 of this book.) The broadest categorization, shared by scientists, sportsfishers, enforcement personnel, and fisherfolk, distinguishes game fish from coarse or rough fish. Local fishermen and marketers differentiate between catfish (including spoonbill) and scale fish.

Ten more or less important commercial species of fish and one commercial turtle species live in the lower Ohio Valley today. The most important commercial fishes in the river are three species of catfishes (*Ictaluridae*): channel cats, flatheads, and blue cats. The states regulate them as both commercial and game fish. Catfish in general are associated with popular stereotypes of lazy rural southerners or midwesterners sitting by a riverbank or pond with a pole. They are popularly believed to be scavengers and are therefore not considered fit food by many people.

People with little catfish experience often erroneously believe that the barbels, the whiskerlike feelers around the fish's snout, are venomous. The three spines that extend from a catfish's dorsal fin and gill covers *can* injure, and they do contain a slightly venomous, or at least irritating, substance, which some people find painful. The folk cure is to rub the wound with slime from elsewhere on the fish's body.

Channel cats prefer a carnivorous diet of smaller fish, insects, and crustaceans, and they will also scavenge. They feed by smell and are attracted to strong-smelling baits such as waste cheese and soured mussel meats. Channel cats prefer large waters, such as the Ohio and the TVA impoundments. Their predictable migration and spawning habits make them easier to understand and thus to catch on a consistent basis. Fully grown channel cats can reach more than sixty pounds and four feet in length, but such large ones are extremely rare today.

The paramount commercial fish in the rivers are young channel cats, known as fiddlers, when less than about fifteen inches long. Fiddlers are easy to distinguish from other young catfish because of their spotted skin. They have the best flavor and texture when they are eight to ten inches long. They are the highest priced commercial fish species on the river.

Another commercial species of catfish is the flathead, mudcat, or yellow cat. Flatheads spawn at the same time in spring and early summer as channel cats. They can be numerous then, but they are rare at other times of the year. Flatheads grow large, up to six feet and more than 120 pounds. Three- and four-footers are still caught. Their unsavory looks and their habit of hiding in hollow logs and old tiles and culverts have caused flatheads to be unfairly maligned. Despite their negative image, flatheads are high-quality table fish. Their quality is ascribed to their purely carnivorous diet, which presumably makes them less subject to off-flavors found in more omnivorous species. A minstrel song once popular in Illinois sings their praises:

> Don't talk to me o' bacon fat
> Or taters, coon, or possum,
> For when I'se hooked a yaller cat,
> I'se got a meal to boss 'em.

Blue cats are the largest species in the river. During aboriginal times, they ran to six feet in length and probably more than two hundred pounds. Retired fisherman Lawrence Wade, who was for years the gatekeeper at the Old Dam Campground on the Wabash near New Harmony, Indiana, liked to tell the common tall tale of a big blue cat he landed on a trotline. He said the fish had so many hooks and sinkers stuck in it that he sold it to a scrap-metal dealer.

Large flatheads and blue cats are the subject of legends throughout the central and southern United States. Monstrous flatheads are reputed to inhabit oxbows, cutoffs, or backwaters, tempting anglers for years. The flathead has a large mouth and is known to hide in holes or hollow logs, mouth open, ready to swallow anything swimming past. A number of cutoffs and oxbows in the Ohio Valley have their legendary monster cats, often bearing names. One is "Cutoff John," who has defied anglers for generations, hiding in the Ribeyre Island Cutoff (a channel connecting an oxbow lake to the Wabash River) across from New Harmony.

Big flatheads and blues have reputedly been caught with various contents in their stomachs, including outboard motors, cats, dogs, and piglets. There are a number of legends of them swallowing humans, or at least pulling unsuspecting humans into the river where they then drown. According to fisherman Vergil Leibenguth of Caseyvile, Kentucky, a large blue cat or flathead was supposedly caught at the mouth of the Tradewater River in the 1960s, containing the remains of a human baby.

Former Kentucky Fish and Wildlife Resources Department director Charles Bowers is skeptical of the stories of man-eaters: "Sure, we have monsters down there, in the Ohio River and elsewhere, and they are big enough to eat a person. If they wanted to, they could tear an arm off, or something like that. But they're not inclined to."

Part of the lore of giant flatheads includes the practice of catching them by "tickling," "noodling," or "hogging." This practice—a traditional display of machismo among young men who live near the river—consists of reaching into hollow logs or under floating debris or overhanging banks to locate a hiding catfish. In some accounts, the tickler strokes the fish, causing it to relax, before grabbing it. He then seizes it, by the lip or gill cover, and hauls it ashore. Some ticklers will even thrust a hand down the fish's throat and grab the gill cover from inside. A callus around the wrist caused by catfish's rough lips is a badge of courage among avid ticklers.

Commercial fishermen Ed and Annie Atwood were sure that they hooked a sixteen-foot blue near their home in Wolf Creek, Kentucky, in 1911, but they turned him loose for fear of his size. Their son Walter, also a fisherman, has landed a hundred-pounder himself in more recent years. He believes that very large catfish, hardly ever encountered by fishermen, live in deep holes for years.

Blue cats were never as common in the Ohio as channels and flatheads. The 1979 completion of the Smithland Lock and Dam created the largest and deepest pool on the river. Blue cats, which prefer such conditions, have now become a common species in that area.

Commercial fishermen land a few other catfish species, including several species known as bullheads. Somewhat confusing are the niggerlippers or coalbolters. Fishermen consider them a separate species, as did biologists until the 1940s. Now they are considered a variant of the channel cat. In the Ohio Valley, they are a late spawn run of channel cat, with distinctive genetic characteristics. Niggerlippers, as they are most commonly called, at least by whites, have no spots and a more massive head than ordinary channel cats.

They are more common in a few localities, and fishermen outside those areas rarely encounter them. Earl and Herbert Sharp of Smithland, Kentucky, often catch them during the late June and early July spawning season at the Cumberland-Ohio confluence. Small niggerlippers and bullheads also retail as fiddlers.

Spoonbill, paddlefish, or spooneys are no relation to the catfish family but count as catfish in the markets of the lower Ohio Valley. Because they have catfishlike flesh and no bones, they are sold as "boneless cat." These unusual-looking fish have sharklike bodies and oarlike snouts that make up one-third of their entire length. They are endangered in Illinois and Indiana, but there are some places in the lowest part of the Ohio and in the TVA lakes where they are still common enough to be commercial fish. Fishermen gill net them, and in the Tennessee waters of Kentucky Lake and Lake Barkley, they catch them on set snaglines.

Spoonbill are called a "living fossil." They have teeth only when very young. The toothless adults are plankton-feeders and are almost never caught by anglers, except when accidentally snagged. They can grow to six feet and two hundred pounds, but even eighty-pounders are rare today. Commercial fishermen regularly catch four-footers in the fifty-pound range.

In the late nineteenth century, spoonbill were caught in seines and sold as "spoonbill cat" along the Ohio River. At that time they and white perch brought the highest price. A market for spoonbill caviar also developed at that time. Liking large, still waters, they increased in numbers after the building of the TVA and other inland river impoundments. Spoonbill fisheries in the 1940s were mostly based on snagging, and they wasted many fish in the quest for caviar.

Perhaps because of their odd appearance and unfamiliarity to the casual angler, spoonbill are believed to be inedible by many area residents. I once witnessed a Cave-in-Rock Fish Market customer express loud revulsion as fisherman Tommy Sherer of nearby Tolu, Kentucky, hauled in a tub of freshly caught spoonbill. "You'll never catch me eating one of those!" he exclaimed with disgust, and promptly purchased thirty pounds of frozen, dressed, packaged "boneless cat" for a family reunion.

Suckers and buffaloes (*Catostomidae*) are another important family of commercial fish in the Ohio Valley. Suckers are bottom-feeding plankton eaters. All are very bony, and most are considered less desirable food fishes. They and two unrelated species, the carp and the locally misnamed "white perch," constitute the classification of fish called scale fish, because, unlike catfish and spoonbill, they have easily visible scales. Sucker species caught or sold for food are almost never called suckers.

Three species of buffalo are the largest suckers. Fishermen distinguish biologically recognized species and subspecies and local variations, but all are marketed simply as "buffalo." Biologist Milton Trautman believes that the term *buffalo* was originally affixed to freshwater drum (white perch) because of their audible grunt but that species confusion transferred the name to large suckers.

Buffalo reach sixty pounds. Examples three feet long weighing twenty to twenty-five pounds are not uncommon. Despite the large buffalo population, anglers rarely encounter them, as these fish do not readily take a hook. Buffalo meat is very bony but white and lean.

A genus of sucker species also called carpsuckers are locally called highfin (pronounced "hyphen") or quillback. They are much smaller than buffalo, rarely exceeding twenty inches and three pounds and often marketed at half that size. In places where they are common, such as the Wabash, they are a year-round bycatch by fishermen seeking catfish in hoop nets. Carpsuckers and buffalo resemble carp superficially, and accounts of carp caught in pioneer days probably referred to those species.

A local variety of the common white sucker, called blackhorse, are occasionally sold commercially in the spring, when they are easy to catch and their flesh is firm and sweet. Willie J. Carver of Old Leavenworth, Indiana, reported that his brother, "Skeet," and family used to spear large numbers of another sucker called redhorse with pitchforks in the nearby Muscatatuck River and market them in Louisville.

One sucker, usually called blue, black, or gourdseed sucker, has a near-legendary status as a rare but fine food fish. Carver remembers a Jewish Louisville fish dealer whom he supplied who always kept the black suckers for himself and his family. In 1882, biologist David Starr Jordan reported them as the premium fish caught at the Falls of the Ohio. They are so rare nowadays that they may well be considered practically extinct in most of the Ohio Valley.

Carp are an exotic species, imported from Germany in the late 1870s in the hopes of starting an aquaculture industry in the United States. They were a successful food fish in Europe and Asia, having first been raised in ponds in China as early as 1000 B.C. In the United States, imported carp were distributed by congressional district at the request of congressmen.

Many midwesterners introduced carp into farm ponds and livestock wallows, where they thrived, being hardy, omnivorous, and able to tolerate low oxygen levels. These prolific but poorly managed fish were of poor eating quality, and this was the origin of the negative attitude most Americans have toward carp. The fish's rooting habit muddies waters where game fish live, increasing the carp's competitive advantage. As more land was put under cultivation, midwestern rivers became increasingly muddy, again favoring carp over native species.

In recent years, another exotic carp species has entered the Ohio Valley. The grass or white carp, a large northeast Asian species, was introduced to rice fields in the South to eat superfluous vegetation. Like its better-known cousin, it adapted to its new environment beyond anyone's expectations, and most states now forbid its importation. It is usually larger than the ordinary carp and has a whiter, finer flesh. Some commercial fishermen praise the grass carp highly and hope that it will increase enough to become an important commercial fish. So far, it only ranges in the southernmost part of the Ohio Valley.

The so-called white perch of the lower Ohio Valley is not a perch at all. It is a freshwater drum. Other names for it include sheepshead (the name most common among African Americans), grunter, gaspergou, croaker, and even buffalo. Lower Ohio Valley fishermen almost universally refer to them as white perch. Most perch are relatively small, weighing one to two pounds.

At one time, white perch were considered a high-quality food fish in the Ohio Valley, at least if caught in cold water. Today they are bought almost exclusively by poorer African Americans in a few localities and are considered a nuisance fish by most commercial fishermen. Fishermen agree that white perch, although still plentiful, have deteriorated remarkably in quality and size. They attribute this to pollution and to the decline of mussels, which were once their primary food.

Most bony fish have two bean-shaped ear bones called otoliths. Those on the white perch are particularly large and have a pearl-like sheen. People in the Midwest and South, especially African Americans, have prized them as trinkets or curiosities. Some individuals carry these "lucky stones" as good-luck charms. Roy Lee

Walls saves the finest ones for a favored customer, a black woman from St. Louis, who periodically stops at his market when she is in the area.

A number of species that were once important commercially are now either so rare that they are not worth trying to catch or are now protected as game species or even as endangered species. Lake sturgeon, which are locally called simply sturgeon, were once relatively common in the Ohio Valley, often attaining a length of more than six feet. They are now a protected endangered species throughout the Midwest. Harold "Pat" Patton of Cave-in Rock remembers dressing out numerous six- to eight-footers during the 1940s. The sturgeon were shipped to New York City and were eventually smoked and sold there. Older marketers have kept photos of enormous sturgeon sold earlier in the century. They were marketed for both their flesh and their caviar, both of which were shipped by rail to large cities.

Today, hackleback or shovelnose sturgeon are the only sturgeon available. They run small, rarely exceeding two feet. In some areas, fishermen do not bother to catch them, as they have low demand. However, in other areas, such as near Paducah, they are still a popular food fish, and fishermen set trammel nets to catch hackleback in early spring and late fall when they are most numerous. During winter, they are sometimes the only fish available.

Gar are rarely eaten in the Ohio Valley. Ira Gene Bushey of Smithland, Kentucky, occasionally catches a large number in his gill nets at the Cumberland-Ohio confluence. He regularly markets fish in St. Louis and occasionally brings gar along, as there is a demand for them there among African Americans from the South.

The final fish species worth considering here is the grinnel or bowfin, a large (up to three feet in length), mud-burrowing, and air-breathing predator, unrelated to any other species of fish. Sportsfishers hate them because they eat young game fish. Game managers, on the other hand, consider grinnel's predation beneficial in overstocked waters.

Grinnel survive drought by digging deep into dried-out mudholes. Some older African Americans in the area between Paducah and Cairo are fond of them. Bob Cox of Golconda remembers as a boy prying grinnel out of dry swamps and selling them to black customers at his father's market. Grinnel must be killed immediately before cooking and eaten right away or their flesh becomes soft and unappetizing.

Bob Cox with carp on the Cox family houseboat, Golconda, Illinois, ca. 1950. (Photographer unknown; photo courtesy of Bob Cox.)

As early as 1912, fisheries economist George W. Miles noted the connection between race and class distinctions and disdain for certain species of fish. Of the dogfish (grinnel), Miles wrote: "Placed under the ban as an outcast, despised by all members of society, and no person who had any care for his good name or reputation dared taste the flesh of one. . . . Children were taught at their mothers' knees that if they would keep their good names and honored places in society, they must not eat the dogfish!"

The common snapping turtle or snapper is an aquatic food resource in some parts of the lower Ohio Valley. These most common aquatic reptiles in North America can be found from the Rockies to the Gulf of Saint Lawrence. Snappers have increased in number since the last century with the proliferation of farm ponds. Snappers are dangerous to handle because of their strength, speed, and sharp beaks. A well-placed snapper bite can sever a finger. Experienced handlers hold them by the rear end of the shell near the tail. People are often glad to have them removed from their ponds, but snappers do help check overcrowding of fish.

The mussels or *Naiades* of the North American rivers are only distantly related to the true mussels of the oceans. Native freshwater mussels are all members of the family *Unionidae* and are actually freshwater clams. Over thirty species have been harvested for their nacre (mother-of-pearl) and pearls. Because of the biological complexity and singular use of these resources, they are covered in detail in the chapter, "Musselling and Pearling."

It is a popular notion that availability of fish and other aquatic resources has declined precipitously and steadily since the beginning of this century. This assessment is not entirely accurate. Undoubtedly, fish landings are nowhere near what they were in 1900. Populations improved after the early 1970s, declining in the early 1980s, improving again by 1990, and then declining again during the early 1990s drought. People close to the river are of the opinion that the worst years for pollution were the 1940s through the 1960s and that after new antipollution laws came into effect, the river's water quality improved, as did the variety and quantity of fish. Several serious spills and low water levels in the early and mid-1980s caused another decline, but conditions improved again later. Also, during the recession of the early 1980s, there was more fishing pressure, as otherwise unemployed and underemployed river people went back to fishing.

Many retired fishermen believe that commercial species of fish are now in short supply. However, those individuals were most active during the worst years. Sweeping complaints by former fishermen testifying to the almost total extinction of food fishes have been quoted for publication. Fisherman Bill Williams of Ragland, Kentucky, a full-time professional fisherman in his early sixties, claims that there are now more fish, especially catfish, than there were in his early days of fishing. Williams is aware of the laments of those who disagree. He suggests that this discrepancy may be caused by the fact that there are fewer active fishermen today but that they are fishing more efficiently. Older fishermen who held on to older techniques became less successful, and thus it seemed to them that the fish were disappearing. A young fisherman, John Farmer of Grayville, Illinois, has succeeded as a fisherman and marketer into the mid-1990s. His experience is that the buffalo, highfin, and catfish that he sells have continued to be plentiful in that part of the Wabash.

There is little doubt that river fish have been, for most of this century, an underutilized food supply. Although environmental degradation has caused a drastic reduction in desirable species, little of the standing crop is harvested. A 1965 study of reservoirs, lakes, and rivers found that for the Ohio and Tennessee River basins, only a small percentage of the available commercial fish crop was actually landed. Snapping turtles have actually increased in numbers.

Will marginal commercial fishing of the type found today in the Ohio River Valley continue? If pollution is kept in check, it is likely that it will. But if studies of toxic substances in the fish lead to a total ban on the sale and commercial landing of river fish, this way of life will be destroyed.

THREE

Watercraft

Most commercial fishermen fish the river from boats. In the earliest years, dugout and plank canoes (or pirogues) were the leading fisherman's crafts. But since the post-Civil War growth of the industry, skiffs, johnboats, houseboats, and floating markets have been the most important boats in the Ohio River fishing industry.

Before the widespread use of the outboard motor, most small boats on the river were skiffs. A 1978 study of midwestern river fishing boats by Malcolm L. Comeaux reveals three types of skiffs: full-fisher, half-fisher, and yawl. These designations describe the boats' rakes and tapers. On the full-fisher, the sides are sharply raked and the bottom planks are less than four inches broad where they meet the rear transom. The half-fisher has less of a rake on the sides, with the aft bottom six to twelve inches broad. The yawl has relatively vertical sides and a bottom only about three feet broad at the transom.

Before the 1950s, almost all boats in the Ohio Valley fisheries were wooden. Professionally built small craft were usually skiffs of the types noted by Comeaux. Leavenworth, Indiana, was one of several communities in which skiff building was a major local industry. Three plants, the D. Lyon Skiff Company, the D. Allen Company, and the Starr Skiff Works, were located there. D. Lyon was established in the 1820s and stayed in business until 1941. D. Lyon skiffs were widely known throughout the Midwest both for their quality and because the Corps of Engineers purchased hundreds of D. Lyon "Leavenworth yawls" for its dam operations. Many of them later found their way into fishermen's hands, and the Leavenworth yawl is still remembered by older fishermen as the best of the commercially made skiffs. The last commercial skiff works on the Ohio was the Weaver Skiff Works of Racine, Ohio, which closed in 1975.

During the time when small boats were powered by oar, the narrower full- and half-fishers were easier to row, although the yawl could carry more weight and was more stable for a net fisherman who regularly had to stand up in the boat. With the exception of the yawl, small skiffs were not practical as powerboats, and few were

Hugh "Duck" Beatty and sons with flathead cat and fisher-type skiff,
Ohio River near Rising Sun, Indiana, 1905. (Photographer unknown;
photo courtesy of Chris McHenry.)

built or used after the 1940s. Later yawls were built to accommo-
date an outboard motor, with broader bottoms aft, modified gunwales, and a transom perpendicular to the bottom.

By the middle of the twentieth century, skiffs were replaced by
flat-bottomed scow-ended boats. Like skiffs, their traditional design
was altered to receive outboard motors. The older, rowed examples
were far narrower, with rarely more than a three-foot beam. They
were also often proportionally longer—a twenty-two-footer was
not uncommon—and they usually had a bottom that raked upward
aft.

Scow-ended, flat-bottomed boats have a number of names
throughout the greater Mississippi River basin, and they are all
variations on a basic type called the flatboat. Those built in the
greater Mississippi basin north of Louisiana are called johnboats or,
occasionally, joeboats or dogboats. Specialized johnboats modified
for musselling and seining also emerged.

The best professionally built skiffs and johnboats were made of cypress, either locally cut or brought in from the South. Cypress grows naturally as far north as the Wabash bottomlands above Vincennes. According to Orval Loven, the old-growth cypress available before 1940 was quite oily and shed water, whereas the later second-growth was not as high in quality. Donald "Dutch" Moore found suitable timber growing in nearby swamps and girdled it. A year later, he felled it and hauled it to a nearby sawmill. He preferred cypress for the sides and old oak flooring from an abandoned house for the bottom. As the supply of cypress dwindled after the 1930s, marine plywood took its place. Many boatbuilders used marine plywood for the bottom and whatever cheap lumber was available from a local lumberyard (usually pine) for the sides. In recent years, most newer home-built johnboats were made of ordinary exterior plywood. To quote Harlan Hubbard, "These johnboats are more or less expendable anyway. They're not supposed to last forever."

Although wooden johnboats are easy to build, there have also been boatbuilding shops that have specialized in their production. One such plant was Kelly's Band Mill of Lawrenceville, Illinois, on the Embarras River. During the 1950s and 1960s, the company built more than five hundred johnboats in ten-, twelve-, fourteen-, and sixteen-foot lengths. All but the sixteen-footers were made with the sportsfisher in mind and fitted with three or four thwarts. Most were built by the owner, Bob Kelly Sr., and Roy Gowan, who started as Kelly's high school student apprentice. Kelly complains that they built them too well and thus never needed replacing. Several are still in use on the Wabash River today. A longtime source of cheap johnboats was Nelson's Planing Mill in Brent, Kentucky (near Cincinnati). From the 1940s through the 1960s, they sold unpainted johnboats out of their plant for one dollar per linear foot.

Most of today's commercial fishermen use sixteen- or eighteen-foot aluminum johnboats. Some still prefer wooden boats for their relative stability and because of a belief that a wooden boat is quieter than an aluminum or fiberglass boat and is thus less likely to scare away fish. Aluminum johnboats can be purchased without the usual three or four thwarts found in a sportsfisher's boat, but many fisherman have modified sportsfishers' johnboats by removing all but the aft thwart or by removing all the thwarts and installing a wooden seat in an aft corner.

Many part-time or semiretired fishermen still make wooden johnboats, as often for the love of the craft as for practical purposes.

Older and more experienced fishermen are the ones more likely to have boatbuilding skills and a clear idea of the requirements for a boat that they may want to custom-build for commercial fishing purposes. Some fishermen can very quickly build simple johnboats. Don Harrington claims that he can build three wooden johnboats for the cost of an equivalent aluminum boat (about one thousand dollars for a sixteen-footer). In his words: "I can take and build a johnboat and in the time I go down to get the papers made up on an aluminum boat and bring it home, I could have my wooden johnboat almost ready to put in the river." Full-time professional fishermen today rarely take the time to build their own boats and usually use commercially built aluminum boats.

Aside from boats specially modified for specific activities, there are two basic types of johnboats built in the Ohio Valley today— those with and those without frames. The former are usually called ribbed because of the riblike frame pieces extending athwart the bottom at two- to four-foot intervals. The ribbed johnboat is usually longer, at least sixteen feet, and it is built to last. This is the type usually built for commercial fishing purposes, as it can carry a substantial load of fish and gear. It usually has beam of about four feet.

Most ribbed johnboats are built the same way, except that some people prefer raked sides and will go to the trouble of bracing the boat's timbers while building it. Others do not bother and leave sides at right angles to the bottom. To rake the sides it is necessary to nail together two temporary forming braces (one fore, one aft) each out of five pieces of scrap timber. Two cross timbers, the upper slightly longer than the lower, and two triangular side pieces nailed to their ends, make an angled brace that will bend the sides outward from the top.

The ribs and knees (tapered timbers extending from bottom to gunwale at each rib) are cut preferably from one-by-four oak but sometimes from cheaper timber. Sides and transom are ideally made from one-by-sixteen planks, but since these are now difficult to find, one-half- or three-quarters-by-eight, -ten, or -twelve planks are often used instead.

Nowadays, most builders use a single large piece of one-half- or three-quarter-inch marine or exterior plywood for the bottom and a smaller piece for the bow. If the boat is to be rowed, the bottom piece is cut in two, and two facing edges are mitered to give a raked bottom aft. The more traditional johnboat has a bottom of crossways

A commercial fisherman's johnboat built by Cecil Harris, Smithland, Kentucky, 1978.

half-by-six or half-by-eight planks. Few take the extra time to build a boat with a plank bottom anymore. One or more strips of one-half-by-two are cut to form a keel or a set of longitudinally parallel skegs (pronounced "skags").

Once the lumber is cut to size, it is assembled, usually on a pair of sawhorses, occasionally on the ground. Sides and ends are nailed together after glue has been spread on connecting edges. This is done around the forming braces, if the builder has chosen to make and use them, so that the sides are raked and tapered. Each rib is fitted with two knees and set and nailed in place to the sides. At each step, connecting edges must be planed to form a tight fit. According to Don Harrington, careful planing can make caulking unnecessary.

The entire assemblage is then turned over and the bottom is nailed to the sides and ribs, again after connecting edges have been glued. The keel or skegs are then nailed on, and the boat is again turned over. Desired seats or thwarts are nailed into place, and the framing braces are removed. The boat is then primed and finished with two coats of exterior enamel.

Most boats seep when new or dried out, but as water expands the lumber, it eventually becomes watertight. Boats with a serious seeping problem may be sunk for a few days to promote maximum swelling or leaking joints may be caulked. This was more of a problem in the days when johnboats were built of planks. Johnboats are usually fastened with galvanized or copper nails. Those making especially fine boats may use brass screws, but this substantially increases labor time and cost of materials.

Smaller boats used by part-timers and casual sportsfishers often have no ribs or knees. They are held together only at the edges of the lumber and derive rigidity from their thwarts. They can be made without framing braces and are box-shaped, except for a rake on the bow.

During the days when seining was common, much larger and more substantial johnboats were specially built as seining barges. A twenty-four footer made of inch-thick lumber was not unusual. They were often fitted with vertical stakes along the gunwales. Planks could be set edge to edge along the stakes, giving the boat a greater capacity in case of a large haul. Such a craft was called a stakeboat. Seining barges often had planks mounted athwart the bow (the seine deck), on which a fisherman stood while pulling a seine or lifting a hoop net. Such a boat had to be large and steady enough not to swamp when so used. In some cases, a hand winch was mounted on two vertical stanchions above the seine deck.

Many fishermen learned to build johnboats from their fathers or other older relatives or neighbors. Some were also self-taught, including Carl Eswine of Shawneetown, who built dozens of johnboats and several skiffs, both for his own use and for sale. "I built them b'guess and b'gosh," he says.

Retired commercial fishermen sometimes use their boatbuilding skills to build elaborate sportsfishing johnboats. Bill Cox built a beautiful fourteen-footer during the 1970s, with built-in tackle drawers and scrolled soffits below the thwarts.

The chief exception to today's prevalent practice of buying aluminum boats occurs among mussellers, most of whom build their own boats or hire an adept neighbor to do so for them. There are, however, some mussellers who modify larger aluminum johnboats to make them into musselling boats, and local welding shops occasionally make steel-hulled musselling boats. These are most common in the lowest part of the Ohio and in Kentucky Lake and Lake Barkley.

Custom-built wooden musselling boats share certain typical characteristics. They are essentially large (sixteen- to twenty-foot) johnboats, usually five-foot beam, often built of inch-thick lumber, with more substantial ribs and knees (often made of two-by-fours), so that they can carry a ton of mussels. For that reason they are often fastened with screws instead of nails.

The most visible characteristic of a musselling boat is its four vertical two-by-four standers extending from the bottom to several feet above the gunwales, two to a side, six to eight feet apart and notched on their top ends. On each is suspended the mussel brail or crowfoot bar. Some, especially those in the TVA impoundments and the lowest part of the Ohio, also have a braced forward stanchion with a small gasoline-motor-powered winch for hauling the brails from deep waters. A musselling boat is also fitted with a "mule," a piece of plywood or braced canvas extending aft that steers the boat across a mussel bed. Some of the larger musselling boats have a canopy covering all or most of the boat. It stretches from four corner posts and is tall enough for a man to stand up under it hauling in mussel brails.

The river houseboat or shantyboat (as it was called by land-dwellers and in literature) is likely a direct descendant of the flatboat used for transportation on the frontier. The term *shantyboat* is generally considered derogatory, and people who lived on them preferred the term *houseboat*.

People no longer live on traditional houseboats in the lower Ohio Valley, and there are very few surviving examples around. Nonetheless, the traditional river houseboat was, for decades, a centerpiece of the river way of life. There are still a few floating markets and fish houses whose design is based on the traditional houseboat model. Howard Durham's floating fish market, still afloat on the Ohio at Old Shawneetown in 1994, was once a houseboat lived in by the Yakely family at Wabash Island.

From the time they were first described by Timothy Flint in the 1830s until the last ones were forced off the river in the 1950s, many thousands were built, usually by their owners. A typical houseboat consisted of a lightly framed cabin superstructure built on a wooden barge. The barge consisted of two long gunwales connected by a frame of ribs, and a bow and a stern covered with planking on the

Howard Durham's floating fish market, formerly the Yakely family
houseboat, Old Shawneetown, Illinois, 1980.

bottom and deck, and very little freeboard. The cabin was typically
as wide as the barge but not as long. Fore and aft were two small
decks, with the roof of the cabin extended over them to make two
small porches. Doors leading inside were built into each end of the
cabin, which was equivalent to a small frame house. It usually had
between one and four rooms, with two windows opposite each other
in each room. If there were two or more rooms, they were always in
a row. Two-room houseboats were most common, with one room
serving as a bedroom and the other as a kitchen, parlor, and work
area. Some of the larger houseboats, particularly those used by fishing families, also had projecting catwalks on both sides along the
cabin. Older houseboats were board-sided. Later on, plywood was
used and was sometimes covered with brick-imprinted tar paper.

Ohio Valley fisherfolk have described houseboats of various dimensions. Harold Weaver lived in a four-room houseboat forty-
seven feet long by eighteen feet wide. Roy Lee Walls once had a
three-room houseboat sixty feet long by fourteen feet wide. The
houseboat on which Maggie Lee Sayre's family lived on the Tennessee River and Kentucky Lake was sixty feet long. Sandra
Cunningham Hartlieb of Indianapolis described her fishing parents'
houseboat at Owensboro, Kentucky, which they used from 1935 to

Harold Weaver's family houseboat on the Ohio River, late 1940s. Harold is seated leaning against the superstructure. His wife, Rikke, is looking out the window. (Photographer unknown; photo courtesy of Sarah Weaver Clark.)

1945, as thirty-six feet long and twelve feet wide, with three rooms and two-foot porches fore and aft. At one end was an adults' bedroom with a double bed, chest of drawers, and a dresser. A room amidships held a child's bed, a woodstove, two chairs, and a corner closet. At the other end was a kitchen, containing a woodstove (with oven), a table and three chairs, a cupboard, a work table, and an icebox.

During the 1950s, most of the houseboats in the Ohio Valley were hauled up on land. There, most were either abandoned or disassembled, but a few continued to be used as dwellings, usually by former river folk. One extant example is a forty-four-by-fourteen-foot two-room houseboat owned by Joe "Bunk" Owens of Metropolis and stranded in his back yard near the waterfront. It is seven feet from deck to ceiling, and has two five-foot porches, one of which is partly enclosed.

One of the very last homemade traditional houseboats built in the area was a one-room, twelve-by-eighteen-foot craft built in 1963 by retired fisherman Ralph Carver on the Clark River at Woodland, east of Paducah. It was hauled ashore in 1977, and he still lived in it in 1980.

The Cunningham family houseboat, Owensboro, Kentucky, ca. 1950.
(Photo courtesy of Sandra Cunningham Hartlieb.)

In the early years, houseboats generally had slightly curved or
shallow gable-end roofs. The last houseboats usually had completely
flat roofs sealed with hot-mopped asphalt, which needed frequent
repair. For most of the period during which houseboats were in use,
they floated on flatboatlike barges. After the 1930s, some were built
on dock platforms buoyed by rows of sealed fifty-five-gallon steel
drums, like today's boat and swimming docks.

Until recently, many sedentary fishermen along the rivers built
floating fish markets. Communities such as Carmi, Cave-in-Rock,
Golconda, Maunie, Metropolis, Old Shawneetown, Paducah, and
Rosiclaire had small floating markets. There were six in Old
Shawneetown during the 1960s. One still remains in 1994. It is
Durham's Fish Market, originally built as a houseboat and open only
sporadically during the summer season. This two-room boat was
originally on a wooden barge. It now stands on a steel barge con-

structed as a ferry for oil-drilling equipment (called a mudboat) of the type used in the Wabash Valley oilfields. One room is a living area and seasonal home for Howard Durham. The other has four freezers out of which Durham sells fish. The boat's dimensions are forty-two by sixteen feet.

More recent fish markets float on the Wabash at Maunie, Illinois, built by Fred and Dennis Lueke. The last of them was assembled in the late 1980s, also on a steel mudboat barge, twenty-eight by twelve feet. It is full of freezers. Next to it are a twelve-by-twelve-foot and another twenty-eight-by-twelve, moored in line, to each other, parallel to the bank. The new barge and the small one are sided with corrugated synthetic material. The older of the large ones is open-sided but covered with a roof. It has two winched steel-cage fish boxes that can be raised and lowered into the river. One is used for carp and the other for other species, because carp will fight and kill other fish with which they are confined.

The largest floating market in the area is the Cave-in-Rock Fish Market, unusual in that it floats on several platforms and is moored perpendicular to the river bank. The Cave-in-Rock market's dimensions are twenty-two by forty-eight feet. The shoreward half consists of the public market and includes counters, fish-dressing benches, and freezers. The riverward half includes a galvanized-steel-lined ice room for fish storage and a marine fueling station, and it opens on a public marina and fueling dock. All of the above markets and docks, with the exception of the two built on mudboats, float on rows of fifty-five-gallon oil drums.

Related to floating markets are smaller floating fish houses. The latter are not usually used directly as retail markets. Instead, they are primarily used only for landing and dressing fish. They represent a traditional type of floating structure still being constructed in the lower Ohio Valley at the end of the twentieth century. They also stand on docks supported by floating oil drums.

Of the six floating fish houses on Bonpas Creek in Grayville, Illinois, in the 1980s, all were either eight-by-ten or eight-by-twelve feet. One was enclosed in aluminum siding and wired for power. Another was completely open, and four others were enclosed but had small porches on their ends. Two belonged to Orval Loven, who built the last one in the winter of 1978–79. All were fitted with at least one fish box, workbenches, and dressing tables that drained into the river. Loven's contained two fish boxes, as he kept a sepa-

Dennis and Fred Lueke at Lueke's Fish Market on the Wabash River at
Maunie, Illinois, 1993.

Floating fish docks at the mouth of Bonpas Creek near the Wabash
River, Grayville, Illinois, 1978.

rate fish box for carp. Jack Emory built and still uses an open three-sided shed on a dock floating in the Little Wabash River, in downtown Carmi, Illinois. Next to it is an open dock with a hand-winched wire-cage fish box. One side of the shed is covered by a huge sign advertising fresh fish, clearly visible from the State Highway 1 bridge.

Fish boxes or live boxes are enclosures that keep fish alive in the river without allowing them to escape. Several varieties are used in the Ohio Valley. At one time, semisubmerged skiff-shaped live cars or tow cars, some with enclosed bulkheads, were towed behind boats to transport living fish.

In this area, most fish boxes are small and rectangular. Some float and others are suspended by a rope or chain on a winch. They range from four-by-four feet to as small as two-by-two. The simplest is a frame of light lumber supporting sides of hardware cloth or chicken wire. One side is hinged, making a door with access to the fish. More elaborate fish boxes are built of wooden slats, sometimes with a frame of welded steel pipe. They may also contain pieces of styrofoam or empty plastic bottles for buoyancy. Some boxes are open on top and suspended, top edge above water surface, often surrounded by the deck of a market or dock.

Since the 1940s, practically all boats used by commercial fishermen are fitted with outboard motors. Before World War II, motors were an exception, and most fishermen rowed. Automobile engines, such as four-cylinder units from Ford Model T's and Model A's served, but their weight was a problem, and boats in which they were mounted often swamped, especially after a rain. Several brands of one-cylinder inboards, such as Sears' Motor-Go, the Fairbanks-Morse, and Evansville Engine Company's Mink, were available, and a few of these are still maintained by their owners as antiques. During the 1920s, single-cylinder Elto and Elto-Evinrude outboards became available. Carl Eswine held the first Evinrude franchise in southern Illinois, and he sold many fishermen their first motors. Most of the earlier outboards were used by sportsfishers and waterfowl hunters.

A commercial fisherman must be a skilled engine mechanic. Orval Loven explains: "If your motor needs a little working, you can't take it off every time and take it to a mechanic and have him just go to it, because they'll charge you till the sky's the limit and maybe two screws is all it takes." Makeshift repairs on outboards are often necessary, and fishermen pride themselves on their ingenuity. Roy Lee

Walls tells of fabricating a hickory connecting rod that did not need replacement for twelve years. A fisherman should be able to rebuild an outboard motor in an afternoon.

Whether a johnboat is home-built or store-bought, it must be outfitted to be used for commercial fishing. An outfitted boat typically contains the following accessories: an outboard motor (typically a large Evinrude) with rudimentary maintenance and repair tools (screwdrivers, wrenches, a nail or piece of stiff wire for poking the carburetor, and replacement propeller pins), an anchor (often homemade from welded steel or cement block), a homemade grappling hook, spare coils of rope, and whatever fishing gear is in use at tnat particular time and place. If the fisherman markets live fish, the boat may trail a wooden and chicken-wire fish box. Fish to be sold dressed are pitched into a bucket, usually the bottom cut from an oil drum. A bailing scoop made from a cut-off bleach bottle, a spare gasoline tank, and a spare oar or two complete the outfit. On his person, the fisherman carries a netting needle for quick repairs and a folding pocketknife.

Ohio Valley fishing craft are designed for utility and ease of building. Perhaps because fishing boats are soon encrusted with a smelly layer of fish slime and spilled bait, they are rarely perceived by river folk as things of beauty.

FOUR

Hoop Net Fishing

An Ohio Valley fisherman must master a wide variety of skills. Most fishing information is either transmitted traditionally or learned through trial and error. Although the tools and techniques are traditional, the fisherman must be flexible enough to innovate if he or she is to succeed. These days, much of the skill and knowledge a fisherman needs concerns the hoop net or barrel net, which is the central artifact of the river fisherman. In the last few decades, the hoop net has regained its prominence as the most important fishing tool of the midwestern commercial river fisherman.

In much of the English-speaking world, including the East Coast of North America, hoop nets are known as *fyke* nets (from the Dutch *fuik*, meaning trap), and that is the term used in the technical literature of fishery science. In England and in the Great Lakes and the rivers of the Midwest and inland South, the term *hoop net* is far more common, especially among the fishers themselves.

Although it covers a small area, the hoop net is easily handled by one person and can be moved about with little effort when its catch declines in a given spot. When the net is set, tail anchored, mouth downstream in flowing water, it holds its shape in the pressure of the current. Its convenience and its adaptability to both baited and baitless fishing make it the ideal tool for the small-scale commercial river fisherman. The hoop net is an efficient device for catching catfish, especially when baited with a strong-smelling substance, such as waste cheese or "soured" (fermented) mussel meats or seedcake. For catfish, bait must be strong-smelling. Waste cheese rind from cheese factories is purchased by the barrel from fishing gear suppliers. Seedcake baits are most effective for scale fish. Fishing regulations favor hoop nets over potentially more efficient gear, such as gill and trammel nets.

Although hoop net fishing is strikingly convenient, success depends upon mastery of knowledge of fish movement, bait preference, and water and bottom conditions. It also depends on such skills as net preparation and repair and, in many places, on the navigational skills necessary to locate unmarked underwater gear.

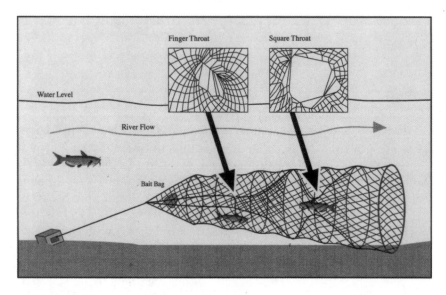

Figure 4.1. Hoop or barrel net, set baited

Orval Loven lifting a hoop net in the Wabash River, near Grayville, Illinois, 1978.

Most lower Ohio Valley fishermen can identify with Matthew Vaughn of Cairo Point, who describes himself as a "hoop net fisherman." Despite seasonal and conditional fluctuations in efficiency, full-time year-round fishermen, such as Tommy Sherer, always keep some hoop nets in the river. In Sherer's words: "It's your bread and butter of your commercial fisherman, is the hoop net. In the river, where you got current all the time, you can't fish anything else. Most of the year I've got them in there all the time."

Most Ohio River fishermen fish blind, but there are many fishermen on the smaller streams, such as Wabash River part-timer Orval Loven of Grayville, Illinois, who mark their nets with bleach-bottle floats. This make them easier to find, reducing the time needed to be on the river. In the past, fishermen all marked the positions of their nets with floats, but the increase in outdoor recreation has brought many more people to the river and a tremendous increase in thievery. The practice of fishing blind is believed by some to have been originally invented to outwit conservation officers. It is practiced many places in the world.

A basic hoop net consists of a set of hoops over which a cylinder of netting is stretched. One end (the tail) is tied in a point, the other end (the mouth or head) is open. Within it are usualy two throats. These are funnels of carefully knitted twine mounted inside the net. Their narrow openings are suspended by two or more lengths of twine at the center of their portions of the net. Fish swim into the wide opening and out the narrow opening and are thus confined inside a closed-off chamber.

Willie J. Carver explains it this way: "They'll go in that first throat and then they'll hit the other throat and go back in there, and the reason they don't get out in there–it's very seldom one gets out after he's in–because they fight the side of that net. They don't hit that hole [in the throat] there. They could if they had sense enough to hit that hole, but they get in there, they fight that side of the net like a redbird in a cage."

Fishermen can purchase complete hoop nets ready-made in various sizes. Many do when they are in a hurry, despite the expense, because of the time it takes to make one's own. More common is the practice of buying ready-made hoops and webbing and then assembling or "hanging" the complete nets, both to save money and to ensure that the nets are made to one's specifications. Most fishermen prefer to knit the all-important throats themselves. Ohio Valley fishermen usually buy supplies by mail-order from Memphis

Net and Twine Company or Nylon Net Company, both of Memphis, Tennessee.

On the Ohio River, all-purpose nets usually have 1½-inch mesh webbing on the tail (the chamber beyond the second throat) and two-inch webbing on the head (the chamber between the two throats). Hoops are usually thirty or thirty-six inches in diameter, and the nets themselves are usually fourteen to sixteen feet in length.

The first or square throat on most hoop nets is mounted on the second hoop and has a square hole secured by tying four strands of twine to the fourth hoop. The second or finger throat is mounted on the fourth hoop and has a flat opening secured by two pieces of twine tied in slip knots at the tail of the net. When the lengths of twine are loosened, they allow the inner throat to fall back, as that portion of the net is raised over the bottom of the boat, letting the fish fall into the head of the net, from which they are easily shaken.

Fishermen categorize the plain and unmodified hoop nets in use on the river. First in importance is the all-purpose net, often called simply a hoop net or barrel net or, if fished baited, a bait net. The typical example has seven hoops and two throats. Second is the much smaller fiddler net, similar in structure but sometimes having as few as four hoops. Smaller fiddler nets have a hoop diameter of from twenty to twenty-four inches and a total length of eight to twelve feet. They usually have from five to seven hoops and the same two throats found on all-purpose nets. Occasionally a fiddler net will have only one throat. The third type of hoop net is the much larger buffalo net, longer with larger hoops and a larger-mesh webbing. Most Ohio Valley examples have the usual seven hoops and two throats. All-purpose nets and buffalo nets are sometimes made with a D-shaped first hoop at the mouth.

Several modifications of the hoop net are occasionally used. Among them are the lead net, which has a long wall of netting or "lead" to lead fish to the opening of one or two hoop nets. Another is the heart net, in which a heart-shaped pen (the "heart") made of walls of netting opens into the hoop net. A third is the heart and lead net, in which an attached lead first directs the fish into the heart. Yet another combination, known as a wing net had two leads extending outward from opposite sides of a hoop net's mouth.

When Orval Loven was a young man, he used to accompany older fishermen on winter brush-clearing operations in nearby bottomlands. The cleared areas were marked with tall stakes, and when spring floods arrived they set leads and hoop nets along the stakes.

They set the leads parallel to the riverbank so that when the water level fell, fish were stranded behind them, an operation that would be illegal today.

For many years, Kentucky prohibited the use of less than a three-inch mesh on hoop nets, effectively shutting off the main stem of the Ohio River, the lower Tennessee and Cumberland Rivers, and northern Kentucky Lake and Lake Barkley from legal commercial fishing for small catfish, except by box trap. Mesh sizes down to one inch were permitted by the early 1990s.

According to fisheries scientist C.H. Augur, hoop nets designed for fishing with bait were patented as early as 1844. They were still a curiosity in the Mississippi basin by 1893, but by 1899, after waste cheese became available, they were common in the Mississippi. Tommy Sherer never saw a baited net in the lower Ohio Valley until 1940, when they appeared in inland Illinois waters. He claims to have brought them to his part of the Ohio.

All-purpose and fiddler nets are usually set baited, although unbaited all-purpose nets sometimes catch catfish quite well during spawning runs. The bait is usually placed in a cheesecloth bag tied inside the tail of the net, with its tie-strings tied to the net itself.

The foul smell of waste-cheese bait permeates docks, boats, nets, and the fishermen and their clothing, so much that the smell of fish is overpowered. Most fishermen are very self-conscious about this and believe that it detracts from their reputation. They are quick to criticize any fellow fisherman whom they do not feel is keeping the odor under control.

Early this century, hoops as large as seven feet in diameter on nets up to thirty feet in length were used on buffalo nets, although five- or six-foot diameters and twenty- to twenty-four-foot lengths were more common. Such nets had to be handled by two or more fishermen. Harold "Pat" Patton remembers that fishermen once installed a pair of rails, or "ways," on the steep bank of the Little Wabash in Carmi, Illinois, for raising them.

Today buffalo nets are rare. Four feet is the largest hoop diameter, and sixteen to twenty feet is the range of length. Most have 2- to 2½-inch-mesh netting. Buffalo nets usually use only square throats, with the inner throat fastened with enough slack to turn itself inside out when the net is raised, letting the fish fall out. They are not set baited, and the fish enter them, presumably for shelter or to seek mates during "spawn run."

Fishing with hoop nets consists of running a line of nets along a stretch of river. A line is the set of nets that are fished at one time, and a rig is the entire stock of nets, including those out of use for repair or change in season. Numbers in a line or rig vary substantially. During the 1940s, an average fisherman kept a rig of ten to twelve nets. Roy Lee Walls's uncle had a rig of twenty-two nets in 1927, which made him a "big fisherman." After widespread adoption of outboard motors in the 1940s and low-maintenance nylon in the 1950s, rigs got larger: forty to sixty were common. Harold Weaver remembered running a line of one hundred fiddler nets in the Ohio in the early 1960s. Tommy Sherer maintains that a full-time professional fisherman needs a rig of between forty and sixty hoop nets, two-thirds all-purpose and the rest fiddler nets. About five or six buffalo nets will supply any sudden demand for scale fish. Part-timer Orval Loven, who fishes the Wabash, runs a much smaller rig. The following is a typical evening net run in the Wabash River in the early fall:

➤ On a warm day in October, Orval Loven leaves work on a floating sand dredge on the Wabash River at 4 P.M. He motors a sixteen-foot aluminum johnboat from the dredge to the mouth of Bonpas Creek at the foot of Main Street, Grayville, Illinois. Tied up along the bank of the creek are seven small floating sheds–fish docks. Each one has at least one live box raised and lowered by a winch through its deck. Two have hand-lettered signs advertising fish for sale. One of these, obviously closed up and no longer in use, is connected to a power line and displays a large sign.

Loven ties up his boat to one of the fish docks, walks ashore across a narrow plank, climbs in his pickup and drives home for dinner. An hour later he is back at the creek bank. Unlocking the door of the fish dock, he scoops up a load of cheese scraps from a pasteboard barrel and dumps them into a five-gallon bucket. He loads the bucket and a gas can into the boat. Out of the bed of the pickup, he hauls three newly hung hoop nets attached to homemade anchors he made by bending and welding pieces of steel concrete-reinforcement bars. Already in the boat are a clutch of bleach- and antifreeze-bottle floats, coils of nylon rope, and the lower half of a large plastic drum. Loven starts his motor and heads downriver toward the tall concrete pilings of the Interstate 64 bridge. The sound of the motor drowns out the chugging of several small oil wells on the floodplain on the Indiana side of the river, but not the sound of semis tearing over the bridge. He speaks loudly over the noise of the motor and the highway. "River's low for this time of the year. We usually start getting some rain by now. We will soon, I'm sure. Seems like it gets them to spawning. Then we won't need to bait the nets. They'll just come right in then."

A short distance downstream from the bridge, he cuts the engine. Using an oar to steer, he drifts up to a floating bleach bottle, catches it by hand, and begins to pull in the rope that was a hoop net's tail-line. Eventually it hauls up the closed, pointed tail-end of a hoop net. He drags the whole net aboard and unties the twine that holds the tension on the net's throat. He shakes his head in dismay. "Three carp! Who needs 'em? I eat a few once in awhile. They're really quite good if they're fresh, but hardly nobody'll buy 'em. Trouble is, a few of them get in the net and the catfish don't wanna come in."

Loven puts fresh bait in the bag, reties it and the end of the net and the throat, and feeds the net back into the river, pointing the closed end upstream. He lets it out one hoop at a time, stretching the mesh between hoops, so that the current will catch it and hold the net open, mouth downstream.

Orval starts his motor and heads a little further upstream until he is under the Interstate bridge. Here he catches another float and hauls in another net. This time it contains a few small catfish. One of the hoops has broken and partly collapsed. This net is loaded into the boat and one of the new ones he has brought from shore is baited and set in its place. As Loven works his way up the river to Grayville, he hauls eight nets and lands a total of twenty marketable catfish. Eighteen are "fiddlers," immature channel cats, and three tasty but ugly flatheads. He spends about an hour and a half on the river.

Lately, Loven has been selling most of his fish to neighbors and acquaintances in town, dressed and frozen, so he is not using the live box that he lowers into the creek through the inside deck of his fish dock. On its outside deck is another live box, also out of use, that he has made for carp, which cannot be kept together with other species or the carp will kill them. At times tavern-owners and fish-marketers further south have bought them, but not in the last few years. After landing, Loven dresses and skins the fish on a little drain-fitted table inside the fish dock. Above the table is suspended a hook on which he hangs the fish by its gill cover while he skins it with a pair of fisherman's tongs. He then drops the dressed fish into a plastic sack to bring home and put in his freezer. He leaves the fish dock, and heads home. ◖◀

Hoop net fishing in the lower Ohio Valley varies with season. Sherer, who fishes the Ohio and some of its chutes in the Cave-in-Rock vicinity, indicates that there are regular seasonal changes. The regular channel cat and fiddler run starts in mid-May and lasts until about the beginning of July. At that time, he sets all-purpose nets without bait, mouth downstream. Most effective are waters near rocky banks, where fish search for hiding places. Sherer sometimes puts a male in the net to decoy females or "sows." Other fishermen use a sow to lure males.

Highfin are also spawning then, so if one seeks them, one places the nets on muddy bottoms. During July, Sherer gradually starts baiting his nets. Fishermen believe that catfish are not attracted to bait until water temperatures reach 60°F. On a day in late July, Sherer explains:

> As soon as the catfish spawn's over, that's when I go over to the bait net. You have to bait the fiddler [and all-purpose] nets then to be effective. I just gradually start baiting a few of them as I go along, moving them around and getting them in the good places where I know the channel catfish frequent more. Most of the time, you try to work the head of the bars, where there's good, clean, hard gravel bottom. This time of year, it seems the channel cats prefer that to anything else. I don't know whether it's because of the microscopic organisms that grow in the gravel or what it is, but they prefer that bottom to any other type. I baited four last week. So far, I've got just a few fish out of them, but I hadn't had time to move them around to locate a place to really catch them. This morning I raised a net that I'd been catching spawning fish in, and it had two nice channel cat in it that had already spawned. I dropped a big bag full of cheese in there this morning. Now, probably the next time I run that net, if the channel cat are there and work in on the bottom, I'll have several channel cats in there when I pick up the nets.

During late summer, when the temperature reaches into the nineties, catfish stop feeding and become dormant. Hoop nets are then relatively useless, unless a batch of fresh water, such as from an upstream storm, flows into the area. As the water cools in autumn, baited-net fishing again succeeds. This is also a good time to set unbaited buffalo nets, as buffalo begin seeking shelter. All-purpose nets set in deep holes and along rocky banks catch many flatheads. This period of fishing is called the fall shelter run.

Because of danger and uncertain return, most fishermen cease fishing in winter. High prices inspire a few to continue. Sherer reports winter success baiting nets with well-rotted shad. Roy Lee Walls explains that fiddlers will bunch up in certain areas during very cold weather and that carefully placed nets occasionally bring large hauls. He runs lines of ten to fifteen hoop nets all winter and reports about two good hauls per week at that time.

In early spring, buffalo and carp spawn, and fishermen with a demand for scale fish will then set buffalo and unbaited all-purpose nets where the fish are trying to get into the shallows. Leads, hearts, and wings are then most effective.

Tommy Sherer is a firm believer that detailed knowledge of bottom and water conditions is indispensable:

> Right now I can go out there and put out ten nets, and tell you exactly what kind of fish I'll catch out of every one of them, if I put them in different localities. Put them close to the bank this time of year, all you get is some game fish, bluegill, crappie, and bass–stuff like that. You go on a mud bottom, throw a little cottonseed in them, you catch a fill of white carp [highfin] or carp, just like that, and a few white perch. Ordinarily your perch are a clean bottom fish . . . the same as your roachback buffalo. . . . Channel cats prefer clean bottom. . . . Now, you do have sand reefs, where sand will reef up maybe four feet high. As soon as the river pools out, then you work those reefs. It mixes oxygen in it, same as it will going through wickets in a dam. That's the reason there's so many fish there in the summertime. The water is oxygenated real heavy. And when the river gets dead in the summertime, you'll find those places where the river's rolling over, because it's mixing oxygen in it all the time. It's churning that-a-way. . . . The more prolific places is where there's more oxygen in the water. You must have that oxygen in the water, to have a concentration of fish, because you can't have a heavy concentration if you don't have enough oxygen to support them.

Because the newer high-lift dams do not oxygenate the water, fishermen now run their nets no less than every twenty-four hours, as mandated by law. During warm weather, they may run them every twelve hours. During very cold weather, they can be left for three or four days without killing fish.

Raising a net full of fish without damaging the net, losing the fish, or injuring oneself takes skill. Matthew Vaughn explains:

> If you don't know how to do it, you'll break every hoop in it. . . . You gotta roll them in, and that saves your hoops and is easier on you, too. There's a sleight to any of them, if you can get them. . . . You go down the front. That's to keep your fish from getting out. Start there and go to roll, just about two hoops at a time, then you go gather up another one, until you get down to the fish in the back. And you get to them, and maybe the other guy'll have to help you lift them in, but, as I say, I've lifted in some pretty good ones myself, because I knew how to do it.

Because hoop nets are so similar in appearance, many fishermen modify them for identification. A lost net may thus be recovered. Orval Loven has a unique knot that he uses for knitting, repairing, and attaching netting to hoops. Roy Lee Walls reports that on his part of the Ohio, he and other fishermen use distinctive colors of nylon rope on their nets' anchor lines.

Since the introduction of nylon in the late 1940s and early 1950s, fishermen no longer have to undertake the tedious, strenuous, and dangerous task of coating nets with hot tar every two or three weeks. Vats of tar were melted over an open fire, carefully, to avoid a conflagration. Splashing bits of tar burned the skin as the nets were lowered, one by one, by block and tackle, into the vat, lifted out and shaken or beaten to shake off the excess tar before it hardened. In the words of fisherman Bill Williams, "That nylon was the best friend the fisherman ever had." Nowadays nets are periodically coated with a solution of tar in mineral spirits, marketed as "Texaco Netcoat." This helps keep the knots tight, strengthens the fibers against abrasion, and blackens the netting, making a hoop net seem more like a natural object on the riverbottom. Willie J. Carver explains: "If you don't tar them nets, you don't catch no fish anyways. If you put it out there, just white twine, you ain't catching well, they see that thing, but if you tar that son-of-a-bitch, they just think it's a damned old log and go right in."

Local retired fishermen and the wives and daughters of fishermen sometimes specialize in netmaking. Herbert Sharp's daughter, Cindy, used to make them for members of her family and would be paid a share of the proceeds from the catch of each of her nets. Most local netmakers buy finished machine-knit webbing and attach it to hoops, either bought or homemade. Almost all make their own throats. During slow times, some fishermen knit their own webbing from twine. Thus the skill of net-knitting is still alive in the Ohio Valley. Specialized hoop nets, such as Smithland fisherman Ira Gene Bushey's turtle traps, are usually locally made from twine.

The most exacting part of hanging nets, as their assembly is called, is making (called knitting) the throats, usually a square and a crowfoot on each all-purpose hoop net. The knitter must know how to taper the throat correctly, depending on hoop size, throat length, and type of throat. In the words of Emil Bushey (Ira Gene's father), "The throat of a net is the main thing. If you don't get a good throat, you don't catch good." Many fishermen maintain that the throats on the purchased ready-made hoop nets are inferior. Harold Weaver believed that the longer throats made in recent decades are an important innovation, "Make a long throat, and once he gets in there, he'll stay in there."

The skill of knitting is also especially important for the repair of inevitable tears in the nets, as Orval Loven can attest:

► On a crisp sunny Saturday afternoon in early November, Orval Loven sits on a stool in his back yard. Suspended from a tree limb above him are three large all-purpose hoop nets, sixteen feet in length, and four feet in diameter. Two of them are black, having been treated with Texaco Netcoat. They have seven hoops apiece. They show signs of wear and have obviously been in use. The third is white and untreated and has only five hoops. Loven is seated by the white net. On the ground next to him are two homemade, olive-colored, four-foot-diameter, fiberglass hoops and a homemade throat. His skillful hands hold a wooden netting needle, a universal fisherman's tool resembling a weaver's shuttle or bobbin, loaded with fine multifilament nylon twine. With the needle, he ties the webbing of the net to the lowest of the five hoops. As he completes the job, he ties a knot and pulls out a cigarette lighter. With it, he melts the frayed ends of the nylon twine. "Just two to go, now, and I got me another net, soon as I get that throat in there. Now, the reason we call this an all-purpose net is that you can bait them and catch catfish in them, and the mesh is small enough to hold fiddlers too, but you can also set them for buffalo and other scale fish. It's got a big enough throat."

The net has only one throat in it, its mouth attached to the

An all-purpose hoop
net in Orval Loven's
back yard, Grayville,
Illinois, 1978.

fourth hoop down and its tail end tied to the tail end of the net.
Like many fishermen who hang their own nets, Loven prefers
to knit his own throats from twine in order to get the dimensions and tension that he has found most successful in the
waters where he fishes. "Sure, I can knit a net as good by hand
as they can by machine, but why should I? Takes too long!
Sometimes, in the winter, if I haven't got enough to do, I'll knit
webbing. Course that's the way the old timers used to do it. . . .
It'll be a while before I get this next throat hung up in there
right and the rest of them hoops on there too. I'm going to need
those other two nets on Monday, so I better get to fixing them."
    Loven picks up his stool and moves it a few feet so it is next
to one of the black hoop nets. The line holding its tail is draped

Orval Loven fastening webbing to the hoop on a hoop net, Grayville, Illinois, 1977.

over the limb and its free end is tied around the trunk of the tree. He unties it, lowers the net about half of its length, and ties the line to the tree again.

He picks up another netting needle, with lighter gauge twine. He also picks up a "block," a small block of smooth-sanded, rounded-cornered wood about one-half inch thick, exactly one and one-half inches wide and about two and one-half inches long. The block is used as a gauge to make sure that the mesh is consistently the right size, one and one half inches. He lays the tools on the ground, within easy reach.

Loven turns the net a bit until he faces a round hole about eight inches in diameter. With a sharp pocketknife, he trims loose ends of webbing twine back to their knots. He explains how one must start by trimming back to a three-strand knot, then proceed around the edge, trimming further back to produce a circle of two-strand knots and then end with another three-strand. That corrects the tension, as you knit the mend. Loven says, "Now, I've fooled with ropes all my life, and with strings and tying. If I've been tying and I've seen somebody else tying a knot, I've learned how to tie it."

Loven picks up the needle in his right hand and begins to tie it to the first three-strand knot. With his left hand, he picks up the block, inserts it in the space next to the knot, and ties the twine around it. Traditionally, net-knitting knots are square or reef knots, but since the introduction of nylon, which is much slipperier than cotton or linen, the square knot is no longer reliable. Instead, Loven and other fishermen usually tie the more complicated sheetbend, which they call a mesh knot or fisherman's knot. He works his way down the hole, moving the needle and the block along the way. At the junction with the old webbing, he adds an extra loop, making it a double knot. After a little more than five minutes, the whole tear is closed. The black net now has a white panel knitted into it. Again using his lighter, Loven seals the loose strands where the new webbing was tied to the old. He then raises the repaired net up in the tree and lowers the next one that he will be working on. ▰◀

Hoop nets must be cleaned regularly. If they are too full of leaves and trash, fish will not enter them. The fisherman hoists the net up in a tree and beats it gently with a carpet beater or a broom. Infestations of sand fleas can be overcome by placing the nets in deep anaerobic mudholes for a few days. Buildups of organic debris can be removed by soaking the nets in a weak lye solution.

Most hoop nets in the lower Ohio Valley are made with split white oak or fiberglass hoops. The ones installed in ready-made nets are usually fiberglass, and cottage craftspeople make fiberglass hoops (which first appeared in the late 1960s). Orval Loven fabricated his own motor-powered machine, consisting of a set of axle-mounted plywood dies upon which he molded the fiberglass. He learned this by visiting several hoopmakers' shops in West Memphis, Arkansas.

Occasionally hoop nets are made with metal hoops, usually hollow galvanized-steel tubing. Some fishermen make their own with heavy-gauge wire. Metal hoops are more common in small fiddler nets and in turtle traps.

Many fishermen prefer wooden hoops. They are of the opinion that the fiberglass ones are subject to abrasion from the river bottom when used in current. The rough surface of the abraded hoop then, in turn, abrades the webbing itself, causing it to weaken or tear.

Most commercially sold wooden hoops are made by craftspeople in the White River Valley of Arkansas. Making wooden hoops is a specialized craft that only a few fishermen bother to master. James "Harry" Linville of New Harmony remembered a houseboat family who floated down the Wabash seasonally during the 1920s and 1930s preparing rived wooden hoops. which they sold to other fishing families. Harold Weaver and his father did the same, floating down the Ohio. Until 1977, Virgil Gray of Princeton, Indiana, operated a small net shop where he also made split white oak hoops. Before 1970, most of the hoops used in the area from Cave-in-Rock to Cairo were made by O.B. Cash of Wickliffe, Kentucky. His operation is still legendary, because he used a mule to pull splints through a die in order to smooth their edges. Emil Bushey had a motor-powered die that did the same thing.

When Harold Weaver retired, he taught hoopmaking to his friend, Owen Miller of Rosiclaire, Illinois, and left him his tools:

►● Owen Miller loves to remember the days when Harold Weaver lived in Cave-in-Rock. Miller has been a fisherman, on and off, most of his life, but he also works in the local fluorspar and zinc mines.

His next-door neighbor, Walter Ramsey, was also a lifetime fisherman, but because of poor health, he turned over his gear to his son, who sometimes fishes with Miller. Miller learned most of his fishing knowledge from Weaver and Ramsey. "Weaver was a good old buddy. `Bring along a six-pack of beer,' he'd always say. He built that shaving horse. Told me which kinds of wood to choose. . . . I'd take him along in the boat and he'd tell me right where to fish."

During Weaver's later years, he fished less frequently and spent much of his time preparing gear. It is not only Weaver's fishing and gear-making knowledge that Miller misses. It is also his ability to entertain. Weaver had a reputation, from Old Shawneetown to Paducah, as the finest story and joke teller, singer, and all-around raconteur on the river.

This June morning, Miller is making white oak hoops for hoop nets. He is working second shift in the mine, so he has to get as much work done as possible by midafternoon. On the ground are several old galvanized house gutters. In them, covered with water, are five-foot lengths of quartered white oak log, which he will rive further to make hoops. He explains the type of wood to choose for this process, as he had learned from Harold Weaver. "They've got to be paper-bark white oak, in pretty good timber. Occasionally you find a good one. It's gotta be straight as a gun barrel. Can't have knots."

He explains a controversy about whether northern or southern exposure timber is best. In his opinion, the northside wood is easier to split evenly, but the southern wood is tougher. He definitely prefers wooden hoops to fiberglass, believing their elasticity holds the netting at the right tension.

Miller is also an experienced smith, a skill he learned in the mines. At the fluorspar mine where he is presently working, they let him fabricate some of his own tools in their shop, and he makes several drawknives there, as well as some steel hoops which he uses as forms for shaping wooden hoops. The wood he is working today is several weeks old. To keep it from seasoning prematurely, he keeps it under water. "You gotta make them with green wood and cure them. They don't bend when they're dry. . . . The idea of riving them out and whittling them with a drawknife [is] you don't cut across the grain. You cut across that grain and bend them, you break them."

He stands one of the quarter logs diagonally in the space within the riving horse, which is shaped like a capital A tipped on its side. Miller beats the frow into the timber with his maul, first separating off the heartwood, which he discards. The hoops are made from sapwood. As the frow works downward, he grabs the upper piece of wood that is splitting off and pulls at it to tear it free, the rest of its length. He is left with two lengths, one quarter-circular, the other roughly square.

He then stands the square length in the horse and attacks it with the frow and maul. Again, after working the maul part way downward, he pulls the pieces apart with his bare hands. For the next hour and a half, Miller repeats this process, until he has about thirty rough splints (called splits). He puts them back in the gutters to keep them wet.

After a break for a cold pop, Miller takes one of the splits out of the gutter and places it on his shaving bench. He sits on its seat with his foot on the hinged lower timber that in turn pulls the upper piece downward, holding the split in place, as he

Owen Miller splitting white oak for hoops, with a frow and maul,
Rosiclaire, Illinois, 1978.

shaves it with his drawknife. When it is smoothed to his satisfaction, he lines it up with a mark on the bench and trims off a
few inches of extra length with a hatchet. He then carefully
tapers each end with the drawknife. Each split is half the
circumference of a hoop. When its ends are joined, the tapered
ends overlap, without overhangs, which could hang up the net.
For the next couple of hours, Miller works at the shaving bench,
producing a supply of smooth, even splits. At times when he is
making a larger quantity of hoops, he uses an electric planer to
do much of the work, but it does not do as precise a job as a
drawknife.

Miller begins the job of bending splits into hoops. These
hoops are for an all-purpose net, with a four-foot diameter
mouth. He pulls out two splits, places them against a block of
wood on the shaving bench, and lines up the tapered ends so
they overlap exactly. Holding them in place with one hand, he

puts two small finishing nails through the overlapped joint, turns it over, and clinches the ends. He then bends the two splits into a circle and joins the free ends the same way. He now has a green oak hoop, four feet in diameter.

With a few taps of the hammer, he forces the hoop snugly into a steel hoop only slightly larger than the wooden one. He has about a half hour left before he has to grab his lunch and leave for work. In that time, he makes two more hoops, each one slightly smaller than the previous, and forces them inside each other. When he has seven concentric wooden hoops inside the steel outer hoop, the assembly is set aside to cure for a week, before the hoops are taken out to be hung into nets. "Weaver made the prettiest hoops," says Miller, "perfectly round and evenly thick." ◀●▶

Tommy Sherer makes hoops together with his Tolu neighbor, Bill Tinsley, but he prepares his white-oak hoops somewhat differently. Tinsley has permission from a Hurricane Island property owner to fell an occasional straight, knotless, white oak tree, the best kind for hoopmaking. He bucks them into five-foot lengths, hauls them back to Tolu, and then quarters them with a frow and maul, before working them into splits. Sherer and Tinsley make each hoop from two splits. Instead of using a steel hoop as a die, they form them around circular sets of blocks that are nailed to a wooden table. The bundles of half hoops are set aside to season for several weeks. After they are seasoned and toughened, they will be nailed together into full-circle hoops. Held in a circular position while seasoning, they will be quite rigid when they are ready to use.

Fishermen also often make their own net anchors and grappling hooks. Steel concrete-reinforcement bars are a common raw material used to make these items.

A completely different type of hoop net, called a turtle trap, is used for catching turtles in swamps and farm ponds. They are legal only in Kentucky. One variety consists of three or four round four-foot-diameter hoops and a single square throat. A more efficient model was invented by Ira Gene Bushey. It consists of four rectangular steel-wire hoops and a single square throat. He says that it is less likely to be moved by the thrashing of a load of turtles than are the round traps. He and his father, Emil, make the traps together. They are like hoop nets but with rectangular steel-wire hoops and heavy-gauge webbing, which his father knit into two-inch mesh

Tommy Sherer at the shaving bench, smoothing splits for hoops, Tolu, Kentucky, 1978

from coarse nylon twine. Commercial webbing is not strong enough to withstand the powerful snapping turtles. Here is how Ira Gene Bushey runs his turtle traps:

➤ At about eleven o'clock in the morning, Ira Gene Bushey drives his pickup to Chestnut Lake Swamp near Ledbetter, Kentucky, just east of Paducah. In the bed of the pickup is the empty lower half of a fifty-five-gallon drum, a pair of hip boots, and a plastic bucket containing about a dozen carp. Early this morning, he removed the carp from several gill nets set in the Ohio River below Smithland Lock and Dam. The swamp is near the point at the confluence of the Tennessee and Ohio Rivers, but neither river is visible in the heavily wooded area. It is a typical southern cypress swamp, with tapered trunks, great roots, and cypress knees protruding above the water upon which floats a green scum of duckweed.

Bushey parks the pickup on a bank next to the swamp, gets

out, and pulls on the hip boots. He scans the swamp and points out a few places where a bit of netting tied to a cypress knee or root or a stake shows above the water: "You can see them just jerking around a little bit. They've got turtles in them, all right."

Bushey is running a line of net turtle traps he set the day before. He wades into the uninviting swamp and heads for the first trap. He unties it from the tree root, pulled up the stakes holding down its mouth, and hauls it toward shore. From a distance, one can see several large, black objects moving around in the trap. From the strain showing on Bushey's face, it is obvious that the trap and its contents are heavy. Bushey steps ashore and hauls the trap after him. In it are three large, vicious-looking snapping turtles, clawing and hissing. He pulls it a few yards from the bank to the rear end of his truck. Then he unties the closed end of the trap, picks it up by the throat end, and shakes it out. Three angry turtles tumble out on the ground, hissing and snapping. Bushey deftly picks them up, one by one, from the rear of the shell, and drops them into the half drum.

He then selects one of the carp, slashes its side to make it bleed, puts it in the trap, and closes the trap's end. He wades back into the swamp, attaches the trap at a new location, and wades to the next trap, hauling it ashore. In about an hour, he has run eight traps. One is empty, and one contains six. He has caught eleven turtles. The largest is about three feet long. While he is picking up one of the turtles and explaining how to handle it safely, it rears back and bites him on a finger. Before going back into the swamp, he improvises a bandage by tearing a piece of rag and tying it around the finger to stop the bleeding. One of the nets is damaged, so he stows it in the truck bed. Soon he is driving back to Smithland.

In the back yard of his house is a large, round galvanized tub, the type used for watering cattle, which contains eight turtles from the previous day's haul in nearby farm ponds. He care-fully moves all eleven into the pen, one by one. With nineteen turtles, he is now ready to drive to St. Louis to market them, about a four-hour drive each way, a trip he usually makes about once a week. He gets between eighty cents and a dollar per pound for live turtles, and he estimates that he has between 400 and 450 pounds of turtle in this load. In Bushey's words, "You can handle that money a lot easier than you can handle them turtles." ◄►

Ira Gene Bushey dumping snapping turtles from a net turtle trap, Chestnut Lake Swamp, near Ledbetter, Kentucky, 1978.

Many fishermen never use any gear other than the hoop net, and it is unlikely that a fisherman could succeed at any but the most marginal part-time fishing without mastering its preparation, use, and repair. Those who master the hoop net are the only fishermen likely to be able to continue the traditional occupation of commercial river fishing.

FIVE
Fishing with
Hooks and Lines

Fishing with hooks and lines is an ancient and universal practice. It involves some of the most modern techniques used in commercial fishing, as well as practically all sportsfishing. In its simplest form, it consists of a baited hook attached to a piece of line held in the hand. Stanley Murphy of Metropolis, Illinois, occasionally fishes buffalo in the Ohio with doughball-baited handlines during spawn runs. Hooked baited lines are also attached to overhanging tree limbs or roots, in which case they are called droplines, bushlines, or limblines.

Use and abandonment by casual part-time commercial fishermen causes serious problems for other river users. Tommy Sherer explains that a change in water level can leave hooks hanging at face level, where they can injure anyone riding by in an open boat. Asked if he ever fished with bushlines, Sherer replied, "I haven't stooped that low yet." At times when chemical or fuel spills into the Ohio have driven many of the fish into small tributaries and fishing in the main river is closed anyway, some serious commercial fishermen will resort to bushline fishing.

When fishing for turtles, some fishermen employ the equivalent of droplines. They attach large hooks, sometimes hand-forged, to pieces of rope and bait them with scraps of meat or chicken.

Fishermen sometimes attach hooks and lines to floats and set them adrift in the river, retrieving them later. These are called juglines when hollow floats are used, or blocklines when floating blocks of wood are used. Retired Coast Guard light-tender Carl Eswine of Shawneetown used to drift as many as seventy-two juglines while tending navigation lights from an open skiff. Turk Curtis, a fisherman and marketer in Cairo, still puts out juglines when running hoop nets and picks them up on the way back. The Ohio has very little current in that area, so the jugs do not drift very far. He uses number five vegetable cans, soldered shut and painted black.

Angling is fishing by holding a pole with a hook and line attached to it. When running hoop nets in the fall, Sherer may angle for catfish near submerged or floating logs. Laurel Millis of Golconda used to angle with cane poles for skipjack at an old Corps of Engineers dam, back when these fish made an annual spawn run in the Ohio. He remembers catching a washtub full an hour. Dennis Lueke sets rows of poles on the Wabash River's steep banks during the early part of the spring catfish run.

Ohio Valley fishermen may also deploy rods and reels for commercial river fishing. They use short fiberglass rods, one or two feet in length, to catch fiddlers during the summer. Two fishermen in a boat can sometimes catch hundreds of pounds in a day. Many short-rod anglers are seasonal part-timers who fish the Cumberland and Tennessee Rivers below Barkley and Kentucky Lake Dams' spillways.

The most characteristic form of commercial hook-and-line fishing in the lower Ohio Valley is the use of the multihooked set jumperline or jumpline, as done by Herbert and Earl Sharp near Smithland, Kentucky:

►● Herbert and Bonnie Sharp and their son, Earl, live in a large old house on the riverbank. Like many riverbank people, they fish, trap, and do other seasonal work. During much of the year, Herbert and Earl are full-time commercial fishermen, working together as a team. Both Herbert's and his wife's parents were nomadic river fisherfolk. "I'm a houseboat girl!" Mrs. Sharp says proudly. "I've traveled up and down the river for about five years in one. Right along here, up the Tennessee and up the Cumberland."

What is unusual about their fishing is that they often use jumperlines, common enough among part-timers and subsistence and recreational fishermen, but rare among full-timers. They have found a way to make the method work for them, despite its being considered uneconomical by most professionals.

One of the economic drawbacks of jumperline fishing is the cost of bait. Another is the fact that fish are not necessarily biting. This is especially the case when longer periods of extreme cold or warm weather make them dormant. "Right now, they're just laying," says Herbert. Late July is usually not a particularly productive season for the line fisherman. But the Sharps find that live bait would sometimes entice even the

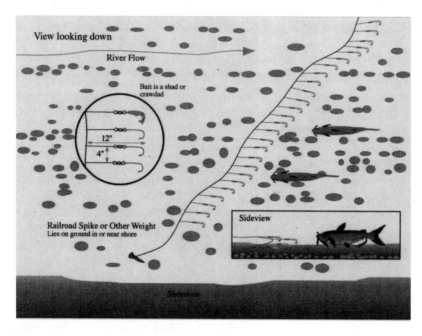

Figure 5.1 Jumperline (portable trotline)

Earl Sharp rowing, Herbert Sharp holding a jumperline, Cumberland Island Chute, Ohio River, near Smithland, Kentucky, 1978.

laziest fish. Lately they have used crawdads (crayfish), which are expensive to buy, but the Sharps have access to ready sources by seining nearby swamps and farm ponds. In the spring they use shad guts to attract hackleback. "Them hackleback look just like a damn lizard, but they sure are good eating, and Jackson's market'll buy all we can catch," Herbert says. When the fish stop biting on one bait, they change to whatever other bait is available. The Sharps used to catch lake sturgeon in the spring, before they became locally extinct.

The Sharps start out at about 4:30 A.M. Finishing their coffee, they head out the back door toward the river, carrying a pair of oars, a grappling hook, and a life jacket. They pull their sixteen-foot wooden johnboat down the steep, muddy bank. Two days ago, Barkley Dam had released a large flow of water from last week's thunderstorms. When the Sharps landed the boat, the river had been considerably higher. Now it is low again. After the boat hits the river, Herbert straps on his life jacket and climbs in, sitting down on the bow thwart. Earl stows the oars, climbs aboard, picks up one oar, and shoves off. Then he sets the oars in their locks and proceeds to row downstream along the shore. They are in the Cumberland Island Chute, with Kentucky aport and Cumberland Island to starboard. After about twenty minutes of rowing, they reach a wide place in the chute. The sky starts to turn bright red in the direction from which they came. Earl rows across the chute. "I see it over there," says his father.

The falling water level exposes the shoreward end of a jumperline, including a stake and three hooks. Earl rows over to the bank, and his father grabs the line with one hand and picks up a piece of lumber from the bottom of the boat with the other. As Earl rows away from shore again, Herbert slowly pulls the line aboard, avoiding the hooks, all of them bare, and winds the line around the piece of wood. The sky lightens a bit more and everything is bathed in beautiful orange. After a few yards, the line starts to wiggle. "I got something there, now!" says Herbert. A few hooks later, a two-foot-long catfish breaks the water's surface. Herbert dislodges the hook and throws the fish in the bottom of the boat. As he works his way up the ninety hooks on the line, he finds six more catfish, all of them smaller. At the far end of the line is a railroad spike sinker.

By now, it is almost six o'clock and the sun has risen, although it is not yet visible above the trees on the wooded shore. The fog is lifting from the river, which looks as if it is steaming. "Pretty out here on the river, ain't it?" remarks Herbert Sharp. One can hear the churning of diesel engines from a river tug, coming from beyond the island.

The boat crosses the chute several times as the Sharps work their way back eastward toward Smithland. They take in six lines. When a fish appears to be on a hook, Earl grabs a large homemade dip net and plunges it into the water below the fish before his father hauls it out of the water. He then lands the fish using the net. By eight o'clock, the sun shines brightly, haze has replaced mist, and the Sharps have landed thirty-two catfish and an eel. One of the cats is almost three feet long, and another is scarcely smaller. "That's got to be at least a twenty-pounder!" declares Earl. As they haul the boat ashore, Herbert talks about keeping costs down.

"Lot of fishermen think they got to have this, have that, just to fish. You know, we can get around just as easy in this here chute with a pair of oars, as with a big outboard motor. Lot cheaper too. Now, we'll use it when we go out net-fishing in the river, but most of the time, this is all we do."

Today's catch consists mainly of channel cats, two flatheads, which the Sharps call yellow cats, and one of the catfish that are locally called niggerlippers. Sharp says he sells most of the last to his older brother, who resells them in Old Shawneetown.

Bonnie Sharp and two grandchildren come out to look at the catch. Herbert dangles the eel at his grandson and teases him. "There he is, Herb! Herb, look at that! There's that snake! Get him! He's trying to bite!"

"You ever fry one of them eels in beer?" asks Mrs. Sharp. "You get you up a batter with beer and let it set up a little while, then you roll them in it and deep fry them. Just a batter, sort of like a flour batter. I never used to eat any at all, until he had me fix them like that and it's really good."

Then they start talking about getting some more carp and white perch, which they feed to their hogs. They explain how hogs acquire a strong fishy taste when fed fish. They must take the hogs off their fish diet several weeks before butchering them. They use most of the carp and white perch they catch as hog feed. Later in the day, Herbert and Earl go to Paducah to sell fish to Roy Jackson's market.

A jumpbox and jumperline baited with "minnows" (shad fry), Saline
Landing, Illinois, 1978

In the evening they sit in the kitchen, taking crawdads out of
a picnic cooler and attaching them to the hooks on six jumperlines. Each line is carefully mounted on a square, notched box
called a jumpbox, with a hook dangling down from each notch.
By now, several hundred hooks are each graced with the wig-
gling body of a crawdad. As twilight approaches, they head out
on the chute again.

After Earl rows a little way up the shore, Herbert picks up
one of the jumpboxes. Unlike many jumperline fishermen, he
does not really "jump" the line, that is, he does not toss a
weighted end into the water and let it pull the line after it.
Instead, Earl rows up the beach and Herbert gets out. With a
piece of scrap wood, Herbert stakes the end of the line in the
sand and feeds out part of the line. The first ten or so hooks are

empty. As Earl rows away from shore, Herbert carefully feeds out line until they came to the end, about three hundred feet from land. The end of the line is tied to a railroad spike, which he tosses overboard. The next morning at dawn, they run the lines again. ◣◀

When Herbert and Earl Sharp fish with their jumperlines and jumpboxes, they use a variant of the device that fishery literature calls a longline or trotline. The fisherman using only a few lines can dispense with the jumpbox. Ohio Valley people call them simply trotlines (locally pronounced "troutlines") when they are not used with a jumpbox. Some net fishermen will set trotlines or jumperlines here and there while running other gear, because baited hooks will sometimes catch catfish at times when few are going into nets. Barney Bass Sr. of Vincennes ties trotlines to bushes or tree roots along the Wabash and White Rivers at times when they are more efficient catfish catchers than his usual hoop nets. He does not jump them from a jumpbox. Instead he feeds the already-baited lines from coils called birdsnests.

Although the Sharps propelled their boat with oars, most jumperline fishermen use a motor, and many say that jumperline fishing became far more efficient after the widespread motorization of boats after World War II. Some fishermen used to notch the gunwales of their boats in order to jump a line. Jumpboxes and similar devices are used throughout the world. A variant of the jumpbox used in the Midwest is tray-shaped, about four feet in length and a foot wide, with one outwardly slanted side, which has the notches. Some say that it does a better job of keeping the lines in order, but it is awkward to carry more than a few at a time in a boat. Ira Gene Bushey still prefers trays, but he sets his jumperlines a few at a time, while running other gear.

The trotline and jumperline consist of a mainline or headline, to which shorter lines, called stages, are attached. One hears other terms for stages, such as *stagings, droppers, offshoots,* and *tugs.* A freeturning swivel attaches each hook to a stage. Nowadays swivels are purchased commercially. In the past, fishermen made their own by bending two nails together, or they did not use a swivel at all. Without a swivel, a trotline or jumperline is much less efficient. Serious commercial fishermen who use jumperlines buy their own nylon twine, swivels, and hooks and assemble them themselves. They also make the jumpboxes out of plywood and one-by-two-inch lumber.

The lines are weighted with railroad spikes or large machine nuts. Some fishermen mark them with floats, but this risks theft. Fishermen usually set lines on the bottom at a right angle to the current. Laurel Millis sets a zigzag line of jumperlines across a navigation channel, with lines connecting them, so that he can run them in succession.

Hooks and lines of any kind are simply not economical for fishermen who have to purchase their own bait. Only when bait is freely available is it worth it for the commercial fisherman to use hooks and lines. Serious jumperline fishermen use store-bought minnow-seines, and some make their own scoop nets from hardware cloth, all for catching bait. Two fishermen will seine a sandbar in the big river for so-called minnows (actually gizzard shad fry) or a farm pond for crawdads. In late June and early July, there are often many "catalpa worms" (larvae of the catalpa sphinx moth) available, and in late August, grasshoppers are caught by dragging a minnow seine through a grassy meadow. Another bait sometimes used is cut bait, cubed pieces of nonmarketable fish, such as carp or white perch. After musselling season, "soured" (fermented) mussel meats can be used as bait.

Tommy Sherer fishes with a jumperline in the early spring, when the water is high and the fish are avidly biting. At that time earthworms are also easy to procure. He will occasionally set jumperlines in July during catalpa worm season.

It is also possible to outfit a jumperline with tufts of untwisted nylon rope fibers, for use as lures. These are called fuzzy tugs. Harold Weaver, who retired to Antioch Harbor, Tennessee, used fuzzy-tug-mounted jumperlines in Kentucky Lake. He said that they were especially attractive to large blue cats, who feed by sight.

Some fishermen believe that various locally concocted liquid baits will attract fish to a hook, sometimes even obviating the need for real bait. Most commercial fishermen consider liquid bait, or doodle oil, as it is often called locally, to be a hoax; some, such as Weaver, have made their own concoctions and sold them to unsuspecting part-timers and sportsfishers. Interestingly enough, a copy of the famous nineteenth-century Pennsylvania-German conjuring book, *The Long Lost Friend,* found in Cave-in-Rock, contains a liquid bait recipe guaranteed to attract fish to "hook, nets, or the fisherman's hand."

Many, if not most, jumperline fishermen are part-timers, and their efforts are not taken seriously by full-time professional fishermen.

Sherer's words summarize this view: "They're fishing for the fun
of it, anyway. They go out there, and put out ten or twelve lines,
and when part of them get tired of running them and go home, why
the rest of them pick them up, run them, bait them. That's just the
way they operate."

However, consistent successful jumperline fishing also takes a
great deal of skill and knowledge. Not only does the fisherman need
to know how to fish, he or she must also know how to obtain bait
and prepare and maintain gear. On a cool gray day in April, Clifford
Durham of Old Shawneetown, Illinois, taught his daughter-in-law,
Charlotte, how to manage jumperlines and jumpboxes:

> ►● Durham's Fish Market, which floats on a barge in the Ohio
> River beyond the Old Shawneetown levee, is owned by
> Clifford's brother, Howard. Clifford, like his brother, used to
> fish for a living. As he got older, he turned over much of his
> gear to his son, John, and his daughter-in-law, Charlotte, whom
> he calls "Pinky." Many river fishermen got their start by setting
> and running lines for more experienced members of their
> families.
>
> Hanging from a tree limb in Clifford's yard are several large
> hoop nets suspended above a vat containing hardened black
> preservative. On the top of an old steel drum is a pile of
> jumpboxes with twine and hooks hanging in a jumble. On
> another drum, Charlotte does her best to untangle a snarl of
> nylon twine, rusty fishhooks, and railroad spikes. Clifford
> inquires of her, "Got them straightened out?" Charlotte re-
> sponds, "Yeah, I hope so," adding, "Some of the kids knocked
> them all over and, boy, they got them in a mess."
>
> Charlotte and her husband intend to use fishing to supple-
> ment the income from his regular job. She says, "We're just
> starting in, mostly, me and my husband and his sons. Just been
> trying the rigs and trying to start making it on this." She then
> talks about the difference between the efficient jumperline and
> the casual fisherman's trotline. "Yeah, you bait them up and put
> them out. This [jumpbox] makes it easy for them to go out.
> Clifford made the frames. He's the fisherman, mostly, around
> here. Makes it easy to throw out. John wants to put them out
> today at suppertime. Clifford made the whole works, line and
> all."
>
> Clifford observes that it takes time to prepare a jumperline.

An experienced gearmaker, however, can make two or three a day. "Like what they always say, 'Hook, line, and sinker.' Get about six, seven, or eight of these [lines] and you got to be pretty fast to get them all done. I put about ninety hooks on each."

Charlotte hopes for a good catch because a local politician, who just won an election, plans a fish fry at nearby Big Lake. "Him [Clifford] and his brother [Howard] are furnishing the fish. Right man got it, he said he'd have a fish fry for us, and the right man got it. He's gonna have catfish, that's what we're hoping for. Hope for fiddlers. They're best kind of fish we can get. I hope it's plumb full of catfish. . . . Ninety fish out of ninety hooks, that'd be a pretty good day."

Clifford says, "If you're fishing pretty heavy, sometimes you get across them, sometimes you'll get one on every hook for maybe four or five hooks and then you might go out there on twenty-five more hooks before you catch another one and then get more after that. . . . The longer you're at it, the better you get."

They discuss the bait they use for the lines—crawdads, worms, cut bait, and even, in the past when it was available, P&G Laundry Soap. Clifford comments, "They say that fishing is a lazy man's job, but they're wrong about it."

Charlotte pulls up another jumpbox, one that has obviously not been in use for some time. It needs new hooks, as the ones already on it are rusted beyond redemption. "Got to get some stuff to make some new lines for it, too." she observes. "Swivels is rusting off too."

She painstakingly untangles the disarray of lines, hooks, and sinkers. She talks about heading for the river with her husband in the evening and trying to supplement their net catch with the lines that will be ready, by setting the lines farther out in the river channel. Clifford explains how it is done. "Well, you got to watch the current on them. You give them too much current, they get away from you, they go on downriver. There's a lot of drift in the bottom of the river. Leaves and trash, fish, logs too, big logs, and a lot of that stuff when you get it out in the current, that stuff's all moving down the stream. You get enough on one of them lines and he goes, it'll break them. . . ."

Clifford muses about the shortcomings of cotton, as opposed to the virtues of nylon. "Fishing steady, about every three, four weeks, we had to take them up and let them dry during the day, before we put them out. We just leave them, why they'd rot out in a week or two."

He complains about the rising costs of commercial licenses: "Yeah, you got to have a license, cost you fifty dollars, then it's fifteen dollars for what they call a block of tags. But you get ten tags with it. And if you want any more tags, it costs fifteen dollars for ten more tags, you can't get them one at a time, either. First day of January you got to fix you up with a license again. Yeah, it costs me, I expect, a hundred dollars."

A car drives by, and a man waves. It is John Durham returning from work. Charlotte sets the two unscrambled jumpboxes aside and starts out for home. ◂●▸

Hooked lines can also be used to snag fish, without any bait or lure. The simplest method of all is jerking or grabhooking. When fish are very numerous in a particular place, such as during a buffalo spawn run or when a shoal of spoonbill are feeding, a fisherman can drag a jerking rig through the water and catch fish. A jerking rig consists of a weighted main line about eighteen feet long, to which five to ten shorter lines, called hangers, are attached. During the coldest part of winter, when fish are not feeding but are bunched up in deep holes, jerking can be a way of catching fish to meet sudden demand. Laurel Millis has been quite successful jerking spoonbill in the summer, sometimes bringing in several hundred pounds in an evening. Some fishermen use a heavy, saltwater-type rod and reel to aid with raising and lowering. Some part-timers use a rod and reel to jerk for fiddlers, when they are numerous in the summer below dam spillways.

Far more efficient than jerking is the use of a set snagline. A snagline is similar in structure but different in dimensions from a jumperline. Its hangers are usually about two feet long, and they are most efficient when spaced four to nine inches apart. The fisherman sets them across a current or from the bank out into deeper water so that they make a curtain of sharp hooks through which fish have to swim. Their depth depends on the species sought. One end is often tied to a root or a piling and the other anchored. Baiting a snagline is illegal, but some fishermen will occasionally bait about every fifth or tenth hook.

Snaglines are legal only in the larger waters of Kentucky and Tennessee, and they are prohibited entirely in Illinois and Indiana. Ken-

Harold Weaver with a
snagline, Antioch Harbor,
near Paris Landing,
Tennessee, 1978.

tucky law mandates that hangers be eighteen inches apart. This renders them inefficient, so they are rarely used in the lower Ohio Valley, except in the Tennessee waters of Kentucky Lake, where they can be closely spaced.

In the Ohio, buffalo lines are sometimes worth using. They are short snaglines, weighted to lie on the bottom, with short (usually six-inch) hangers set apart at the legal eighteen-inch distance, and fitted with triple hooks. Stanley Murphy has used them profitably in the Ohio, during buffalo spawn runs. As buffalo root on the bottom, expelling inedible objects from their gills, they become entangled. Murphy has caught nearly five hundred dressed pounds of buffalo in a week using this method. It only works in very slow current, such as is found in Kentucky Lake or the lowest part of the Ohio.

Like jumperlines, snaglines must be moved about. This can be done using a jumpbox, but it is more common to use a thin steel rod, from which the hangers are fed, when it is set. Fishermen run their snaglines several times a day, as fish die soon after snagging. Many fishermen consider snaglining too dangerous and labor-intensive to bother with. Herbert Sharp comments on its hazards: "I'll tell you, that's a dangerous way of fishing. You get one of them big cats on there on a line pulling with them hooks about eight inches apart, like I did. He'd have you dodging hooks over there. It could take me about an hour and a half to get him. Had one had sixteen hooks in him."

Set snagline-fishing, like jerking, is most useful for catching species such as buffalo and spoonbill that do not usually bite a hook. Large blue cats, which are attracted to shiny objects, will sometimes bite on an unbaited snagline hook.

Although hook-and-line fishing is more commonly pursued by part-timers, like Charlotte and John Durham, there are some full-time fishermen, like the Sharps, who can consistently make it pay, provided they have a regular supply of bait. However, even they must use other methods as well, as seasons and conditions change. The combination of jumperline and jumpbox has increased the efficiency of the casual fisherman's traditional trotline. And, under certain conditions, the snagline, where it is legal, can be a very efficient fishing device.

SIX

Rigid Traps and
Walls of Netting

Lower Ohio Valley fishermen use other devices besides hoop nets and hooks and lines to catch fish. These devices fall into two general categories: rigid traps and walls of netting. All are based on a combination of tradition and innovation in both fabrication and use. These fishing methods, like hoop net and hook-and-line fishing, are learned and communicated informally.

Throated fish traps made of wooden splints are ancient devices. On inland American rivers, especially in the South, fishermen wove rigid basket traps of split oak, and slave fishermen made and used them, sometimes to feed a whole plantation. Many travelers' accounts refer to fish baskets used in the pioneer Ohio Valley. Most of today's rigid traps are boxes or cylinders nailed together from wooden slats, usually called slat traps, box traps, or baskets.

In 1899, C.H. Townsend of the U.S. Fish Commission reported that Mississippi Valley fishermen used fyke nets of copper mesh, and he remarked on their long-lasting properties. Steel chicken wire or hardware-cloth traps were widely used during the 1920s and 1930s. Chicken wire was cheaper than the equivalent amount of twine needed to construct a comparable hoop net. Today wire traps are strictly illegal, but poachers still use them on a small scale.

Catfish fishermen still use cylindrical and rectangular slat or box traps, especially in the Ohio Valley. Most fishermen have made them at various times in their careers but today usually purchase them ready-made from the Memphis suppliers, who buy them from craftspeople in eastern Arkansas. The traps themselves are usually made of two-inch-wide slats of white or red oak.

The typical cylindrical trap used in the lower Ohio Valley is five or six feet long and eighteen inches in diameter. The rectangular type is five feet long, one foot tall, and one foot wide. Both types have one closed end and one open, and enclose two open cones of tapered inward-pointing sassafras slats called finger throats. Along

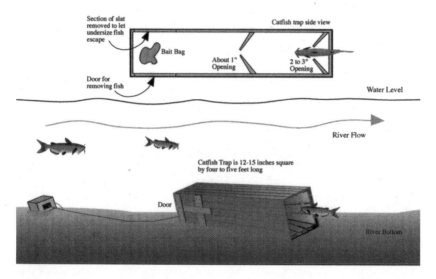

Figure 6.1. Box or slat trap

the side at the closed end is a removable door, held in place by a sliding wooden pin, out of which the captured fish are dumped. The major structural difference between the cylindrical and rectangular traps is that the latter's slats are nailed on to a supporting frame, whereas the former's are held in place by eight hoops, each made from a strip of wood. Four hoops are visible on the outside, with corresponding, slightly smaller diameter hoops in the same positions on the inside. Conservation laws require the removal of part of a slat on the side near the closed end, opposite the door, to allow undersized fish to escape.

The finger throats are the key element of a slat trap. Almost all fishermen agree that sassafras makes the best throats, and supply catalogues advertise that their traps have such. Fishermen believe that the odor of sassafras attracts catfish.

A finger throat consists of between ten and twenty-five carefully tapered slats, called fingers, whittled to a point. The wide ends are carefully carved to specific angles so that when they are fastened to the hoops or frame of the trap, they form two flexible cones. The opening on the outer throat is about three inches in diameter, the inner one, just under one inch. Catfish force their way through the opening. Some homemade traps have only one throat, or even a wire or netting throat, but most use two finger throats. Slat trap users believe that throatmaking is an exact art. Some fishermen rebuild the throats on store-bought traps, claiming success only with their own homemade throats. Emil Bushey explains: "Right there you can take a man making one of them baskets. He can take a piece of that wood and work it with his hands, feel of it. He can tell whether it's a good piece to put in the throat and *the throat's the main thing*. When you get that throat so you got it right, that thing's gonna catch fish, and if it ain't right, it ain't gonna catch them. You can hardly put them in there!"

Experienced slat trap users agree that the traps must be seasoned before they will catch fish. This is usually done by weighing them down and keeping them under water long enough to darken the wood. A new slat trap will not catch fish. According to Donald "Dutch" Moore of Cave-in-Rock, this is because of the acid (presumably tannin) in the wood.

Studies by wildlife agencies have found slat traps to be both highly efficient and highly selective devices, chiefly catching small fiddlers and flatheads. Bill Williams recalls raising traps literally bulging with catfish. However, some fishermen believe them to succeed only in certain waters. Orval Loven explains: "What'll work in one place ain't worth a dime in another. Right out here in the Little Wabash, the Whitstones, they fished out there for years. I made them four hundred dollars' worth of wood traps to catch the catfish in, well, they worked just fine. So I decided I'd make me some. I laid in and made me some, and they ain't worth the time it takes to make them in the big Wabash."

Slat traps are usually fished in the spring and fall. A fisherman runs a line of traps, as he does with jumperlines or hoop nets. Because of their bulk, it is difficult to run more than twelve at a time, if very many of them need to be moved. Their bulk, especially compared with collapsible hoop nets, is the main reason that more fishermen do not use them.

Fishermen usually run slat traps once a day in cooler weather, twice a day in warmer weather or if fish are plentiful. The trap itself is weighed down with a few rocks and tied to an anchor line, throat downstream. A trap is usually baited with a bag of cheese, soy, or cottonseed bait in the closed end. During the spawn run this is not necessary, especially once a sow catfish is in the trap.

Ira Gene Bushey is one fisherman who uses slat traps for fiddler fishing:

Bill Williams and a
box trap, Ragland,
Kentucky, 1978.

►● On a hot morning in early August, Bushey motors his johnboat away from the bank. The boat heads out the mouth of the
Cumberland River into the Cumberland Island Chute and
across the main channel of the Ohio, past the Smithland Lock
and Dam, to the mouth of Dog Island Creek, on the Illinois
side. He is in a hurry, wanting to run ten box traps, haul them
aboard, run four gill nets, and still have time to go turtling in a
swamp near Paducah, and if he gets a good haul of turtles, to
take them to market in St. Louis and still get home to Smithland before midnight.

"This'll be the last haul on those box traps. When it's hot like
this, it's like the fish, they just go dormant. I pretty much switch
over to just catching turtles, when it's like this. It means more
drives to St. Louie, but they'll buy all I can bring them."

The boat motors up the creek a few hundred yards. Looking

Ira Gene Bushey emptying a box trap, Dog Island Creek, Illinois,
near Smithland Lock and Dam 18, 1978.

for marks on the bank, Bushey casts a grappling hook a few
times, eventually snagging an anchor line. Pulling the line
brings in a five-foot-long rectangular box trap. After the trap is
in the boat, he opens the sliding. Six small catfish tumble out.
"I'm surprised there are any in there at all." After running five
traps in the creek and at its mouth and landing a total of fifteen
marketable fish, he heads upstream along the Illinois bank of
the Ohio. He carefully stacks the traps on the bow. Along the
shore he raises more traps. Here he is more successful, bringing
in about thirty marketable fiddlers.

"Water's deeper, colder out here," he says. "Usually we get
more in the creek, but not when it's hot like this. They just don't
seem to feed much in this kind of weather." Bushey rebaits the
five traps and resets them in the river. "Might as well see if
they'll catch me a few more fish." He then heads back downstream to run his gill nets.

Seining is dragging a wall of vertical netting through the water to
concentrate and encircle fish. The fish in the seine are then hauled

ashore or into a boat, or the concentrated fish are removed by hand
or with a dip net. It is one of the oldest and most widespread fishing methods.

Seining was once a major fishing technique on the inland rivers.
The typical river seine consists of a corkline or floatline, fitted with
cork or plastic floats, floating a wall of netting, which was, in turn,
attached to a leadline (pronounced "ledline"). The leadline is
weighted either by a lead core or a series of sinkers or leads (pronounced "leds") and the combination of the leadline and corkline
keeps the net vertical. The ratio of floats to sinkers determines to
what extent the whole net floats or sinks.

A number of factors have contributed to the decline in seining in
the lower Ohio Valley. One is the decrease in demand for scale fish.
Another is the decline in the spoonbill population, as almost all the
warm-weather seining was for that species. The building of high-
lift dams has moderated the depth fluctuations that once made seining convenient. The exertion needed to pull a seine and the fact that
it was always at least a two-person job has also contributed to its
demise. "It wasn't nothing but mule work," remembers Tommy
Sherer. Roy Lee Walls remembers a preacher-fisherman from
Olmsted, Illinois, who "pulled himself blind" hauling a seine in the
Ohio River.

A number of different sizes of seines were used in the lower Ohio
Valley. Early in the century, Ohio Valley seines were small, usually
one hundred yards by twelve feet. Some were even as small as fifty
or thirty yards in length, especially those used in smaller tributaries and overflow lakes. During the last years of seining's importance
(the late 1940s and early 1950s), seines as long as three hundred
yards and occasionally as deep as twenty-two feet were used. Finer
mesh seines caught more fish but were far harder to pull, and regulations usually set a minimum mesh size of two to five inches, depending on the locality and the dimensions of the seine. In this century, fishermen almost always purchased the seine-webbing and
then tied it to the floatlines and leadlines.

Until the late 1940s, seines were usually made of cotton and preserved every few weeks with a mixture of five parts crude oil and
one part coal tar. The last seines in use were nylon and needed only
an application of Netcoat preservative once or twice a season. Nylon seines had to be kept wet to maintain strength and durability
and were often stored weighed down in the river.

The use of seines necessitated keeping certain areas, designated

Oscar D. Weaver seining on the Ohio River, ca. 1930. Weaver is the man holding the net. (Photographer unknown; photo courtesy Sarah Weaver Clark.)

seine hauls, clear of debris to prevent seines from hanging up. The hauls were informally considered to be the private fishing grounds of those who cleared them, and other fishermen avoided setting gear there. Said Tommy Sherer, "If it were a regularly established seine haul, you didn't fish with other gear in it. You stayed out of it. I mean it was a common practice. Wasn't nothing against it or a law or anything like that, but it was just common practice, a courtesy, to stay out of a seine haul." Fishermen seeking scale fish sometimes "chummed" a seine haul with cracked corn or wheat a few days before seining.

Several different techniques of seining were described by lower Ohio Valley fishermen. Most typical was a team of three fishermen using a one-hundred-yard by twelve-foot seine and two boats. One of the boats was usually mounted with a platform, called a seine deck, across the bow, flush with the gunwales.

Quiet was extremely important. One motored only to the vicinity of the haul. Then one used oars, often muffled with burlap. A sealine was fastened ashore, and one fisherman stayed on the bank with a tied-up boat to hold and transport the fish. The other boat— the one mounted with the seine deck—had the seine carefully piled on the deck. It was rowed out to deeper water upstream from the haul. As the boat floated downstream, the fisherman on the bank let out extra sealine. As it reached the deepest part of the haul, a fisherman standing on the seine deck began "shooting" the seine, that is, letting it out, and the fisherman ashore began pulling on the landward sealine to bring the free end of the seine closer to the bank.

When the seine was played out, the third fisherman began rowing vigorously upstream toward the starting point, making a circle of the net and the sealine. Meanwhile, the fisherman on the deck shot the outer sealine as the boat continued toward the starting point. Once it was played out and the boat was still being rowed toward the starting point, the circle diminished in size. Rowing was then very difficult, and the fisherman on the seine deck tied his sealine to a cathead, sat down, and began rowing with a second set of oars. As the two fishermen in the boat rowed, the one ashore hauled his line. All three fishermen were by then exerting themselves to the utmost. Once the boat was close enough to the bank, one of the fishermen in the boat jumped or waded ashore with the boat's line. The two fishermen ashore alternately pulled the two sealines, diminishing the circle until they got to the net. One remained ashore to stack the net as the two got into the water and alternately pulled one, then the other end up on the bank.

Once the fish were concentrated and started jumping about and straining at the net, a fisherman fetched the other boat and brought it alongside. Fish were scooped out with a dip net or grabbed by hand and pitched into the boat. Experienced fishermen could station themselves a few feet apart and pull upward on the leadline, making a pocket of netting from which the third fisherman could grab fish and pitch them into the boat. As the two holding the net moved closer together, they raised a small pocket of fish and turned it over, dumping its contents into the boat. Eventually they pulled the seine ashore and carefully stacked it. The net was then carefully restacked on the seine deck of the first boat. This required coordination, one man stacking the corkline, another, the leadline, the third, the webbing. Were it done without tangling, the seine was ready for reuse.

Two fishermen could handle smaller seines. One tied the first sealine to a tree. Very large seines in use in the 1940s and 1950s often had additional sealines along the length of the net, to facilitate pulling each section ashore. Hanging up, or snagging on underwater debris, was a serious problem. It tore the net and released fish. Were the water deep, the fisherman had to dive underwater and attempt to free the net, a very dangerous task. Harold Weaver described one such instance:

> I'd just tie the boat to my corkline and pull all of my clothes off and jump overboard and go down there and get it loose from that hang. And I come nigh near about two, three times, getting tangled up in that webbing. One time I had barely enough breath to get to the top. I went down there with my clothes on, see? And I got the buttons caught and I guess them buttons are still in the bottom of the river down there. I tore them loose and I got the belt on my britches even hung up in it. Well, I put my foot on the webbing and just tore it loose. And I told them, I said, "I ain't never going down there anymore with my clothes on."

Under-ice seining, important in the colder waters of the Illinois and upper Mississippi Rivers, was rare in the Ohio Valley because the rivers there hardly ever froze over completely. When they did, a few fishermen such as the Busheys, who had learned the technique elsewhere, were able to take advantage of this difficult but highly productive technique.

Seining was seasonal. The relatively shallow water that made seining easier was more common in late summer. Overflow lakes could be seined most times of year, but they mostly yielded buffalo. Low-water periods in summer were good for seining spoonbill, especially at night, when they were concentrated in feeding shoals. One of the best times in summer was when the river was low, but the water was beginning to rise because of an upstream storm. Fish then crowded the banks to avoid the increase in current in the deeper water. In early spring, when chunks of ice floated downstream, fish of every species crowded the banks. However, seining was very difficult if ice chunks floated into the haul.

The tendency of fish to congregate in shoals along the banks during cold weather made winter seining highly productive for those willing to brave it. Winter seiners made large hauls of buffalo and carp. Even catfish, which normally avoided seines by burrowing into the mud, could be harvested in great numbers by cold-weather seiners. Harold Weaver remembered keeping a large lard can of boiling water over a nearby fire. Just before shooting the seine, he poured boiling water over it to thaw it enough to make it flexible to handle. Weaver recalled winter seining as being extremely painful.

Stories of great hauls of fish persist among older fishermen. Ohio

River fishermen remember 1,800-pound hauls of spoonbill and 6,500-pound hauls of mixed carp and buffalo.

Another important aspect of the memory of seining is that most older and middle-aged fishermen began their careers helping their fathers, older relatives, or neighbors seine. A child's first responsibility in the fishing trade was often rowing the boat that carried the fish from a seine haul. Present-day seining is largely limited to two people hauling a fine-mesh ten- or twenty-foot minnow seine through shallow water for bait.

A few lower Ohio Valley fishermen still seine under specific conditions. Bill Harrington, who operates a small market in Russellville, Illinois, sometimes seines the Wabash with his brother Don, if conditions are right and there is a large order for scale fish. Don explains: "You could seine anytime as long as the water's right and you got an order for fish. Ain't no use in you going out and catching a bunch of fish if you can't sell them. Somebody wants a big order, we just throw the seine on the boat and go up and catch them. If he can't catch that order through his hoop nets, we'll just take his seine and help them, see?" Roy Lee Walls and his son Jerry sometimes seine the scale-fish-rich Cache River and the shallows in the lowest parts of the Ohio.

Gill nets and trammel nets entangle fish as they try to swim through them, snagging gill-covers and forward fins. The fish are unable to go forward or back. The fisherman hauls the net aboard and removes the fish individually.

A gill net is a wall of netting with fine filament knitted in slack mesh, suspended vertically by a corkline (or floatline) and a leadline. On a trammel net, the lines suspend three separate walls of mesh, an inner one of fine slack mesh, like a gill net, and two outer layers of larger mesh, called walling. As the fish tries to swim through the larger mesh, it creates a pocket of the fine webbing in which it is entangled.

Gill nets of twine and plant fibers were used by both pioneers and Native Americans, and both gill and trammel nets appear in early Fish Commission surveys of inland rivers. They were not very effective until machine-knitting made mesh-size uniform. Because of the stiffness of natural fibers, their high cost, and the maintenance they demanded, they were uncompetitive against hoop nets and lines until the invention of nylon in the 1940s. The introduction of polyamide monofilament in the 1950s made them so efficient that

Jack Coker, Sr. and Jr., seining the Ohio River for shad jumperline bait, near Saline Landing, Illinois, 1978. *Below,* Ira Gene Bushey with a trammel net, Smithland, Kentucky, 1993.

they were outlawed in most areas. Today they are illegal in Illinois and Indiana. Gill and trammel nets (multifilament only) are legal in the Kentucky waters of the Ohio, Cumberland, and Tennessee Rivers. They were legalized at the urging of fishermen after the building of the large TVA impoundments, because other gear was less effective in still deep waters. Tommy Sherer noted, "That's the reason I put a personal push on the gill and trammel nets in this area myself, because I felt that in the wintertime they were needed for a man to make a living. They have helped considerably too."

Gill and trammel nets are easier to use than seines in the winter and are effective in catching spoonbill in large, open areas of water. The disadvantage of gill and trammel nets is that they have usually killed the fish by time the fisherman runs the net, except in very cold weather, so most of the year they cannot be used to catch fish marketed live.

Older fishermen using gill and trammel nets today remember when they first became common in the area. Some first encountered them fishing in the upper Mississippi or the Osage River of Missouri. Roy Lee Walls began using trammel nets in the early 1950s. He remembers some Wickliffe, Kentucky, fishermen knitting cotton trammel nets in the 1930s. He learned the techniques from a Wickliffe fisherman when contracted by the state to remove rough fish from Horseshoe Lake near Cairo.

Some fishermen buy gill and trammel nets "pre-hung" (assembled). Others hang the nets themselves, so they can be assured of proper dimensions, tension, and balance. Correctly hanging a gill or, especially, a trammel net, is far more difficult than assembling a hoop net.

Gill and trammel nets can be made in any practical dimensions, but regulations usually determine limits. Most trammel nets in the lower Ohio Valley are fifty or one hundred yards long and six, eight, or ten feet deep. Gill nets tend to be smaller, usually twenty-five feet long if fished set or anywhere from fifty feet to one hundred yards if drifted. They are, however, often ten or more feet deep. Minimum legal mesh size is four inches for gill nets and inner mesh of trammel nets. Outer walling of trammel nets is usually twelve- or sixteen-inch mesh.

For the sake of efficiency, most gill nets and some trammel nets are hung tied down, with vertical lines connecting the corkline to the leadline, across the webbing. Typically, a twelve-foot-deep wall of webbing is tied down with ten-foot lines (ties), creating considerable slack, called bagging. Most common is using ties three-quarters as long as the depth of the net. Because this slacks about half the depth of the net, fishermen call it "hung on a half basis." Tommy Sherer explains the advantages of tied-down nets: "It puts slack in that webbing. A fish hits it and it's not tight, he won't tear through or bounce off of it and go the other way, 'cause there's enough slack in it that he hits it, it'll pocket him or it will swirl around him and hold him." Depending on the fishing method to be used, lines attached to anchors and floats connect to the four corners of the net to anchor it below and mark it above.

Hanging a gill or trammel net is usually done on a nice day in a large open area. The fisherman purchases gill webbing or, for trammel nets, inner mesh and walling. Hanging a gill net begins with preparing corklines and leadlines in the proper weight ratio. Depending upon its use, a net is hung "to sink" (in other words, leadline on the bottom and corkline midwater) or "to float" (corkline nearer the surface and leadline midwater). One stretches the lines between two trees or posts and ties the webbing to them. Tommy Sherer believes it is rarely worthwhile for an active fisherman to hang his own gill and trammel nets: "You can knit them yourself and save a little money, but if you're going into it, if you're talking about an initial investment and going into it to start, you're better off to buy it already hung, 'cause you get to dilly-dallying around and it takes time to hang them, and the first thing you know, you haven't got your nets all hung and the fishing season passes you by."

Hanging gill nets is an important source of income for retired fishermen like Bill Tinsley, who have areas in their yards set up for the task:

▶● About four in the afternoon, on a hot, humid summer day, after helping Sherer make hoops, Bill Tinsley sets to work hanging hundred-yard tied-down gill nets for Sherer and his partner, Jim "Stoney" Stone, of Crayne, Kentucky, to use drifting for spoonbill on the Ohio River. Tinsley uncoils nylon rope from a cardboard spool, walks it to the proper length, and cuts it off. From another spool, he uncoils a length of lead-cored leadline and cuts it off. He ties the pair of lines between two trees. Each is about one hundred yards long, but the trees are only about half that distance apart, so he first hangs one half of the net, then the other. The webbing that Sherer uncrated in the morning was packed in an accordion fold. Tinsley carefully pulls out the flimsy four-inch-mesh and lays it out on the ground parallel to the lines.

He picks up a large plastic netting needle loaded with thin-gauge twine, grabs the far end of the webbing, and, using the needle, ties the edge of the webbing to one of the lines. He makes the ties at the apex of each mesh. To give them the desired slack, he ties them about three inches apart. Over the next hour or so, he works his way down the fifty yards of line. After a Coke break, he goes back to the beginning and starts hanging the other line.

When the entire net is hung with webbing, it is time to "tie it down." He attaches vertical lines every fourteen inches to both corklines and leadlines. Each is only two-thirds as long as the webbing is deep, thus slacking the webbing by about a third. Completing that, he fastens a set of plastic floats to the corkline, so that the completed net will hang vertically from the water's surface. The process takes approximately three hours. ◀█◀

Trammel nets, with their complex structure, are far harder to hang. Especially difficult is hanging the middle layer of gill webbing. The netmaker must tie with extreme care so that points of contact of all three layers correspond exactly and do not slip out of position. If this is not done correctly and the layers do not stay in place, meshes will not be parallel and slack pockets will not form. Such a net is said to have slipped, and it will not catch well. It must then be disassembled and completely rehung.

There are two basic techniques for fishing with gill and trammel nets. One is the set net method, in which nets are left in a particular place for a period of time and then visited periodically to remove whatever fish they have caught. The other method, called drifting, is similar to seining in that a fisherman uses a net to surround, enclose, and ultimately entangle a shoal of fish. The net is then brought aboard or ashore and the fish removed.

Fishermen use several methods of fishing with set gill and trammel nets. They are not effective in strong current and are most useful in lakes and large open impoundments. Fishermen use them when state conservation agencies issue special permits to remove rough fish from sportsfishing lakes. They can also be efficient in slack bays of flooded bottomlands during spring flood season and at points of confluence of great rivers. Matthew Vaughn set trammel

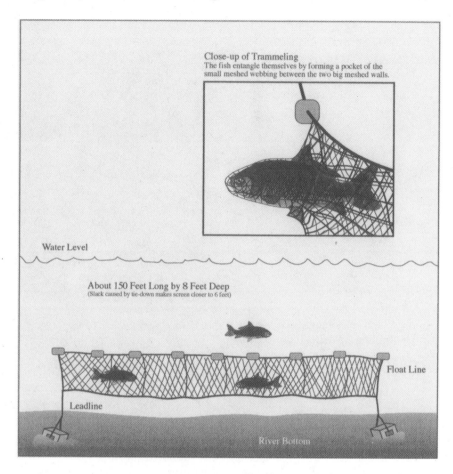

Figure 6.2. Set trammel net, hung to sink

nets with great success at the Ohio-Mississippi confluence at Cairo Point for years. Long, narrow overflow lakes are often fished with trammel nets. The fisherman sets a row of nets at one end of the lake. He then approaches the nets by boat from the other end of the lake, beating the water with a drain plunger to frighten the fish toward the nets.

They can also set the nets in deep holes in winter and early spring if current is not too strong. This is especially effective for catching buffalo, and for midwinter catches of catfish, which are otherwise nearly impossible to catch in very cold weather. When it is cold, nets are set close to the bottom, and as the temperature rises, fish-

Bill Tinsley hanging a
gill net to drift, Tolu,
Kentucky, 1978.

ermen redistribute floats and leads to fish closer to the surface. Bot-
tom-set gill or trammel nets are also effective for catching buffalo
during the fall migration season. In midsummer, Ira Gene Bushey
catches carp in floating gill nets in the Ohio to bait turtle traps. When
gill and trammel nets are set to float, the corkline must float a few
feet below the water's surface in order for the line to avoid snagging the propellers of boats passing overhead.

Although trammel nets are more efficient than gill nets, fishermen sometimes prefer the latter. They are cheaper. Being single-
walled, they are easier to handle and to untangle. It is also easier to
remove fish from individual mesh than from pockets of mesh that
form in the trammel net. Trammel netters carry a small dull pocketknife to help slip the fish out of their pockets. Sherer remembers
that an old-fashioned shoebutton hook was especially handy for that
purpose. In very clear water, fish are more likely to see and avoid a
trammel net, because of its two walls of heavier filament.

Drifting with a gill or trammel net (which is also sometimes called seining) is usually done by a team of two fishermen in separate boats. The method is most commonly used these days to catch shoals of spoonbill in the summer. Fishermen typically use a tied-down gill net, hung as if to sink, but with plastic jug floats added to give buoyancy to the ends. The middle of the net is kept at the water's surface by the tension of the two boats pulling against each other. Hackleback sturgeon are also drifted, but usually with a trammel net, as they do not easily entangle in a gill net.

Here is what a typical midsummer spoonbill-drift is like:

About 7:30, on a warm summer evening in late August, Tommy Sherer and Jim "Stoney" Stone stand on the dock of the Cave-in-Rock Fish Market. They load two eighteen-foot aluminum johnboats with gear. Into one of them goes two nylon 100-yard four-inch-mesh gill nets, which Sherer and his neighbor, Bill Tinsley, had specially hung the previous week. Every few yards, along the corkline, an antifreeze-bottle float is attached for visibility. Also loaded are two lanterns, gas cans, a spotlight, grappling hooks, a pair of binoculars, anchors, extra antifreeze-bottle floats, several large filleting knives, a large galvanized washtub, a water bottle, and an oar in each boat.

"Beautiful night," remarks Sherer, as he looks in the direction of the reddening sky. The river is unusually calm and quiet, and there is no breeze at all. One barge train passed, but its wake has already dispersed and the summer sportsfishers and speedboaters have long since tied up at marinas and docks. Sherer and Stone climb into the two boats, cast off, and sit down.

The quiet of the night is pierced by the noise of the two starting outboard engines. The pair of boats head southwest, full-throttle, crossing the main channel of the Ohio River, toward Hurricane Island. Between the island and the Kentucky shore is another channel, about half as wide as the Ohio itself, known as Hurricane Island Chute. After about twenty minutes of motoring, the boats enter the chute and immediately throttle down. After another ten minutes at slow speed, both cut their engines and begin to drift. Eddies turn the boats and begin to drift them toward the upstream end of the chute. Sherer stands up and scans the river with his binoculars. Stone is a few hundred yards closer to the mainland shore. No one says a word. After about ten more minutes, Sherer suddenly speaks loudly in

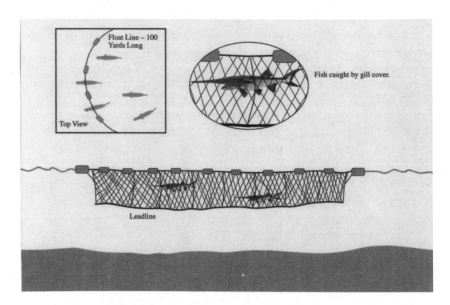

Figure 6.3. Drifted gill net, hung to float

Stone's direction. "See them up there, towards the point?" Stone nods vigorously. Less than a quarter mile back toward the chute entrance, but closer to the island shore, the water is filled with small, irregular ripples and an occasional dark object projected above the waterline. The activity is scarcely visible and not at all noticeable without the binoculars.

Both engines start, and the boats proceed, at low throttle, in the direction of the action. About two thirds of the way, Sherer cuts the engine and drifts for a moment. He notices that at this point the boat again drifts downstream. He gestures to Stone and restarts the engine. At slow speed, the two boats pull close together and give a wide berth around the place of all the activity, which seems to disappear. A few minutes later, they are upstream from it, and they cut their engines. Sherer hands Stone a line. As Stone pulls it aboard, with it comes an anti-freeze-bottle float and one end of the gill net. Sherer starts his engine and slowly motors toward the island shore, carefully feeding out the net. When he reaches the end, he cuts the motor again. Both boats now drift downstream. All is quiet for several minutes.

Suddenly there is commotion on the water again. Now they

can see the oarlike snouts of spoonbill breaking the surface, particularly when their lighter undersides show. Sherer picks up an oar and begins to paddle, standing up. The boat turns toward Stone's, and the net gradually makes a large arc around the fish. The bobbing of the floats indicates that the fish are making contact. Once the net is tightly stretched, both men start to haul their ends of the net aboard. Every few feet at first and then about every few inches, a spoonbill is entangled in the fine webbing of the net. Deft hands untangle them, occasionally resorting to the knife to clear an especially entangled fish. Unlike fish caught in a hoop net, the spoonbill are dead after being removed from the net. Sherer explains: "It's like they just give up as soon as they hit the net. They get real quiet. By the time we untangle them, they're about dead!"

The boats gradually pull together. They meet near the middle of the net, and the men finish removing its contents. Each boat now has a substantial pile of fish. "This is a good haul!" remarks Sherer. He estimates that they caught more than six hundred pounds of spoonbill in a single haul, an unusually good catch. Many of the fish are more than four feet long from snout-end to tail.

By now it is twilight, almost nine o'clock. Sherer and Stone cruise along the chute for about half an hour, shining spotlights out over the water. "We usually get a couple of hauls of an evening like this," comments Sherer. By 9:30, it is dark. "Let's quit!" shouts Sherer, and both boats motor toward the Kentucky shore. At Tolu Landing, there is a small barge tied up at a private ferry slip. Standing in their respective boats and using the barge deck as a dressing table, the two men behead and gut the fish and toss them into the washtub in Sherer's boat. Although it is now pitch dark, the landing is well-lit by a bright overhead security light. There are about eighty fish, and the tub is overflowing. Stone ties up his boat at a nearby dock and goes ashore, bidding us good night, as he gets into his pickup and drives home to Crayne. Sherer motors back across the Ohio to the fish market and hauls the tub of fish into a room in the market that is piled with crushed ice. He then locks up the market, gets back in his boat, and heads home to Tolu. ◀█

During cold weather, fish stay close to the bottom in deep water. Fishermen then drift their nets along the bottom. This works espe-

Tommy Sherer and Jim "Stoney" Stone removing spoonbill from a drifted gill net, Hurricane Island Chute, Ohio River, near Tolu, Kentucky, 1978.

cially well when the wind is blowing upstream, which causes fish in shallower water to shoal up and head upstream. But it presents additional problems because of the tendency of the net to hang on debris such as waterlogged tree limbs, boulders, or trash (all called hangs). According to Bill Williams, a gill net is only good for about two or three days of bottom-drifting before it needs to have its webbing completely replaced. For that reason, most fishermen only bottom-drift in areas known to be free of hangs. Some clear an area that they plan to use by dragging an old worthless net across it to locate hangs, which they then remove with a grappling hook. New hangs are often deposited after a precipitous rise in the river's level, necessitating a repeat of the process. Drifting or seining the bottom is usually profitable only in midwinter when wholesale fish prices are high enough to offset the cost of replacing and repairing damaged gear. Because it is almost impossible for one person to remove a snagged net from a hang, bottom-drifting is always done by teams of two.

A few especially skilled fishermen can drift alone. Bill Williams ties a long wooden staff (called a brail) to each end of the net. On the free end of the net, lines tied to the ends of the brail connect to the handles of a steel washtub, called a mule. To the upper handle of the mule he ties an additional line connecting to a float made of several plastic jugs. Careful feeding out of the floats, the mule, and the net itself into the current creates a tension that makes it possible for him to encircle a shoal of fish and haul the net back into the boat from its free end. Sherer can drift without brails or mule in waters that are still near the bank and swift farther out:

> What I do, I tie a jug on one end and run my net out, and put me a good line on the other end. Then I let the jug be in the swiftest water and it'll carry just about as fast as I can back down on the slow water side of my end. So you start at the bank and run your net out, and always on the bank side so you got the slowest water. I just take the inside next to the bank with the motor and keep it in reverse downstream, and the other end out in the swifter water'll carry it pretty evenly.

Ohio Valley fishermen consider gill and trammel net fishing the modern replacement for seining. It is more expensive in materials but cheaper in labor cost. Despite the expense, fishermen with the skills and the market are avid users. By fishing with gill and trammel nets, they avoid the difficulty, danger, and discomfort of wading around in the water pulling a seine. Fishermen agree that seining died out when gill and trammel nets were legalized. In Tommy Sherer's words, "I wouldn't trade one three-hundred-foot trammel net for two thousand yards of seine."

Serious commercial fishermen rarely engage in poaching or "outlawing" because the penalties are too high and would jeopardize their licenses. They do, however, often bend the rules regarding such matters as mesh size, number or spacing of hooks on a line, size limits of fish, and the prohibition of fishing after dark. Some part-timers and greedy sportsfishers will occasionally resort to the use of dynamite or M.80 fireworks to catch a mess of fish for a fish fry. Because of the mining industry in the lower Ohio Valley, explosives are relatively easy to acquire.

Commercial fishermen take a dim view of dynamiting because of its wholesale destructiveness, and they will gladly report violators to conservation authorities. In 1910, shell buyer J.F. Boepple complained that much of the Cumberland River had been depleted of fish by a few dynamiters. Despite their disapproval of dynamiting, river fishermen like to tell humorous tales of dynamiters out-

witting conservation officers. One version, collected from a fisherman on the levee in Elizabethtown, Illinois, goes, as follows:

> There's this bunch of old boys been fishing up in the Saline Creek with
> dynamite, and the conservation officer, he figures he's gonna catch them,
> so he hides up there in his boat and this one boy's got two sticks of dy-
> namite. Just when he's got the fuse lit, the warden comes out and says,
> "Hey!" So he hands him the dynamite and the fuse is still burning. He
> just takes one look at it and you know how nine times out of ten some-
> body hand you something, you'll take it without even looking at it? So
> he heaves it overboard and boom! Fish fly all over the place. That fellow
> just said, "Don't go getting on us for dynamiting no more, when you
> just done it yourself."

Spearing or gigging fish was once a major commercial method, but
it is rarely profitable for the commercial fisherman today. Donald
"Dutch" Moore used to gig carp for market from horseback with a
spear made from a boathook handle with a sharpened spike attached
to it.

It is illegal to shoot turtles, but this is also sometimes done by
those bringing snappers to market. Snappers hibernate in winter
and during summer droughts. At those times they are easily gaffed,
that is, pried from the mud with a hooked steel "gaffing bar," usually made from a concrete-reinforcement bar and sometimes bent
into a hook at the end. When ponds are low or dried out, one wades
into the mud and searches for the shells with the gaff, feeling about
in the mud until he hears a hollow thud made by striking a shell.
The turtle is then pried out of the mud by hand or with the end of
the gaff. Most of the turtles sold for stew in the German Catholic
areas of southern Indiana are acquired by gaffing.

Turtles are also trapped by placing a weighed-down and baited
barrel in shallow water, with a plank leading up to its edge. The
turtle climbs up the plank and drops into the barrel.

Use of conical cast nets was once an important fishing method in
some localities. As far back as the beginning of the century, they
were available from Sears catalogs. Willie J. Carver remembers how,
during the 1930s, he and his neighbors used to cast nets off the old
wicket dam at Leavenworth and sometimes bring in enough catfish, skipjack, and white perch to flood the nearby Louisville market.

At the peak of a cast net is a cork or plastic foam ball. Along its
circular lower edge is a leadline to which is attached a row of metal

rings. A purse line passes through the rings all around the net. Casting the net involves the whole body. After finding a visible shoal of fish, one holds the lower edge of the net at opposing points and the ball in one's mouth. One casts with a coordinated motion of the whole body, letting the ball go at a precise moment and quickly pulling the purse line shut to close off the fish's escape route. Assuming it has been done correctly, one then hauls in a load of fish.

Fred Killius of Olmsted, Illinois, may be the one of last fishermen to use the cast net, and he uses it only for bait fish for his jumperlines. He learned the technique on the Tennessee River in the 1960s and brought it to the Ohio.

Other techniques appear in the valley from time to time with limited success. Innovation among Ohio Valley fishermen occurs sporadically, and it is often "nipped in the bud" by conservation authorities, if it seems too efficient or insufficiently selective. Those fishermen who are least successful economically are often those who are most conservative and resistant to new tools and techniques. Successful full-timers are generally quick to adopt a new technique or a new modification of an old technique, once they hear that it works.

SEVEN

Musselling and Pearling

Many lower Ohio Valley fishermen mussel seasonally. A musseller must have an intimate knowledge of the river's mussel beds, knowledge that is often part of a family tradition. Unlike fishing, musselling can produce a substantial return in a short time, when shells are plentiful and prices are high. Mussellers live in or near areas where the resource is available for legal harvest, including portions of the Wabash and East Fork White Rivers, a limited portion of the lowermost Ohio near Metropolis and Joppa, and parts of Kentucky Lake and Lake Barkley.

Those accustomed to steady income from fish alone, usually those with retail markets or with regular wholesale buyers, rarely bother with musselling. Return is uncertain, and the ability to mussel depends on the investment of time, effort, and capital into specialized gear used for only a few weeks or days a year, and in some years not used at all.

Because of the precariousness of the resource, conservation authorities often prohibit musselling in certain areas or even an entire state for years at a time. Japanese mother-of-pearl buyers often prefer shell from other areas and buy Ohio Valley mussels only when other stocks are scarce. In most vicinities, the season extends only from late spring through late summer, during which there may be only a few weeks in which the river level makes musselling practical. These limitations make musselling an uncertain business.

Mussel meats were never part of the diet of local non-Indians, except in emergencies, such as during the Great Depression and by the Confederate Army of the Cumberland during its march along the Tennessee River. Nowadays mussel meat is too polluted to eat, but it is still used as net and line bait and occasionally to feed chickens or hogs. Don Harrington buries the meats in a closed canister and waits a month or more. When the canister is dug up and opened, the meats emit a strong ammonia odor. If the odor is strong enough to burn the eyes and nostrils, the meats are ready for use as bait.

Freshwater mother-of-pearl is thick, solid, and often beautifully iridescent. From the 1890s through the early 1950s, most mother-of-pearl harvested in the Ohio Valley went to make button blanks (buttons without thread-holes, which would be added later at the shirt factory).

There were button plants in many river communities, including Vincennes, Leavenworth, Loogootee, and Madison, Indiana, and Mount Carmel, Illinois. Some individual mussellers owned the tools for cutting blanks and operated a cottage industry. The basic equipment consisted of a motor-driven button saw, much like a small lathe. It operated like a lateral drill press. The cutter held the shell in place with a specialized set of tongs. A lever or a foot pedal drove the sawtoothed end of a hollow tube into the shell, coring out a disk of mother-of-pearl. The operator decided from what portions of the shell to cut the disk, depending on color, thickness, and density. Some of the larger button mills had more automated machinery, which worked on the same principle.

The pearl button industry disappeared in the early 1950s as nylon and polyester buttons became available. Not only were they cheaper but it was easier to drill four evenly spaced holes in a synthetic button. A few pearl buttons are still made in Tennessee for special purposes. Freshwater mother-of-pearl is also still used for handles of fancy pistols, for inlaying stringed musical instruments, and for costume jewelry. The Apco Company of Metropolis manufactures a mother-of-pearl aggregate called Lusterstone, used for aquarium gravel and as birdfeed additive. Apco also casts Lusterstone in polyester resin countertops.

Today, most commercially harvested freshwater mother-of-pearl is exported to Japan, where it is used by the cultured pearl industry. During most of the 1970s and 1980s, very little mother-of-pearl was harvested in the lower Ohio Valley. The Japanese preferred the product from the upper Tennessee and Cumberland Rivers in Alabama and Tennessee and from the Kansas and Missouri Rivers in Kansas. Some of the most desirable species in the Ohio Valley had begun to show discoloration, possibly from pollution. As supplies from outside the Ohio Valley grew scarcer, the market opened again, in 1988 and 1989. Most of the pearl shells from southern Illinois and Indiana are bought by Nelson Cohen of the M.D. Cohen Company of Terre Haute. Cohen operates a wastepaper recycling business and exports mother-of-pearl as a sideline. He is not optimistic about the future of supplies: "The future as it relates to this area is very bleak. We don't know where to go. I think the Japanese are not aware of that, but the American producers are not magicians. So far, we've managed to say, `We're running out,' but then we've come up with new locations, but sooner or later the new locations are going to have to stop."

The Japanese saw the shells into cubes and tumble them to make perfectly round beads, called seeds, about one-half centimeter in diameter. The beads are then placed inside pearl oysters and left there for about three years. Those oysters that survive the insertion leave a one-third-millimeter deposit of mother-of-pearl on the bead. The result is a cultured pearl, more than 90 percent North American freshwater mother-of-pearl by weight. American freshwater mother-of-pearl is the most desirable seed because of its color and density.

Freshwater pearls have also been cultured in recent years, most notably by John Latendresse of Camden, Tennessee, on Kentucky Lake. Latendresse's American Pearl Company markets a high-quality cultured pearl and exports major quantities of American shell to Japan. He and another Camden buyer, the Tennessee Shell Company, export most of the shells gathered from the TVA impoundments and the lower Ohio River, keeping several hundred mussellers active. The Camden weekly *Tennessee Trader* publishes a regular price report on its "Musseller's Corner" page.

Because of the differences in quality and color of mother-of-pearl, mussellers must be familiar with the various species of freshwater mollusks in the area. An elaborate and regionally inconsistent system is used to classify mussel species. Gemologist and pearl expert George Frederick Kunz commented as early as 1898 on the bewildering confusion of names for freshwater mollusks and listed many of them, including several that were racist and sexually explicit. Several lists of names have been published since, but they are not consistent.

The classification system in Appendix 2 of this book is based on interviews with the late Paul McDaniels (president of Apco and owner of Ohio River Shell Company), Nelson Cohen, and musseller Barney Bass Sr. and by consulting the literature. The scientific species categories are those that seem most likely.

The eastern United States once contained more than half of all the freshwater mollusk species in the world, but by 1975 40 percent of the species were extinct. Mussel larvae, or glochidia, parasitize the gills of fish, each species specializing in a particular species of fish. When local populations of fish disappear, so do the mollusks that depend on them. This has been the case with the valuable

A display of freshwater pearl mussels assembled for a high school science fair by Kent McDaniels, son of mother-of-pearl dealer Paul McDaniels, of Metropolis, Illinois, 1978. *Top row, left to right:* buckhorn, buzzard-head, rabbit's foot, mule-ear, monkey face; *second row:* yellow buckhorn, butterfly, stock sand shell; *third row:* niggerhead, eggshell, bullhead, pimple-back, pigtow; *bottom row:* pocketbook, maple leaf, three-ridge, washboard.

niggerhead (more politely called the ebony or black by biologists), which parasitized migratory skipjack, no longer ranging in much of the Ohio Valley. Most freshwater mussel species need the oxygenated water in riffles, so dammed rivers, like the Ohio and the lower Cumberland and Tennessee no longer support a diverse population. A few species, such as the maple-leaf, three-ridge, and washboard, seem to do well in impoundments.

Filter-feeding concentrates pollutants, to which most mollusk species are sensitive. Mussels are usually found in concentrations in certain areas, known as mussel beds, and the experienced musseller keeps track of their locations.

In 1990, musselling and buying shells were closed in Indiana because of a decline in numbers. Nelson Cohen speculated that several years would pass before they would be opened again. Illinois and Kentucky mussels were still being harvested in the early 1990s, and much of the Ohio Valley's musselling was then occurring on Kentucky Lake, Lake Barkley, and a few areas on the lowest part of the Ohio River.

Cohen and his Japanese customers classify exportable shells in two grades. The first is Wabash River maple-leaf, and it consists not only of maple-leaf but also of good quality monkey-face, pistol-grip, pimpleback, and eggshell, most of them rather small but with thick shells. The second grade is the White River washboard. These large shells, occasionally reaching a foot in length, were once a prime export shell, but they have deteriorated in quality. The rest of the species are either too rare, too thin, too low in quality, or too distinctively colored to become part of the export trade. The Camden, Tennessee, exporters use a more complex system, buying niggerheads, three-ridge washboard, pigtoes, and maple-leafs separately, differentiating between Cumberland and Tennessee River washboards, and also buying a "maple leaf mix." When shells are in high demand, Camden buyers will purchase mixed shells in two grades, "lake" and "river" (from impounded and free-flowing waters, respectively). "Lake" grade brings a higher price than river. They may also purchase, at the lowest price, reasonably good shells harvested dead or damaged, which are called "culls" or "scrap."

Discoveries of valuable pearls led to pearl rushes many places in the Midwest, South, and Northeast during the nineteenth and early twentieth centuries. Ohio Valley pearl rushes occurred on the Clinch, Eel, Little Miami, Mississenewa, Tennessee, West Fork White, and both the upper and lower Wabash. Greatest of these was the Wabash pearl rush centered around Vincennes and Mount Carmel, from around 1900 to 1907. Its greatest year was 1905, when $320,000 in pearls and mussel shells were traded in Vincennes alone.

Button blank factories established in the Vincennes area continued to buy and process shells from elsewhere in the lower Ohio Valley on a large scale until the end of the 1920s. Wabash pearls, especially those found earlier in this century, are still said to have the finest luster and greatest value of any midwestern freshwater pearls.

The Wabash pearl still has a legendary status and trade in these jewels is centered around Vincennes. The late Granville "Granny" Palmer of Vincennes acted as an agent for jewelry stores, appraising pearls and buying them from fishermen in southwest Indiana and southeast Illinois. Palmer explained his love for the local freshwater pearls:

People love pearls, the women and some men, but they really like a beautiful pearl, much more than a diamond. There's never two pearls alike in any way. You'll just never see them. They have their own i.d. on them, every one of them and I believe I'll see a pearl I saw four years ago and recognize it, because they're all in my mind. . . . Still, I've perpetuated this for love of what I'm doing. I took the time to do it and I still want to see the fellow on the river get the money for it, because he's the fellow that should get it. That's why I just love to get a real good pearl, give a thousand dollars for it and sell it for a thousand, I love to do that. There's a certain satisfaction in seeing that pearl go to a good home, where it'll stay in that family, maybe, especially if there's girls in the family. They pass them on and after those girls get grown they say, "Well, can I get one for my niece?" "Can I get one for my granddaughter?" People in Vincennes are very conscious of these pearls and with their whole life on the river, really, where they've had publicity on it. For one reason, they're the most beautiful pearls that's ever come along is out of the Wabash. You can't show me anything that pretty.

Palmer remembered the days when pearl buyers came from afar to buy Wabash pearls:

You could always make a living with a plain mussel shell. But if you found a good pearl, that was great, then everybody got drunk in that camp. There's a lot of good pearls came off this river back before my time, and it was eleven countries that was in there buying pearls. That gives you an idea of the quality of the Wabash pearl. Why weren't they down in the Kentucky River? Why weren't they on the White River? You answer the question, they come to the Wabash, because the quality was here. . . . In the heyday, almost every pearl buyer had a bodyguard. Somebody carried a gun with a permit and went with them, and a hell of a lot of times he had to use it, I'm pretty sure, because they just disappeared. They was a rough, tough people. You visualize six hundred boats out here on this Wabash River.

From 1923 until 1985, Simon's Jewelers, a family-owned store in Vincennes, specialized in retailing freshwater pearls from the Wabash and other nearby rivers. The late founder, Leo Simon, became involved in local pearl trade as a young man. The store was later operated by his son and daughter-in-law, Ralph and Marge Simon. Today the local Wabash pearl trade is largely controlled by jeweler Anne Marie Burch, of Jewel Craft, also a downtown Vincennes store, and by Mike Bass and Barney Bass Jr.'s Country Land Gift Shop in Westport, Illinois.

Most natural freshwater pearls are not perfectly round. In fact, in the jeweler's trade, the term *freshwater pearl* is often used synonymously with *baroque* for a pearl of irregular shape. The roundest are the most valuable. Leo Simon explained the differences:

"Most people, when speaking of pearls, think of round pearls. Well, of course, that's true, the best are the round, but there are so many other shapes and they all answer to the name of pearl and the different styles and shapes and sizes and qualities are discernible: All different types, little ones, big ones, irregular shapes, oval shapes, some look good, some don't."

On the other hand, graceful baroques (also called antiques) and other irregulars gain in value from their settings. Ralph Simon explained how this is so: "My wife has taken some pearls, baroques, which are unusual shapes and has designed mountings for them. The mounting must be made around the pearl. It is not something you can just walk in with and find a mounting and fit it in there. The mounting must be custom-made."

One type of large irregular is called a birdwing, and if one has a graceful shape and superior luster, it can bring a high price. Another of the more common shapes that has some value is the teardrop. Mussellers will usually keep them until they have a matching pair, as they bring a better price when they can be mounted as earrings. Pointed elliptical pearls with symmetrical irregularities are called rosebuds, and some, when particularly attractive, are valuable. "Spikes" (narrow cones) are relatively common and do not bring a good price unless they have an unusually appealing color or luster.

The least attractive pearls are called slugs. Mussellers save them in pill bottles until a quantity is collected and then sell them by the ounce to pearl or fur buyers, who often purchase them locally. The slugs are ground for use in cosmetics. Small, high-luster irregulars range in price from ten to one hundred dollars. Small rounds and rosebuds often bring over one hundred dollars apiece if they are beautiful. Beyond that, there are some pearls that bring hundreds of dollars, at least at retail sale, and an occasional large beauty may reach a thousand dollars or more in value.

Ohio Valley pearls, especially those of the Wabash River, figure prominently in local legend. The most persistent of the stories is that of the "Queen Pearl." In brief, the story, which takes place in the 1900s, is of a poor, dissolute pearler named Jumbo Adams (or Jud Owens) from Mount Carmel who found a particularly large and valuable pearl of perfect iridescence and roundness and sold it for $800 to a local physician, who was also a pearl buyer. The physician resold it, for $2,500, to Tiffany's, who later resold it to the Queen of England, and it is supposedly still part of the Crown Jewels.

Freshwater pearls collected by Barney Bass Sr. on the Wabash River and the East Fork of the White River, 1993. Note the black pearls on a cotton wad in the lower right-hand corner.

Adams quickly drank up or otherwise dissipated his earnings. In variants of the legend, it ended up in Queen Mother Alexandra's crown at the coronation of George V in 1910 or as the pendant of Queen Mary's pearl necklace. In a newspaper interview in Vincennes early in the century, P.E. Pepper, a Mount Carmel physician and pearl buyer, claimed to have bought the pearl for $800 and resold it to a French buyer, who, in turn, was to have sold it to British royalty.

The most far-fetched and appealing version of the legend has Adams in prison for a brawl killing a few years later. The Queen of England supposedly intervened to have him paroled because while he was imprisoned the luster on the gem began to fade as Jumbo pined away behind bars. The pearl regained its beautiful iridescence upon his release.

Queen Mary's alleged interference in Illinois justice was actually reported as news in the *Vincennes Commercial* in 1912. In this version, the queen wanted him released so that he could find more pearls for her. A 1973 article claimed that it was Pepper who had secured Adams's release. Inquiries to the Keeper of the Crown Jewels at the Tower of London in 1973 and 1982 indicated that no large American freshwater pearl has ever been part of the collection, but it is possible that a Wabash pearl did find its way into the private collection of a member of the royal family. A 1973 inquiry to the Illinois Bureau of Prisons did, however, indicate that a Jumbo Adams was imprisoned for a killing in the 1900s and later paroled. Adams's descendants, who live in Mount Carmel, are still researching the story.

The origins of the "Queen Pearl" legend are not difficult to infer. First of all, as George Frederick Kunz reports, the pearl is traditionally called the queen gem, and particularly large and beautiful pearls are often called queen pearls. Kunz also reports that a queen pearl found in Notch Brook, near Paterson, New Jersey, in 1857 was sold, by Tiffany's, to Empress Eugénie of France. He includes a photograph of it, labeled "The Queen Pearl," in his 1890 *Gems and Precious Stones of North America*. A 1905 *Vincennes Commercial* reports an Iowa pearler's wife, whose name was Mary, finding a queen pearl in some mussel meats her husband had discarded. She supposedly sold it for seven hundred dollars. The pearl, now called the "Queen Mary," was supposedly resold for fifty thousand dollars (a highly unlikely price) to a Chicago merchant. A queen pearl legend similar to the one on the Wabash also occurs in the White River Valley of Arkansas.

Most of the Wabash "Queen Pearl" legend is pure fiction. However, the persistence of this tale has benefitted those who harvest and deal in Wabash pearls by adding a mystique to the product. Wabash pearls are highly rated by connoisseurs of freshwater pearls because of the high quality of many examples. The "Queen Pearl" legend has likely added to the interest in this brilliant but obscure natural resource.

The simplest way to harvest mussels is to wade in shallow water in known mussel beds, feel for them with one's feet, and then bend over and pick them up. This process is known as polliwogging and was the original method of harvest before the invention of the brail, or crowfoot bar, in the 1890s. Children still practice this method and occasionally pick up pocket money by selling the shells to adult mussellers.

Some wading mussellers use close-tined manure forks to lift the shells off the river bottom. Today few if any mussellers use oyster tongs, but photographs from the pearl rush days indicate that this was once an important technique.

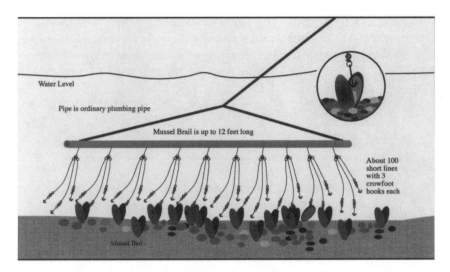

Figure 7.1. Mussel brail with crowfoot hooks

The key traditional musselling technique today is the use of the brail, or crowfoot bar, in combination with a specialized boat. A typical musselling rig consists of a sixteen- or eighteen-foot boat, usually homemade of wood. Aluminum boats are also sometimes used, but they are less stable than the wooden ones. One occasionally sees a homemade steel-hulled musselling boat. About four feet from both ends of the typical musselling boat are mounted pairs of upright two-by-fours called standers, each one with a v-notch in the upper end. Suspended in these notches parallel to the boat are two brails. Each consists of a length of iron pipe, twelve to fifteen feet long, with a length of rope attaching the ends to each other, to which another, much longer rope is tied at midpoint, forming a bridle. Along the full length of the pipe is suspended a row of short lengths of twine or sometimes light chain called stages. They vary in number from as few as twenty to as many as several hundred, with from two to eight crowfoot hooks attached to each stage. Considerable variation exists in the equipment fashioned and used by individual mussellers.

The typical crowfoot hook is homemade and consists of two pieces of heavy-gauge wire bent into a four-pronged hook with upward-pointing ends, like a small grappling iron. It is about four to five inches long from the loop where it is tied to the stage to the lower curve of its hook. In areas where the hooks are used on rocky bottoms, the four ends point downward, and each is melted into a knob with a welding torch to keep from hanging up on the bottom. These hooks are made of thinner, more flexible wire and are called knobby hooks.

Mussellers working in deep water usually mount a motor-driven winch in the boat to help raise the brail. Most boats used in the TVA lakes and the lower Ohio River are fitted with power winches, as sixty- to eighty-foot depths are not uncommon. In shallow water, brails are raised by muscle power alone.

The mollusks lie on the bottom feeding with their shells open. The musseller typically tosses one brail into the water on a mussel bed and floats along. As the crowfoot hooks are dragged over the mollusks, they startle and close their shells, snagging the hooks. When the brail has picked up enough shells to perceptively slow the boat, the musseller raises it and tosses the other brail in the water, continuing along, removing the mollusks from the hooks by hand, measuring them with a gauge, and keeping those of legal size and marketable species.

A boat typically has a high-horsepower outboard motor. In Kentucky and Tennessee waters, the boat may drag its brail under power. This is prohibited in Illinois and Indiana. Instead the musseller uses a homemade sea-anchor about four by five feet, called a mule, which is mounted on a pole or tree limb suspended astern. At one time, mules were made of pieces of canvas, stiffened with sticks of wood. Today, they are usually made of sheets of light plywood or occasionally wood-framed sheet aluminum. The musseller manipulates the mule in the current so that it pulls the boat in the desired direction. A skillful musseller can tack a zigzag course across a bed. Where musselling under power is prohibited, the motor is used only for navigating between the beds and shore.

Here is a typical musselling day on the East Fork of the White River in southwestern Indiana:

>◗● Above Hindustan Falls, the river winds first west, then south, then east, all in a space of five miles. Just before its eastward turn, it flows through a limestone canyon for about a quarter mile. Along the canyon are several shoals where the water ripples and runs shallow. These are the shoals that Barney Bass Sr. drags for mussels. Today, in mid-June, he is in his homemade crowfoot boat, so named for the crowfoot-shaped

hooks on the two homemade devices he uses to harvest the
shells.

Bass camps in a tent on a little island in the river, and he sets
out for a day of "mussel digging," as he calls it. His musselling
boat is a homemade sixteen-foot box-shaped scow, made of
exterior plywood. Each brail has 104 approximately six-inch
lengths of twine suspended from it. Attached to the end of each
length of twine is a light-gauge galvanized steel chain. The
chains alternate in length, every other one being about a foot
and then a foot and a half long. At the end of each chain are
fastened two homemade wire crowfoot hooks.

Bass motors about a quarter mile downriver to a shallow
interrupted by intermittent riffles. "There's a mussel bed here.
Been pretty productive, years past. We'll see what it can do
today. Water's about two feet lower than it ought to be, but
we'll give it a try."

He picks up one of the brails and tosses it into the river. He
grabs hold of the mule's tiller and pushes it astern, resting it on
the transom, thus lowering the mule into the river. Standing in
the boat, he tends the tiller. The boat drifts downstream, but by
manipulating the tiller, he manages to tack back and forth
across the area that he knows to be the mussel bed. This goes on
for about fifteen minutes. Eventually the boat's progress slows,
and the boat begins to hang up in the direction of the submerged brail. Bass raises the mule and starts to haul in the line.
Eventually the brail surfaces. Attached to the hooks are about
thirty large black shells. Bass lays the brail back in its notches
and throws the other brail overboard. He pulls the shells off the
hooks and compares the sizes of smaller ones to a pair of
notches on the gunwale. Those too small he pitches back into
the river. He tosses the others into the bottom of the boat. He
then returns to the tiller and repeats the process. "Musselling's
about the hardest work you can do. It's just like lifting weights
all day long. Every fifteen or twenty minutes, you're lifting
from seventy-five to a hundred, a hundred and fifty, pounds out
of the bottom of the river."

As the day passes, Bass continues his work, gradually filling
up the center of the boat with mussels. Every so often, he floats
downstream past the mussel beds. He then starts up the motor
and heads back upstream above the beds. When he is dragging,
the river is very quiet. The only sounds are the singing of birds,

Barney Bass Sr. removing mussels from a brail, East Fork of the White River, near Hindustan Falls, Indiana. Still from the film *The Pearl Fisher* (1984) by Dillon Bustin and Jens Lund.

the rippling of water over the riffles, and the occasional noises he made as he handles the brails and the mussels.

Early in the afternoon, he motors back to the island to unload shells and have lunch. Sitting on a log, he muses about the years when musselling was most lucrative. "I was dragging shells down on the Wabash, it was back in the sixties. This guy come along up on the highway up from where I was digging. He asked me about the shells and everything, and he was a shell buyer from Camden, Tennessee. He wanted to know if I'd be interested in buying shells for him. He was an exporter to Japan to the pearl industry, and I took him up on the offer and went ahead and at the time the shells was fifty dollars a ton, and him and a local shell-exporter, they got into a shell war and kept a-bouncing the price backwards and forwards to each other and they got up to five-hundred dollars a ton and you could some-times go out and dig a ton a day. It was more fair for the fisherman. I was a fisherman at the time and it helped everybody that was a-doing all the hard work. It kind of phased out the middle man a little bit on the river, he didn't make as much, but the working man made more money on it." ◀◼

After a musseller has a load of shells, he usually heads home to "cook out" and dispose of the mussel meats, sort the shells into marketable piles, and look for pearls. This was how Bass processed the mussels that he collected:

◼▶ On a side street in Vincennes, Barney Bass's pickup pulls around the back of his house into the yard. It is towing a trailer on which rests his crowfoot boat, which contains about five hundred pounds of mussels he has just harvested. His wife, Marge, comes out the back door to meet him.

On the other side of the yard is a specially-built stove used for cooking open the mussels. Below it, partly underground is a fire-box, which Bass stoked yesterday with firewood. It is late afternoon, but he is planning to cook out the mussels by evening. Above the firebox is a rectangular waterproof sheet-metal box. With a garden hose, Bass sprays a little water into the upper box. He lights the fire in the firebox and waits until it is burning well before banking it. With a coal fork, he scoops shells out of the boat and loads them into the stove and covers them with several layers of sacking made of plastic-coated burlap. After about a half hour, the water in the box begins to steam and the burlap puffs up. "These shells don't cook out by boiling them out. It's the steam that cooks them. Whenever it gets puffed up like that, why then we let it set about five minutes and everything gets cooked and they're ready to throw out on the table," Bass says.

With his fork, he catches the corner of the burlap and lifts it off. All the shells have opened, exposing their meats. Bass scoops up the shells, a forkful at a time, and spreads them over a makeshift table, made from an old door, set up near the stove. He shovels some more shells into the stove and covers them with the burlap.

The Basses set to work separating the shells from the meats. Each time they pull a meat from between the shells they carefully squeeze the mantle (which they call the wing) and adja-

Marge and Barney Bass Sr. separating mussel meats from shells,
Vincennes, Indiana, 1984.

cent areas with thumb and forefinger to locate any pearls that
might be present.

As they remove the meats, they sort the shells, by species,
into separate piles. Bass explains the different species as they
turn up: "This here's mixed shell. It's the ones they use to seed
cultured pearls with. Here's one of them there pink pigtoes. It's
a real nice shell. And they use this pink one more or less for
jewelry for necklaces and heart-shaped necklaces for girls.
Here's what they call a butterfly. Looks like a butterfly. That's
where they get the name from. And most of the shells' names
are from what the people think they look like. This is a nice
clean shell here. It's called a maple-leaf. It's really good for
making pearl beads. Here's a pigtoe and there's another butterfly. There's another maple leaf."

Marge Bass remembers a pearl they once found, while

sorting shells. "Barney was digging down on the Wabash and found this just one pearl, and Mr. Palmer came, he offered me fifty dollars for it. I wouldn't take it at the time. Boy, we were really hurting and I should've, but I didn't. I wanted to keep it and make a ring out of it. He said he would like to have the pearl, but he didn't get it."

As they continue sorting, they occasionally find a pearl. Most are poorly shaped and poorly lustered slugs. "Pretty good, this one," says Mrs. Bass, pulling out a small, fine-lustered teardrop shape. Bass explains that if he had a near-identical match to it, the pair could bring as much as a hundred dollars. He talks about the rarity of marketable pearls: "You can usually find about—in the shells from up where these came from—you find about an ounce to the ton, an ounce to an ounce and a half, and them slugs with just no shape at all is worth thirty dollars an ounce, but pearls, they're worth quite a bit of money. There [pointing at the one his wife found], that's what they call an antique pearl."

The pearls and slugs they find are dropped into a plastic pill bottle. One or two good pearls per season, each worth about fifty dollars, is not an unusual haul. Every few years, they can expect to find a really valuable one worth in the hundreds of dollars.

Barney Bass's full-time job is at the local Hamilton-Standard glass plant. During times of unemployment, and at times just to supplement his income, he also commercial fishes on the Wabash and White Rivers. This summer, his nets are put away. He explains that if he were fishing, he would be saving the mussel meats to use as bait. At times, they have given the meats to neighbors who raise chickens or hogs. Today's meats will be buried in the garden.

Bass picks out several of the largest shells and explains that they are called washboards and were once a prime export shell. He points to irregular stains on the mother-of-pearl and explains how these stains, which have been becoming larger and more conspicuous in the last five or ten years, decrease the shells' value. He ponders whether pollution may be the culprit: "And I think it could be some of the stuff they use as liquid fertilizer and stuff they put on the fields and it gets worked into the streams and the river. That's probably what's messing it up, and the washboard seems to be the worst one for it. But you can't stop progress for shells, I guess. You can't stop progress of many for a few, I'll put it that way."

The rest of the late afternoon and early evening is spent cooking out and sorting shells, finding pearls and slugs, and bagging the marketable product. ◂▪

Brailing or dragging for mussels can disrupt and destroy set fishing gear. This has caused major disputes in areas of intensive musselling and commercial fishing, especially in Kentucky Lake and Lake Barkley. In those areas, many of the mussellers are not fishermen, so there is less sympathy between the two competing trades. Attempts have been made to resolve these disputes, such as setting aside certain hours and certain fishing grounds for the respective activities. Nonetheless, there have been times when clashes have erupted into violence.

In the past two decades, scuba diving has become a preferred method of gathering mussels in some areas. It is a "high-tech" version of polliwogging. One finds the mussels and picks them up by hand. Diving for mussels is prohibited in Indiana but allowed in Illinois, Kentucky, and Tennessee. Many mussellers consider it the best method, as it is theoretically possible to choose marketable species and sizes while one is underwater, leaving the others behind. This is important because mussels returned to the river must be replaced in the same position they were in when they were taken or they will usually die. On the other hand, conservation managers worry that it is too efficient, taking every potentially marketable shell. Also, the waters in many of the prime musselling areas, such as the lower Wabash, are very murky, so one ends up grabbing around and hauling up many of the wrong shells anyway. Barney Bass Sr.'s sons, who live on the Illinois side, scuba dive the Wabash near Vincennes, keeping the family enterprise in mussel shell and pearls during Indiana's closed period.

A major threat to all aspects of musselling and pearl culture is the appearance of exotic mussels. The European zebra mussel can live out of water for more than eight days. Aside from other severe environmental damage this organism causes, it also crowds out native mollusks. If permitted to spread throughout North American rivers and lakes, it could totally destroy the native mussel population. A less virulent but still harmful exotic is the Asiatic clam.

As Nelson Cohen observed, the future of musselling is very uncertain. Water quality and careful control of harvest are critical to the survival of this traditional resource-based activity, as is the control of harmful exotics. If these factors can be successfully managed, an American cultured pearl industry in Kentucky Lake may have a bright future, as long as mother-of-pearl shells for seeding are still available. The death knell of musselling and pearling has been sounded many times since George Frederick Kunz first wrote about it in the late nineteenth century.

EIGHT

Marketing, Cooking, and Eating Fish

Early in this century, most commercially caught Ohio Valley fish were shipped by wholesale buyers to urban markets, usually by rail. Harold "Pat" Patton of Cave-in-Rock who operated wholesale and retail markets at both Cave-in-Rock and Old Shawneetown, trucked fish to a railhead in Eldorado, Illinois. From there, iced boxcars took them to Pana, Illinois, where the loads were divided and shipped by main rail lines to Chicago, New York, and other cities. He remembers that much of his fish came from the Cumberland and Green Rivers in Kentucky, where markets employed their own fishermen.

Today, most river fish are marketed locally. Marketing often consists of a fisherman retailing his own catch from a basement or garage freezer or from a live box floating in the river at the dock where he ties his boat. Some fishermen maintain their own floating markets. Others sell all their fish to other markets. Still others maintain fish markets on land, which they and members of their family operate. There are also larger commercial markets that handle wholesale trade, such as restaurants and fish fries. They may supply each other and the smaller fisherman-owned markets during shortfalls. Some also ship fish by truck to urban centers, such as Chicago, Evansville, Louisville, and St. Louis.

A fisherman and a market sometimes maintain an agreement whereby the fisherman will work at the market during business hours at a relatively low wage in exchange for guaranteed sale of his fish at a specific price. In the early summer, sportsfishers who have bought commercial licenses and part-time commercial fishermen may possess large quantities of fiddlers, such as those they catch angling the Tennessee River below Kentucky Lake Dam. These fish can be dumped on the market at a price unprofitable to the professional fisherman. Some marketers, such as Roy Jackson of Paducah, try to give commercial fishermen a worthwhile price, in any case, to ensure a supply of fish at other times of year.

Mann's Tatumsville Fish Market of Tatumsville, Kentucky, specializes in the wholesale fiddler trade. George Williams, owner and operator of the Cave-in-Rock Fish Market, visited Mann's Market to buy fish:

▶● George Williams is short of fiddlers for the upcoming Fourth of July weekend. The little community of Cave-in-Rock, with its nearby state parks, ferry to Kentucky, and convenient marinas, expects to be full of vacationers. Many of them will be frying fish, and fiddlers are always the most in demand.

This morning Williams crosses the river on the ferry in his refrigerated truck and drives the forty-five miles to the dams that impound Lake Barkley and Kentucky Lake. As he crosses over Kentucky Lake Dam, he points out the dozens of anglers in small boats in the Tennessee River directly beneath the spillway. Williams explains that they are seasonal part-timers, catching fiddlers for markets in nearby Gilbertsville, Tatumsville, and Paducah. A son of a friend of his puts himself through Murray State University doing that, he says.

We leave U.S. Route 68 and head for the little village of Tatumsville. On the main road just before entering town is a complex of low tin sheds with a sign in front reading "Mann's Tatumsville Fish Market." Mann's sell both frozen and fresh fiddlers and also handle a substantial quantity of buffalo, practically none of which is bought by retail customers.

Inside the windowless market are at least fifteen tubs of fish on a wet concrete floor, a large walk-in ice room, and several pieces of power equipment. Melvin and Martha Mann and four employees are busy gutting, beheading, and skinning fiddlers.

A butcher's bandsaw is rigged to behead the fish. Martha Mann operates a skinning machine, similar to a power planer. Above the noise of the machines, Williams and Melvin Mann talk quantities and prices. As the machinery screeches intermittently, fishheads, guts and skins are tossed into waiting barrels on one side, and the ready-for-market fiddlers are dropped more carefully into washtubs. After the conversation ends, two young men leave the dressing floor and go into the ice room. There they pile crushed ice on top of three tubs of fish and carry them, one by one, to the open back door of Williams's truck. Williams and Mann step into the office for a few moments. Then they emerge and go their separate ways. Williams climbs into the truck and heads back toward Illinois.

On the way back north, we stop in Gilbertsville at a much smaller fish market run by Gladys and Louis DeFew. The DeFews have invented and marketed a premixed breading for deep-frying river fish, which they call "Fish-N-D-Lit" (pronounced "fishin' delight"). According to the ingredient list on the label, it contains cornmeal, paprika, cayenne pepper, celery powder, and salt. Williams buys fifty twelve-ounce bags. He sells Fish-N-D-Lit at the Cave-in-Rock Market and also uses it to bread the spoonbill fillets his wife prepares for the fish sandwiches they sell in their adjoining lunch counter. Williams and the DeFews chat a while, mostly about the shortage of fiddlers. Louis DeFew says he has ordered some farm-raised fish from Arkansas and hopes that they will arrive before Friday, when the weekend trade will really start to pick up. ◀●

Since some time in the nineteenth century, a Cave-in-Rock Fish Market has operated on a floating barge in the Ohio River at Cave-in-Rock. Fisherman Tommy Sherer of nearby Tolu, Kentucky, regularly works there, dressing and selling fish, and he is also one of the market's main fish suppliers:

●▶ The Cave-in-Rock Fish Market is tied up by a parking lot near the Ohio River ferry landing at the little town of Cave-in-Rock. Its historic namesake cave and surroundings are now a state park. The market's location ensures that it is a popular stopping place for tourists. It is also the major fish market on the Illinois side of the river, and it has its own marina and marine fueling station.

On a Thursday afternoon in late August, George Williams and Tommy Sherer are busy behind the counter, preparing for the weekend trade. Yesterday, Williams trucked in a load of fiddlers from the Tatumsville market. Yesterday evening, Sherer and a fishing partner caught about six hundred pounds of spoonbill. Despite the usual slowness of catfish fishing during this season, Sherer has managed to bring in about fifty pounds of fiddlers this morning because of a flow of fresh water from storms upstream.

Williams has bought the Kentucky fiddlers already dressed and ready to market. Sherer dressed the spoonbill last night, right after catching them, but they need filleting to turn them into marketable "boneless cats." The men help each other carry

Cave-in-Rock Fish Market, Cave-in-Rock, Illinois, 1980.

out two tubs of fish, one of freshly caught fiddlers, the other of dressed spoonbill.

A set of stainless steel counters extend along the wall behind the retail counter. On one side is a hook suspended from the ceiling. Sherer picks fiddlers out of the tub, one by one, and lays them on a cutting board. He slits their bellies and pulls out their entrails by hand, finally scraping the waste off the board to a piece of butcher paper on the counter on the left and pushing the gutted fish to the right. Fish larger than the norm he puts in a separate pile.

As Sherer works the catfish, Williams picks out the dressed spoonbill, also one by one, and lays them on his cutting board. He holds the fish with a rag in one hand and pulls the skins off each side, separately, with a pair of fisherman's pinchers. Then, with a very sharp filleting knife, he cuts a thin fillet of white meat off each side of each fish. What remains is not only the cartilaginous skeleton but also the darker meat in the middle of the fish. This waste goes into a bucket on the floor, and the fillets go into a pile beside the cutting board.

Sherer and Williams carry on a relaxed conversation, mostly about the unusually large spoonbill catch of the night before. Sherer muses about the days when spoonbill and its roe were exported to New York. He laughs as he remembers a time when he "grossed out" some customers while dressing a mess of spoonbill. "Couple of kids, barely out of their teens were here. We were dressing a mess of them, quite a few sows, full of eggs. Kids standing here watching me. `What're they?' they say. `Mmmm, they're eggs!' I says, and I scoop up a big handful of them, shove them in my mouth, and chow them down. Ha, ha! Thought they were like to gag to death! Should have seen them!"

Sherer finishes gutting the catfish. One by one he hangs them by their gill slits on a suspended hook. With the pinchers, he pulls off their skins. One of them is a completely different color, dark yellowish brown with a flat head. It is a flathead. Sherer expresses his opinion of them: "I think these are the best eating of all. We just sell them as fiddlers. I think they're more carnivorous, not a scavenger, like your channel cat. Sure taste good, though." After he skins all the fish, he beheads them. The larger fish in a separate pile, several of which are over two feet long, he chops into steaks with a cleaver.

While Williams continues filleting the spoonbill, Sherer fetches a couple of clean plastic washbasins, puts the fiddlers in them, and carries them back to the ice room. Then he wraps up the steaks in butcher paper, drops the packages into a plastic sack, and puts the sack into a freezer. Just then, more customers come in, and Sherer takes over the retail counter. ◆◄

Roy Lee Walls operates a typical fisherman-owned market. His wife and son stand in for him when he is on the river. Unlike the Cave-in-Rock Market, which has a large tourist trade, his market sells almost all its fish to local customers:

▶● Walls's market is located next to his house, in a small white-painted, cinder-block building beside Illinois State Highway 37. On its side is a large, hand-lettered yellow sign reading. "Please leave all alcohol and foul language out!" For several decades, he owned and operated the Cairo Point Fish Market, south of Cairo, just a few yards from the Ohio-Mississippi River confluence. He sold it in the mid-1970s and moved his business to his own property in Urbandale. While he was at Cairo Point, he appeared in a 1977 *National Geographic* article. He is proud that he has been a lifelong fisherman (and sometime carpenter) who grew up on a houseboat on the Ohio, Mississippi, and Tennessee Rivers.

Although small, Walls's market is a busy place. Walls opens it when he returns from fishing, usually in the late morning. Customers come and go all afternoon. Some are fish marketers themselves. Others own small restaurants or taverns. Most of his retail customers are African Americans from nearby Cairo, Future City, and Mound City. Some of his regular black customers come from as far away as Sikeston, Missouri. Walls makes sure to keep a supply of scale fish that many older local African Americans prefer.

Although he has several hundred pounds of fish to dress, he finds time to chat with all of his customers and with his friend Eugene Droge, an Illinois conservation officer, who stops by to shoot the breeze. He hands Droge a Coke. The officer sits down, and the two engage in animated conservation about some proposed changes in mesh-size regulations. Unlike many marketers, Walls dresses his fish using only hand tools. Like many fish markets, Walls's has a sheet-metal-lined room, fitted with a drain and piled about a quarter full of crushed ice, for keeping unfrozen fish fresh. It also has several dressing tables, freezers, and large sinks. On the wall is a hand-lettered price list:

Fiddlers	$1.60 pound
Buffalo	$1
Large cat	$1
Carp	60¢
White perch	60¢

A middle-aged black man stops in to pick up an order. He and Walls haul out several styrofoam coolers of frozen fish from the ice room and load them in the trunk of the man's car, a big Chevrolet with Missouri plates. The man presents Walls with a wad of cash, and the two chat about the hot dry spell that has been hanging on for more than a month. "It's gonna be hard to catch them fish, especially the cats, if this goes on, sir," says Walls. After the man leaves, Walls says, "One of my regulars. Has a lunch counter over in Charleston."

Droge finishes his Coke, waves goodbye, and gets in his cruiser. Walls continues dressing fish. After gutting a pile of fiddlers, he hangs them by their gill covers on a hook over the table and skins them with a pair of pinchers.

A few minutes later an elderly white couple come in. The woman speaks. "We want to order about a hundred pounds of catfish for next Saturday. Having a fish fry at the family reunion." Walls replies, "Don't know if I can do that. Been coming up short on the little cats lately. I may be able to get some in from another market by then, though. Why don't you leave me your number and I can get back to you tomorrow or the next day." After they leave, Walls says, "Bet I can get some from the market at the point. I know they been bringing some in from over Kentucky Lake. Things get real short and we can probably get some farm-raised from Arkansas way. Kind of short notice, though. I'd generally be able to have it by the end of the week, but this darn weather!" ◖◀

Years ago, river fish, especially scale fish, were often sold locally out of the backs of trucks by peddlers. Some of the markets had their own trucks, and the owner or an employee made the rounds of small communities hawking fish. Today there are a few peddlers left. They make the rounds of some of the more inland African-American communities in Illinois.

Highfin are the only commercial scale fish not principally part of the African-American diet. Although very bony, they have a sweet flavor, and some people prefer them to catfish. They are usually served as fish sandwiches in taverns. In order for the fillets to be edible, they must be scored. Dennis Lueke of Lueke's Fish Market in Maunie, Illinois, on the Wabash River, explains: "Now, take a look at this. The little bones are right in that meat, but if I score them, little scores about a quarter inch apart, that makes them short. Then when you fry them, the little pieces of the bones just kind of curl up and you don't even notice them while you eat them. It kind of fries them out."

Mounted on a workbench in his and his father Fred's floating market is Dennis's own invention, an ingenious little machine. It is a power scorer, an axle mounted with seventy round, sharpened, spinning disks exactly one-quarter inch apart. A pulley wheel at one end of the axle is hooked to a small electric motor with a drive belt. Lueke pushes the fillets, one by one, under the spinning disks by

The interior of Fred and Dennis Lueke's floating fish market, Wabash River, Maunie, Illinois, 1979. Dennis Lueke is at the workbench.

placing them on a grooved wooden board, which slides under the disks along a slot in the workbench.

Marketers prepare different species and sizes of fish in different ways for retail marketing. They usually steak large catfish. They fillet mid-sized ones and behead, gut, and skin fiddlers. Marketers prepare locally sold spoonbill as skinless fillets of the outer white meat. They sell highfin as scored fillets, usually with skin. Catfish, spoonbill, and highfin may be sold fresh or frozen. Buffalo and carp are usually sold live or fresh. If dressed, they may be gutted and skinned, or filleted and scored. The markets usually sell hackleback sturgeon as fillets, fresh or frozen.

The eating of fish by lower Ohio Valley people is influenced by complex and subtle cultural factors. Social and economic status of a food and of the people who choose to eat it profoundly affect the use of a food resource. As early as 1851, naturalist Jared P. Kirtland noted that sturgeon were eaten only by "certain classes of people." In 1912, George W. Miles offered this hypothesis for the varying status of different species of freshwater fish. Early midwestern waters were so full of game fish that only the hard to catch, such as large pike, pickerel, and muskellunge, were offered to guests, "because of the vanity of the master of the household." Bluegill, crappie, bullhead, and perch were "for women and children to catch . . . admitted to the table on ordinary occasions" and "apologized for if a guest was on board." Traditional prejudices excluded the cheaper commercial species because of their place in the African-American diet since slavery days.

Anthropologist John W. Bennett's study of food customs in riverside southern Illinois during the 1940s found that by then, all fish and game were despised food. He hypothesized that this was owing to two factors. The first was racial, as African Americans had only recently been driven out of some of the areas where he did his research. The other had to do with the stereotype of the indolent fisherman. He found that many people liked fish very much but either denied eating it or apologized for it if he discovered it on their tables. Farmers and white-collar workers were most vocal in their disdain for fish.

In recent decades, the growth of leisure time and higher wages has resulted in a revival of interest in fishing and hunting among blue-collar white men. This has raised the status of fish and game as food, and many men in the lower Ohio Valley now express a fondness for fiddlers.

Commercial scale fish, however, are still low status. To what extent this is owing to their being "poor people's food" and to what extent racial factors influence this hierarchy are uncertain. The order of status is, as follows:

> Largemouth bass (sporting game fish)
> Crappie, sauger, white and yellow bass (panfish/gamefish)
> Farm-raised fiddlers
> Bluegill, fiddlers (kids' panfish)
> Fiddlers (gamefish/commercial)
> All other catfish, bullheads, and "boneless cat"
> Highfin (scale fish eaten by whites in taverns)
> Buffalo and white perch (fish, other than carp, eaten by
>   African Americans and disdained by whites)
> Carp
> Gar, grinnel (fish eaten only by a few African
>   Americans)

John Farmer weighing buffalo at Hard Times Fish Market, Grayville, Illinois, 1993.

Hackleback is difficult to place in this hierarchy, except to say that it is relatively low but well liked by those who try it. Snapping turtle also stands outside of the list, not so much because it is a reptile and not a fish as because its status is dependent upon context of preparation and eating.

Whites in the lower Ohio Valley still rarely cook fish at home. Certain area restaurants, such as Kaylor's Cafe in Cave-in-Rock, specialize in "fiddler plates." On a Saturday evening a few years ago, owner and chef Charlie Patton fried fiddlers for his customers:

▶● Kaylor's Cafe seats about fifty, and there are at least forty customers present. The outside wall facing the parking lot is painted in big yellow and black letters:

FISH DINNERS

...WITH HOT CORN STICKS...

Served Anytime

Fiddler plates with corn sticks, Kaylor's Cafe, Cave-in-Rock, Illinois, 1978.

The fiddler plates consist of three deep-fat-fried breaded fiddlers served with two sticks of cornbread. Most of the fiddlers served at Kaylor's are river-caught and purchased either from the Cave-in-Rock Market or from the Kentucky Lake Dam area. Occasionally, he serves farm-raised fish, but only when river fish are unavailable. Patton, like many people in the area, dislikes farm-raised fish. On the other hand, he does not go out of his way to advertise that the fish are from the nearby rivers, as some people might find that unappetizing.

At least half the customers order fish, so Patton has his hands full. He faces his workbench, and to his left is a tub of dressed fiddlers. Next to that is a bowl of beaten egg, and in front of him is a washbasin with several inches of seasoned cornmeal-and-flour breading. One by one, he picks them up by their tails and dips them in the egg, rolls them in the breading, and deposits them on a tray to his right. Behind him is a stove with several deep-fat fryers sizzling away. Every few minutes he takes out a basket of fried fish, dumps them on a counter covered with paper towels, drops several breaded raw fish into the basket, and lowers the basket back into the grease. Every so often he takes out pans of corn sticks from the oven below and replaces them with pans of fresh cornbread batter.

The fried fish are a rich golden color. When cooled enough to touch, he arranges three of them on a plate with a pair of corn sticks. In the dining room, they are served with tubs of cole slaw and tartar sauce. The customers eat their fiddlers like drumsticks, holding them in two hands and nibbling off chunks of meat, until only the bones, fins, and tail remain.

Patton makes his own breading, which he seasons with cayenne pepper and salt. He is an avid fish eater himself and enjoys providing his customers with his own favorite food. He bought the market several years ago, after trying a few other food ventures in the area, and considers it an excellent location. Kaylor's is about one block from the ferry slip, across the street from several souvenir and rock collectors' shops and about one-quarter mile from the entrance to Cave-in-Rock State Park. ◀█

A Village of Ridgway municipal employees' fish fry at the American Legion-V.F.W. Park near Ridgway, Illinois, provides a good look at how catfish are fried on a large scale:

▶● Early summer is community fish fry season, and many extended families hold fries at local parks. So do organizations, such as the Elks and the Veterans of Foreign Wars. Businesses and local governments often sponsored fish fries for their employees.

In the park shelter kitchen, a large vat of vegetable shortening is being heated to deep-fat frying temperature. Chef Jack Dickey, a member of the Village Board, keeps an eye on a frying thermometer as it approaches 375°F. He lets the temperature climb to almost 400°F, explaining that the first batch of fish that he drops in will instantly cool the fat a good thirty degrees or more, bringing it below the optimum temperature. By now, the grease is just beginning to smoke.

Dickey's assistants have been preparing dressed headless fiddlers by rolling them in breading and piling them in a frying basket on the counter next to the stove. There are about twenty-five fish in the basket. "Now!" he says and quickly picks up the basket by its handles and plunges it into the vat of hot grease. As the needle on the thermometer drops down to 365°F, the vat crackles loudly and the smell of frying fish permeates the air. After a few minutes, the loud crackling dies down, and the needle gradually climbs to 375°F. After about five minutes, a few of the fish bob up to the surface, making a hissing noise. A few minutes later, the whole surface of the grease is full of floating fillets, and the temperature is in the 380s. Dickey takes out the basket and dumps the fried fish on a piece of brown paper on the other side of the counter. His assistants have already breaded more fish and laid them in a pile, and he loads another twenty-plus fiddlers into the basket.

The fried fish are allowed to drain for about a minute, and then another assistant picks them up with tongs and places two on each paper plate, passing it out the serving window to people standing in line. ●◄

Small fiddlers are raised in large catfish farms many places in the South, especially in Alabama, Arkansas, and Mississippi. Farm-raised fiddlers are also imported from Brazil. Many of the fiddlers eaten in restaurants and sold in supermarkets in the lower Ohio Valley are raised on southern farms, and some are even sold in Ohio Valley river fish markets. One marketer, who is himself a fisherman and who sells some farm-raised fiddlers, has been rumored to sell Brazilian fiddlers, earning him criticism from other fishermen. Fiddlers are also stocked in pay lakes all over the South and Midwest. The catfish-farming industry carefully manages the catfish's reputation. On the one hand, they debunk the notion of catfish as poor food. On the other, they advertise that *their* product is raised in sanitary ponds on hygienically prepared feed, unlike scavenging river cats.

Catfish connoisseurs disdain farm-raised catfish because of the flavor supposedly imparted by their feed. Farm-raised fish are also said to be weak or "mushy" in texture. Connoisseurs prefer those caught in rivers, which have firmer flesh because of the effect of the current on their muscle tone.

The growth of the farm-raised catfish industry has been a mixed blessing for the river fisherman. Most of the smaller operators feel that they are being driven out of business by farm fish, partly because of the comparison with "unclean" river fish made in advertising as well as the predictability of the farm fish supply. Some even claim that the government publicizes pollution problems in river fish in order to shore up the heavily subsidized farm fish industry. Melvin Mann concurs but also notes that the demand for all catfish has increased substantially with the growth of the farm fish industry: "It cuts both ways."

All catfishes are high in calories, about a thousand per pound of edible portion, comparable to salmon and eel. The fat is most noticeable in larger specimens. Too much fat decreases the value of larger cats and causes the preference for the smaller ones.

Although blue cats and flatheads are usually fried, they are also sometimes barbecued in the fashion typical of the area, which consists of slow roasting over a charcoal fire to which green hickory blocks have been added. Custom barbecuer Rudy Phillips of Shawneetown is occasionally asked to barbecue whole large catfish.

During the tourist season, Mary Williams, wife of George, prepares "boneless cat" sandwiches at a lunch counter in a trailer across the parking lot from the Cave-in-Rock Fish Market. She also deep-fries "boneless cat" fillets that are sold in fish sandwiches by the concession stand in Cave-in-Rock State Park.

Although caviar from spoonbill has been economically important in the Ohio Valley fisheries, it never became part of the local diet. The high prices urban people pay for caviar is a source of amazement to river people. Harold "Pat" Patton was a leading caviar-shipper during the 1940s. Fisherman Herbert Sharp of Smithland, Kentucky told a tale of how Patton was invited by two caviar merchants to visit them in New York:

> They met him at the big depot and they had them a big old Cadillac that they drove him around in and they showed him all the sights and went to a couple of shows and it was all on them. He had a great time. Finally the last night they took him out to a bar and ordered drinks. That first Jew, he ordered a round of beers and a round of caviar sandwiches. That was ten dollars and ten cents. You see, beer was a dime then, but a caviar sandwich cost all of ten dollars. Well, Harold, he was pretty impressed at a sandwich that cost ten dollars. Then the second, he ordered a round of beers and a round of caviar sandwiches. . . . Well, later on, as they were going out, they asked him what he thought of those caviar sandwiches. He thought they were pretty good but that ten dollars was pretty high. Then they told him, "Harold, don't you know that's them same old sour spoonbill eggs you've been shipping us every week?" Well, later on he said that he'd like to have put his finger down his throat at the thought of eating them sour old things. But he was pretty surprised at them getting ten dollars a sandwich for them!

Caviar from hackleback is still occasionally shipped to New York from the lower Ohio Valley. During the 1980s, Tom and Jane Tislow's Fish Market in Vincennes shipped hundreds of pounds of caviar, prepared from fish caught by Tom Tislow, to several restaurants in New York.

During the 1940s, midwestern fishermen developed a method of dressing spoonbill called New Yorking. A New Yorked spoonbill was a large fish that had been beheaded and skinned and had its cartilaginous skeleton and surrounding dark meat cut out and discarded. In this form it was shipped to northeastern cities, where it was smoked and sold as sturgeon. More recently, smoked spoonbill has been sold under its real name in the Chicago area. It is the white outer meat that is sold locally today as "boneless cat."

Buffalo are the freshwater fish species most traditionally associated with the African-American diet, and this may go all the way back to slavery days, when riverside plantations used them as a cheap food supply. Buffalo have numerous small forked bones in the fillet, which makes much of the meat difficult to eat. They have a wide rib cage, and rib steaks can be cut from the bigger fish. Roy Lee Walls, most of whose retail customers are African American, reports that 80 percent of his fish sales are buffalo.

In places with large African-American populations, black fish-eaters patronize white fishermen and marketers knowing that they will get a fresh product, a reasonable price, and courteous service. The lower Ohio Valley, especially the Cairo area, has a history of poor race relations, but the white fisherman-marketer whose business depends on a good market for scale fish is likely to be far more easy and comfortable with his or her African-American customers than many other area retailers.

African-American taverns and restaurants in Cairo and Paducah feature deep-fried buffalo rib-steaks on weekends. One of them is Happy's Chili Parlor, in an African-American neighborhood in Paducah:

➤ It is a Friday afternoon in August at Happy's. Proprietor and chef Eugene "Happy" Thomas has just returned from the Paducah Fish Market with a dozen large buffalo for the weekend house special.

Thomas's teenaged son finishes sweeping the floor and wipes the counter. Several large pots of chili steam on the range for the Friday evening regulars. Thomas lays out about five buffalo, scales the forward parts of their bodies, and cuts off their heads, gill covers, and pectoral fins. He makes a diagonal cut from the anal fin to the spiny part of the dorsal fin. The fish's heads, fins, and hindquarters he throws into a bucket on the floor. He slices each remaining fish body into a three-quarter-inch-thick steak. After rinsing off blood, slime, and loose scales, he drops them into a large bowl of salted water.

By five o'clock, they have soaked for over two hours. A few customers drift into Happy's for an after-work beer. Thomas says, "It's mostly the older folks who order fish. The younger ones like their chili or burgers. We usually sell a few fish plates on Friday evening, but mostly it's some of the old-timers who come in on a Saturday afternoon who want them."

About an hour later, as the place is filling up and almost every table has a bowl or two of chili on it, someone orders one of Thomas's buffalo-rib plates. The deep-fat frier built into the stove is used for french fries. The fish are fried in a deep skillet of hot lard. Thomas pours the brine out of the bowl and puts in some fresh water, in which he rinses all the rib steaks, and then pours out the rinse water. He takes out two of the rib steaks and puts the bowl in the refrigerator. He rinses the two steaks again and pats them dry with a paper towel. In another bowl, he breaks two eggs and beats them slightly. He pours some corn-meal out on a plate and shakes salt and pepper into it. The buffalo ribs are first dipped in the egg, then in the cornmeal mixture, and then dropped into the deep-fat fryer. After they have cooked a few minutes, Thomas drops a portion of precut potatoes into the other fryer. When the fries float, he scoops them out, followed by the fish steaks, and lays it all on a paper towel to drain. He puts the fish and the fries on a dinner plate and two slices of toast on a small plate. His son brings the meal out to a table, together with a bottle of hot sauce and a cold bottle of beer. ◀━◀

Buffalo are the most nutritious river fish. Attempts at farming them in Arkansas failed because of the lack of a market for small buffalo. Dressed buffalo usually retail at about one-quarter to one-half of the price of fiddlers. Influencing buffalo's place in the hierarchy of desirability is its many small bones.

Carp were an important part of the diet of Jewish immigrants from central and eastern Europe, and they were also popular among

Eugene "Happy"
Thomas preparing
deep-fried buffalo ribs
at Happy's Chili Parlor,
Paducah, Kentucky,
1978.

Germans and Slavs, especially Catholics who needed fish for fast-day meals. The increase in demand for carp by immigrants in midwestern cities led to a major increase in commercial fishing in the late nineteenth century. Assimilation among the second generation led to a decline in demand for carp as early as the 1920s. Carp, along with buffalo and white perch, have come to be associated with the diet of poor people. They do not freeze well and taste best if kept alive just before they are killed and eaten. As late as the 1940s, Ohio Valley carp were shipped alive in tank cars to the East Coast. Today few carp are sold as human food, except to Asian immigrants and some African Americans. Large numbers are still fished in the Illinois and upper Mississippi for use as pet food and fish meal.

Despite carp's low reputation, there are, among river people, some real connoisseurs of this fish. Some local people claim that carp, if caught in cold clear water, are the best-tasting fish in the river.

Carp eaters generally score the fillet portions and cut the rib portions into steaks to render the many small bones less troublesome. Some local people pressure-can carp with vinegar, which softens the smaller bones. Roy Lee Walls attributes low demand for carp and buffalo to the laziness of present-day fish eaters, who do not want to contend with bones. Some marketers recommend soaking carp in brine overnight before cooking them, sometimes after bleeding the fish. Others advise removing the prominent vein, which they call the mud vein, which runs along each side of the fish's body. The most common method of cooking carp is to dip them in batter and deep-fry them.

Turtle fanciers are probably a small minority in the lower Ohio Valley. Few area African Americans eat turtle meat, although some older blacks with deep southern roots have a taste for it. Many German-Catholic parishes in southwest Indiana and western Kentucky have turtle barbecues or turtle-stew feasts. The taste for turtle in some midwestern Catholic communities is probably owing to turtle meat having been classified with fish and excluded from the fast-day ban on meat. Nowadays, turtle stew is a mixture of beef, turtle, vegetables, and chicken, often with only a small proportion of turtle meat. In southwestern Indiana, Catholic church suppers featuring turtle stew are an advertised local specialty with boosterish overtones.

Dressed turtle meat freezes well and keeps well frozen. Packages of frozen turtle meat are sold by the pound and bring a high price, often more than five dollars per pound. Almost all retail turtle meat is sold in two- to three-pound bags of frozen chunks of meat and bone from the animal's neck, limbs, and tail, which are the only edible parts. Some fishermen-marketers in southwest Indiana specialize in catching and dressing turtles and retailing the frozen meat. Fisherman Jim Parish lives and operates a market on U.S. Route 41 near Hazleton, Indiana. He and his wife sell packaged dressed turtle meat and display the shells of unusually large specimens on the walls in the market's retail area.

Dressing turtles is a messy and difficult task that few people care to undertake. The high price of dressed turtle meat reflects labor cost. The strength and bad temper of snappers make fishermen eager to dress or market them as soon as possible.

Connoisseurs of turtle meat agree that the snapper has a wide variety of flavors, textures, and colors. "There are seven different kinds of meat on a turtle" is an expression often heard among turtle fanciers. Portions of the meat are compared to beef, chicken, duck, opossum, pork, squirrel, and venison. Most turtle eaters make a soup or stew or dip the chunks in cornmeal breading and fry them like chicken.

The interplay between hierarchical status and personal choice is complex. There are many African Americans who, like most whites, disdain all river fish except fiddlers and game fish. There are also some whites who are glad to eat a fresh carp or buffalo. However, very few well-off whites, whether urban or rural, will eat any freshwater fish other than the most esteemed game species and farm-raised fiddlers.

Educated people, in particular, fear the effects of pollution, and if they do eat freshwater fish, it is usually farm-raised fiddlers. A librarian in Mount Vernon, Indiana, to whom I explained my research, gagged audibly and proceeded to change the subject. A State of Illinois Historic Site manager in Old Shawneetown insisted that there was no commercial fishing in the Ohio, despite nearly a dozen signs around this tiny village offering river fish for sale.

Area fish recipes vary little. Traditionally, most fish were breaded and deep-fried or panfried in lard, although vegetable shortening has largely taken lard's place in the last few decades. Deep-frying is primarily done in restaurants and at fish fries, panfrying at home. Panfrying is also the chief method used by vacationers and sportsfishers.

Most recent regional, organizational, homemakers' or Extension Service cookbooks do not include any recipes for freshwater fish. Fish recipes, if present at all, usually call for frozen fillets of ocean fish. However, a few cookbooks from Louisville and Paducah contain both fried catfish and baked carp recipes. Baked carp was both a Jewish and a German delicacy, so these books may represent their respective cities' central European immigrant heritage.

The frying of fish in the lower Ohio Valley is a traditional, informally communicated skill. The methods used at the Village of Ridgway municipal employees' fish fry, at Kaylor's, and by Mary Williams and Happy Thomas are practically identical and typical of the lower Ohio Valley. The only substantial difference in the way blacks and whites eat fish is that blacks often add pepper sauce, such as Tabasco or Louisiana Hot. One white restaurateur told me that the reason he had hot sauce on the tables was because "we get a lot of colored customers who stop in here for fish dinners, and they like that hot sauce!"

Jane and Michael Stern's guide to regional foodways, *Roadfood*, lists the "fiddler plate" as a regional specialty in the Paducah area. *The American Heritage Cookbook*, 1964 edition, gives a deep-fried catfish recipe essentially identical to that of the lower Ohio Valley, although it ascribes the recipe's origins to the South. Harriette Simpson Arnow's account of the settling of south-central Kentucky, *Seedtime on the Cumberland*, celebrates fried catfish as a delicacy among the pioneers. Whether eaten by blacks or whites, breaded fried catfish, panfried at home or deep-fried in a restaurant or at a fish fry, is related to the tradition of fried chicken in the South. It is a Sunday meal or delicacy and not an everyday fare.

NINE
River Folklore

Early travelers' accounts noted the river people's propensity for storytelling, singing, and musical performance. Some literary accounts portrayed raconteurs and musicians among the river people, as well as situations in which performance occurred. Some of today's fisherfolk are still deeply interested in the oral culture of their forebears and cultivate legends, tall tales, jokes, and songs that they consider traditional. These same individuals are often great first-person storytellers, recounting tales about the river, the fish, and their work as fishermen. Much of their oral culture establishes and maintains river folk identity, both as a source of pride and as a defense against negative stereotypes. There are also fishermen who are, in effect, self-elected curators of jokes, tales, songs, and similar material inherited from the days of nomadic houseboat life.

Circumstances in which traditional performance occurs are rarer today than they were a generation or two ago. They do, however, persist, especially in the cases in which a given fisherman has a reputation as a performer or raconteur. Roy Lee Walls's shop on the state highway is a congenial stop for tourists, conservation officers, and fish customers, at least in part because of Walls' stories and songs. When Tommy Sherer worked at the Cave-in-Rock Fish Market, locals and tourists alike would linger for his humorous tales of river life. Sherer, in turn, enjoyed getting together with Raymond "Bunk" Burke to hear his stories. For Owen Miller, Harold Weaver's songs and stories were as much a part of Miller's learning to be a river fisherman as was careful instruction in riving hoops and making nets, and he, like some of his neighbors, cherished the cassettes of tales and songs that Weaver mailed to them long after leaving the area. Most of the tale-telling and singing sessions that I witnessed (apart from those I induced by asking for performance material) occurred at fish markets. The ones I heard about secondhand were usually associated with fishermen teaching each other gear preparation and maintenance over a six-pack of beer or a jar of moonshine.

Tall tale telling is popularly associated with fishing, but it is more common to sportsfishers than to commercial fishers. Many tales heard from river folk today are well-known tall tales and other traditional humorous stories. The continuing appeal of these tales may be owing to the perception that they are part of "pioneer heritage," as is the work and way of life on the river. Almost all the people interviewed knew some of these narratives when asked about them.

A few individuals have cultivated a substantial repertoire that they like to perform. Roy Lee Walls and Harold Weaver are examples of raconteurs from the transitional generation of houseboaters who became sedentary fishermen. Similar reputations are attributed to Raymond "Bunk" Burke, Donald "Dutch" Moore, and Lawrence Wade. Other fishermen are raconteurs of fishing narratives. Tommy Sherer, Curtis Lang, Bill Williams, Roland Causey of Solitude, Indiana, and Orval Loven are leading narrators of the river-fishing way of life.

The large proportions of some Ohio Valley fish has been the subject of many narratives of personal experience. Although fish size may have increased with successive tellings, these narratives are intended to be not humorous tall tales but recollections of wonder at the magnitude of the fish. Donald "Dutch" Moore tells a story of seeing a farmer hand-grab a huge buffalo in a nearby ditch:

> Right on the bottom, there'd be brush all in there and those fish would come in there feeding, see? There was big ditches all in there because the farmers just took an old crude outfit and tried to get to that lowland where it goes out to this lake, and then goes back in the river. They'd get right alongside one of those ditches and they'd have on hip boots. This big fellow, a farmer, oh, he must have been six-foot-three or four and weighed about two-hundred fifty pounds. There was a big old buffalo come up, and the fellow got out and he got his fingers in that thing and it weighed about fifty pounds. I was just a kid about fourteen years old.

Moore also recalled when he and his son hooked but failed to land a giant catfish by the Cave-in-Rock ferry landing:

> My boy and me, we was running lines. We had one right across the ferry landing and we picked it up and it just started right up to the bank, and I said, "A boat's dragging this one, Bubby." And it was going right up to the ferry landing, oh, maybe forty, fifty feet from me, and we shut the motor off and there wasn't any current in the river, see? People got out of a car and come over to the river. The old baby boy (he must have been sixteen or seventeen years old then) he saw the fish and said,

"Daddy, that's a dandy." I said, "I'll tell you what. Since you're left-handed, it'll come just right for you to lift it, now. I want you to catch a big one," and directly that damn fish's tail came up. I just turned loose of the motor and got the oars. I got off the back seat and got up in the middle, and that fish's tail come right up past them oarlocks. Must have been five feet long. I said, "Get that damn fish, Bubby!" And he got excited and scared the damn fish, and it went down and got off. He said he saw the fish, all right. He bragged it. He said it was a *big* fish. Of course, *I* never did go in for any records.

Humorous tales and jokes are the most common form of stories performed by river raconteurs. Harold Weaver was able to supply quite a few tall tales:

A guy one time said he had a dog. He said, "That dog would watch me, and anything I done, he'd do too." He said, "If I want to go rabbit hunting, I'd just go out in a field and go kicking on a brush pile, and he wouldn't outrun anything but rabbits. If I wanted to go squirrel hunting," he said, "I'd just go out in the woods and look up in the trees and he wouldn't tree nothing but squirrels." He said, "A fellow wanted to go quail hunting, I'd just go walking out through a meadow. He'd get the idea quick and he wouldn't flush nothing but quail."
He said, "One day I thought I'd go a-fishing." He said, "Oh, I got him now. He won't know what I'm doing now." He said he started rigging him up a pole and line. He said he put a string on it, put a float on it, put a hook on it, put a sinker on it and he had to go down to the chicken house to go to the creek. He said he got down there and he heard something down by the henhouse there, and he looked, and that old dog, he done dug himself a can full of worms.

One time I got tired of commercial fishing and I thought, "Oh, well, I'll go crappie fishing." I went and bought me a hundred minnows, and I had to pass by a guy that made moonshine. I stopped there and got me a gallon of whiskey, and I said, "Well, I'll have a little fun out there anyway," and I put that whiskey in a great big-mouthed jug.
I got on down and got to a boat and went to a tree and tied up. I baited my hook, shouldered over the jug, and took a drink, and about the time I looked back and let the jug down, my cork was coming up and I jerked and didn't get nothing. Well, I sat there and every time I put on a minner, I'd take a drink and look and see my cork coming up. I done fished ninety-nine of them minners and just had one left. I said, "I ain't gonna drink, this time." Now I started to put that minner on my hook, and he flopped out of my hand and went in that moonshine. I reached down in there and got him out, and I could tell he was drunk by looking at him, and I put him on my hook and threw him over the

side, and sit there, and I sit there about fifteen minutes, and finally my cork went under and hooked something and I rassled around there about thirty minutes, and I got it over in the boat, and it was a fifty-four-pound yellow cat. And I got down a-straddle him for to get the hook out of him and he didn't have no hook in his mouth. That minner had that catfish by the nap' of the neck.

A guy one time told about catching a fish in the creek and said it weighed a hundred and ten pounds, and he said he caught it on a pole and line. Course the guy he was telling it to didn't believe him. He [the other man] said, "Tell you what *I* done. I was down there at that same creek a-fishing one time, and that was five years ago, and I was back down there a-fishing tonight, where I dropped my lantern in the river." He said, "I was down there today a-fishing and I caught that lantern, that same lantern, and brought it out and it was still burning."

This guy that told the fish story said, "Wait a minute, now!" He said, "Well, I'll tell you what I'll do. If you'll knock about seventy-five or a hundred pounds off of that fish," he said, "I'll blow my lantern out."

One time there was two guys went a-fishing and they rented a boat off a guy and they went out in the middle of a very big lake, and it wasn't long before they'd caught their limit. Boy, them fish was really biting. This guy says, "We ought to mark this place and come back later. This is a good fishing place."

After they got back to the car, the guy said, "Did you mark the place? I forgot it."

"Yeah," he said. "I marked it."

"How'd you mark it," he said.

"I put a x-mark on the side of the boat."

"X-mark on the side of the boat? That's the craziest damn thing I ever heard of. Well, what if we don't get the same boat next time?"

Along the river, there is a whole cycle of jokes about the stupidity or backwardness of people from Arkansas. This has been the case at least since Mark Twain incorporated some of them into his writings. Here is one of the milder examples, also told by Weaver:

Down in Arkansas one time there was a poor family lived, and they had eight kids had to go about four miles to school, and they was eight, nine, or ten years old afore they got to go to school. One of them went in and teacher says, "Come up here, honey. I want you to give me your name and where you live at."

And she went up, and she told the teacher, said, "I live down there in the holler. I don't know where it is, but about three miles from here." And she said her name is "Snotty Nose."

Teacher said, "No, now come on. Give me your real name. I gotta put it down on the register, so I'll know who you is."

These kids in Arkansas, they didn't know what's their whole name till they get big enough to get married, and then they'd tell them. They'd just call them a nickname. She said, "My name's Snotty Nose," and the teacher said, "I see I won't be getting nothing out of you. I'll just write your parents a note." And she wrote a little note and told her to send this here little girl's name back, so that she could put it on the register. The girl went by her kid brother and said, "Come on, Shitty Britches. She ain't gonna believe you either."

Since World War II, commercial music, such as country-western, rock, and bluegrass, have replaced traditional music in the lower Ohio Valley. Because of their cultivated interest in older rural traditions, several of the older river folk still maintain a repertoire of traditional songs. Some of the longer ballads are recited instead of sung. Weaver called them "say songs."

Although a number of individuals know a song or two, the most extensive repertoires are those of Roy Lee Walls and Harold Weaver. As with the traditional tales, those songs that survive tend to be those that are humorous, such as the old minstrel song, "Freckle-Faced Consumption Sarah Jane," which both Walls and Weaver knew.

One of Harold Weaver's humorous songs, "The Juice of the Forbidden Fruit," is related to the well-known ballad "Jesse James." Weaver also liked to perform the British broadside murder ballad "The Oxford Girl," today better known as the bluegrass standard "The Knoxville Girl." It describes a murder committed beside a river.

Weaver learned some of his repertoire from John Lambert Sr. while he and his father lived at Saline Landing, Illinois. He sings the old stage song, "I Was Born About Four Thousand Years Ago" in the context of remembering Old John Lambert, a riverbank squatter who made net hoops, hewed ties, and did other seasonal work in the area:

Old man John Lambert, Dick's daddy, he used to work all week and make ties. (I got to get this in there: He had the seven sons and old man John Lambert is a seventh son. So Dick Lambert is a seventh son of a seventh son.) And every Saturday night and Sunday, that old man'd go to the river and buy the biggest catfish he could get. I'd see him buy them that weighed fifty and sixty pounds. And he'd always carry that jug of whiskey with him. He wasn't very tight then. He'd carry that jug of whiskey in one hand, that catfish over his shoulder, and he'd always sing that song, "I Was Born About Four Thousand Years Ago." You heard it ain't you? And he'd sing:

I was born a-bout four thou-sand years a-go _____

And there's no-thing in the world I don't know _____ I saw

Pe-ter, Paul and Mo-ses play-in' Ring A-round the Ro-ses I can

Original final note F

whup the man that says it is-n't so _____

I saw Satan when he searched the Garden o'er,
I saw Adam and Eve driven from the door,
From the bushes I was peeping, and the apple he
was eating,
I can swear that I'm the guy that ate the core.

I saw Noah when he built his famous ark,
I declare it was night, it was dark,
I saw Jonah swallow the whale, and I pulled the
lion's tail,
And I crossed the land of Canaan on a log.

Queen Elizabeth fell dead in love with me,
We were married in Milwaukee secretly,
And I fooled arou' and shook 'er and I went
with General Hooker
To fight mosquitoes down in Tennessee.

Every time he'd get drunk, that old man'd sing that. He fell in the river and drowned, drunk. Him and Cal Craig'd been over at Caseyville, and came back in a johnboat, and landed the boat, and they found old man John Lambert's coat laying in the boat and Dick Weaver up on the bank in a tent, and they couldn't find him, and he took a pike pole and the next morning, that old man, he was laying right on the side of that boat. He used to make net hoops, ties, rails. He claimed he made enough rails to fence Hardin County.

Harold Weaver also learned part of his repertoire from his father, including the traditional American ballad, "The State of Arkansas," which concurs with the river people's disparaging humor about Arkansas. Weaver performed it as a "say song."

Roy Lee Walls was once an accomplished guitarist before a hand injury limited his abilities. When he is on the river alone, many of his old songs come back to him, but sometimes only as fragments. Being on the river reminds him of his kinship with generations of river people who told stories and sang songs when they socialized. One song Walls still loves to perform is "Travellin' Man From Tennessee," a version of the minstrel song, "Tennessee Coon." It is a favorite because it reminds him of the itinerant ways of his houseboat-dwelling forebears and, in his words, "how they could be there one day and be gone the next."

Walls also sings a sentimental waltz from around World War I, "Blue-Eyed Soldier Boy." He performs many of standard songs of the hillbilly and early country repertoire, such as "My Bucket's Got a Hole in It" and "Wabash Cannonball." The latter he sometimes sings as his own off-color parody, satirizing Cairo's onetime reputation as a vice center.

Roy Lee Walls is especially proud of his mastery of "hollering," a form of communication found in various places in the rural South and often associated with rivers. He reports that as late as the 1960s, people who worked in open boats used loud yodel-like cries to communicate long-distance. A fisherman uncle of his usually won the hollering contest held annually at a fair in Mounds, Illinois. He calls them "yodeling" or "Tennessee nigger hoots." "Nigger hollers," "nigger hoots," and similarly named cries, usually performed by whites, were once common all over the South. The name may indicate African-American origin, or it may be a term of disparagement.

Another lower Ohio Valley hollerer is Red "Buck" Estes, who lives

Travellin' Man From Tennessee

As sung by Roy Lee Walls

I tell all you peo-ple I'm a tra-vel-in' man was born in Ten-nes-see Trade was stea-lin' chi-ckens while an-y thing could see The p'lice got af-ter this boy He cer'n-ly got o'-er the road Makes no diff'rence a fast a freight train go that fool would get on board Oh Lord was-n't he a

Original final note Ab

trav'lin' man? Oh Lord was-n't he a trav'lin' man?

He went down to a spring just to get a pail o'
    water,
The distance to the spring was just twelve miles
    and a quarter.
On his way back he stumbled and fell down,
But he run back home and got another pail, and
    caught the water 'fore it hit the ground.
(REPEAT REFRAIN)

and works on the Green River, near Mammoth Cave, Kentucky. Estes hollered a "nigger whoop" on the commercial recording *"I'm On My Journey Home"* in 1978. Folklorist W. Lynwood Montell reports that on the upper Cumberland, people used "nigger hollers" to signal local ferry operators.

Walls recalled how hollering was used for communication on the rivers:

> We lived here at what we called Holloway Landing and he lived at Joe Romaine's Landing, we called it, which is three miles by water, and if we come out on the river at night, we yodeled, and if he was out there, he'd answer us. We could hear each other. That sound would travel that far, just as plain. My dad and grandfather and him could talk to one another that far, and understand one another, what they was saying, when they spoke and hollered each word at a time, give it a chance to go in separate. Like, if they was going to ask him if he was gonna be in town next day, they'd say:

See? Separated the words, and each word would come in that way. Now, in case, like, if we wanted to get ahold of him, or him get ahold of us, along late in the evening, they'd come out with that "Tennessee nigger hoot":

would be what they'd do, you see, and then wait for a few minutes. But if we ever heard it, then which ever one was hollerin', the other ones'd go down to the river and get in their boat and go out in the river, and then they'd start talking to one another.

Roy Lee Walls still practices the full yodels or hollers himself, while out on the river. One of them he calls simply, *"the* Tennessee Nigger Hoot." He uses it to express gladness or vitality:

Another holler he still performs he calls the "'Stress Yell," mean-ing "distress yell." It is a traditional SOS call among area river folk:

Many fisherfolk of the lower Ohio Valley deliberately conserve traditional lore of river life. Parts of it are connected to the experi-ence of fishing itself, such as game warden stories or reminiscences about outstanding river characters. There was indeed a time when many people could make a sparse but adequate living pursuing the cycle of river activities on a full-time basis. Those times are now gone, but they are still remembered fondly. Also remembered fondly by many are the days when thousands of people lived independent, nomadic, natural resource-based lives on houseboats throughout the midwestern and southern inland river systems. Today's fishermen's ties to that era are in their work and in their memories of tales, songs, jokes, and hollers. For that reason, fishermen with direct familial or experiential ties to the houseboat era often continue to cultivate its otherwise moribund verbal lore.

TEN

Learning, Custom, and Identity

Commercial river fishermen endure insecurity, low return, and physical adversity for the satisfaction of being independent and feeling close to the river and its environment. In other words, fishermen get something intangible and desirable from their labors, as do sportspeople, artists, and hobbyists.

Participation in the culture of the river folk gives joy to fishermen and keeps them on the river. They have preserved portions of the culture of the nomadic houseboaters who were their parents and grandparents, but they have also inherited some of the negative images that beset the houseboaters.

Individuals enter and exit the profession of commercial fishing, depending on economic, environmental, and licensing factors. Newcomers try out fishing. Part-timers and sportsfishers buy commercial licenses. These people are not usually considered to be "real fishermen" by lifelong full-timers. There are also long-time commercial fishermen who take other work for various reasons, usually economic. They may return to the river if conditions change, or they may stay with a job that offers benefits and security and resume fishing only part-time.

Orval Loven is a part-time fisherman. Although he would rather fish, he feels a need for the security he gets from his "day job" on the sand dredge. A day when he only catches twenty fish reminds him of why he does not choose to become a full-time Wabash River fisherman: "Fishing is just like everything else. If I could devote my entire time to it and had the business, I believe I could make a living at it, but there's a lot of guys can't. They think they can, but they can't."

Loven's heroes are those few who do manage to fish full-time. His negative example is the case of two young men from nearby Carmi who came to Grayville a few years ago with a bank loan, a new fish dock full of freezers, a power hookup, and a couple of boats. They were out of business in ten months. "I know I could do it, if I put my mind to it. I've learned what I need to know. But I need that check." He nods in the direction of their dock, as he cranks his boat up on a boat trailer that he has kept parked next to the landing at the foot of Main Street.

Loven likes to talk about the full-time fishermen, many of whom are retired and how he learned from them:

> I've learned from every man in this part of the country that you can imagine that's ever fished, I've learnt something from him. I've learned from Albert Lauder. Roland Causey, over by Mount Vernon, Indiana, learned me a lot of stuff. He's a successful fisherman. A lot of times, when I was first starting, if I wanted advice, I'd go to a guy like that. Ain't no need to go to anybody didn't know any more than I did. Well, that's years ago. Well, I soaked right up what he could tell me. Now Howard Durham of Shawneetown, I know him. Howard, he showed me some things. . . . Any time I saw a guy doing something that I thought was different from mine, I thought was better, I'd say, "Hold on a minute! Show me that, if you will," and when they showed me, why I'd just change it.

In the days of nomadic fishing, most fishermen also collected driftwood lumber to sell (called drifting), trapped furbearers, and pursued other "self-help occupations." Roy Lee Walls and his father cut timber and cleared new ground, and Roy later worked as a carpenter. Even back then, many people took temporary work on land, when it was necessary and available.

Harold Weaver and his father Oscar hewed railroad ties and sold them to the railroads. Oscar Weaver was also an itinerant preacher, who set up brush arbors (locally called bush harbors) along the river and held fish fry revival meetings after large catches of fish. Weaver tells of his father addressing a crowd, "I told you that you could have a fish fry, and the Lord saw fit to fill our fish boxes!" "I dragged that trammel net up and down the river all night trying to catch them fish," remembers Harold. The elder Weaver conducted Pentecostal missions along the river at Saline Landing, Cave-in-Rock, and Elizabethtown, Illinois. He eventually settled on the high bluff called Lover's Leap, overlooking the Ohio River near Olmsted, Illinois, where he conducted camp meetings for many years and preached in area Pentecostal churches, supporting his ministry by fishing and by making gear.

Many of today's river fishermen are still avid trappers, and some earn much of their capital for fishing equipment and operation during the relatively brief trapping season. Short-term heavy construction projects such as those of the Corps of Engineers and the Department of Energy are also sources of capital.

River fishing is a "folk occupation" because it is learned, informally, face-to-face, and across generations. River fishermen are an identity-conscious group who share occupational customs, beliefs, and expressions. Fishing knowledge, technique, and custom are orally transmitted from one generation of fishermen to the next. Today's fishermen are usually alone when fishing. Thus they acquire much of their experience on an individual basis. Their circumstances are usually similar enough that fishermen end up sharing a common body of knowledge and technique.

Fishermen consider learning a lifelong process, based in large part on experience. But almost all of them learned the basic techniques from older fishermen in the area, usually during childhood or youth.

Running jumperlines, rowing boatloads of fish from a seine-haul or a gill-net drift, and helping prepare and repair nets were the usual early responsibilities of a young person learning from an older fisherman. Later, one learned more complex tasks, such as net-knitting and net-hanging, handling complex gear, such as gill and trammel nets, and the subtleties of knowing where and when to fish for desired species. Carl Eswine of Shawneetown remembers how he prevailed upon older fishermen to teach him how to fish and make gear: "As a rule, I got mine [instruction] from some of the old-timers. I used to worry the life out of them. I even got one old man to show me how to knit these nets and he did. He took time off and showed me. And the same way about your fishing, he'd tell you. It seems like they took more of an interest in the kids in them days. They'd explain things to you."

Owen Miller learned white-oak hoopmaking and knitting and hanging nets directly from Harold Weaver. Stanley Murphy speaks of Joe Ed Clanky of nearby Brookport as his fishing mentor, and Walter Ramsey attributes much of his knowledge to early apprenticeship to Raymond "Bunk" Burke of Carrsville, Kentucky.

No one has a monopoly on fishing knowledge, and a wise fisherman knows that one can learn something from practically every other fisherman. Roy Lee Walls uses a variant of a traditional humorous tale to explain how this is so:

My dad told me when I was pretty small, he said, "Don't never think you know it all. Regardless of how foolish a man seems to be or anything or crazy," he says, "he sets down to give you some advice, you listen to every bit, 'cause somewhere along the line, some part of it's gonna help you," and I've found it to be true.

We got, as they say, a "bughouse" here at Anna [Illinois], an asylum,

A flathead or mudcat on display at Metropolis, Illinois, ca. 1950. (Photographer unknown; photo courtesy of Curtis Lang.)

yeah, a state hospital. There's a fellow driving along there one day and a wheel fell off of his car. He was standing there wondering what to do next. And this fellow's standing there looking over the fence at him. He says, "What's the matter, sir?"

"Well, sir, my wheel fell off. They got no lug nuts on them. I gotta walk in to town and get some."

"Well, you know, sir, if it was me," he says, "I'd go around the other wheels and take a nut off each one of them, put that wheel back on there and drive in to town."

That fellow says, "You know, you're supposed to be on the outside and me inside."

And so it works that way. Now see that fellow is supposed to have good knowledge and good brains, and that other fellow's inside there 'cause he's supposed to been crazy. But he told that guy something to help.

Looking at the careers of fishermen revealed in interviews, it seems likely that those who can continue to learn from others and innovate based on their own experience are those who can continue to make a living at fishing. Those who are too tradition-bound eventually give up. Bill Williams explains:

There's a lot of fishermen that don't make much money fishing. They maybe got one way to do it, there's no other way and that's the way. Probably their dad taught them and everything. Well, you find that's true in a lot of things. They got one way of doing it, that's the only way they'll ever do it. There's a lot of people just won't change with the times. Nobody knows all there is about fishing, but a fellow that "knows it all," he's not gonna learn something else. I tried a lot of things that didn't work. I tried a lot of things that did work.

One source of innovation is experience with fishing outside of the immediate locale. The introduction of such gear as slat traps, snaglines, and under-ice seines by fishermen coming in from other places in the Midwest has already been addressed. Fishermen interviewed listed many places where they had acquired fishing experience, including Florida, the Gulf of Mexico, and the North Pacific. Harold Weaver lived for two years with his son in Washington State during the mid-1970s. There he briefly tried fishing in Puget Sound. He found its expanse of water frightening: "I don't like it out there. There's too much water there. Like the colored fellow said when he seen the ocean, he said that's the only time he ever seen anything that there was enough of!"

Full-time commercial fishermen are very conscious of their occupational identity in contrast with other groups. These include landbound people in general, especially farmers and middle-class town dwellers; conservation authorities; sportsfishers; and most specifically, part-time fishermen, especially those who are seen as primarily fishing for sport but also engaging in some commercial sale of fish. Many of the stories fishermen tell most willingly concern some aspect of *differential identity*, involving conflicts with authorities, sportsfishers, or part-timers. And in many stories, they defend the fisherman against negative stereotypes perceived to be held by outsiders.

Those fishermen descended from the houseboat subculture still identify with that population as its descendants and think of themselves as "river people." Houseboaters and river people have been both romanticized and disparaged. The fisherfolk, for obvious reasons, identify with the positive image, but they are also aware of the negative stereotypes of laziness, alcohol abuse, and larceny. The houseboater-fisherman hero of Cormac McCarthy's novel, *Suttree*, is a brawling, licentious drunk. Physician Carl R. Bogardus of Austin, Indiana, devoted his entire book, *Shantyboat*, to characterizing

Oscar Weaver's family houseboat on the Ohio River, ca. 1930. *Left to right:* Mary Melissa Weaver, Sarah Weaver, Marcy Weaver, and Oscar Weaver. (Photo courtesy Sarah Weaver Clark.)

houseboater life as a continual round of loafing and stealing. But Harlan Hubbard's *Shantyboat: A River Way of Life*, Lois Lenski's *Houseboat Girl*, and the works of Ben Lucien Burman exalt the independence, resourcefulness, and strong family ties of river folk.

Some people who are not themselves commercial fishermen but who live and work with them agree with the positive image of the fisherman as independent and resourceful. Marketer Harold "Pat" Patton, who was never a fisherman himself, expressed these thoughts: "Fisherman's got more nerve and more ambition than any other denomination of workmen in the world, in my opinion, because if they go out today and don't catch, then it's, 'We *gotta* catch them tomorrow!' That's the way they look at it." The late Metropolis mussel-shell dealer and processor Paul McDaniels described his plant superintendent, fisherman Curtis Lang thus: "One of the best on the river was my superintendent out there. His name is Curt Lang and he used to produce a lot here. He was one of the top men out there. He's a man for all seasons, just like a lot of those commercial fishermen were. They can repair a boat, they can do plumbing, they

can repair an engine, that's why they were successful. Henry Story—
that's "Abe Foster" in that book, *Houseboat Girl*—could do all of that.
He could build his own houseboat. That's a way of life. They enjoyed that."

Local poet Theodore Weatherford, of Point Township, Indiana,
at the Wabash-Ohio confluence, romanticized a fisherman neighbor
in his 1970 poem "The River Rat":

> He told of his life on the river,
> And how he had made his way,
> How he had worked his nets and lines,
> To earn his daily pay.
> He had been through high waters,
> He had rode his boat through the storm.
> No one thought the River Rat
> Could come to any harm.

On the other hand, former houseboater Roy Lee Walls loves to
tell the story of a pair of larcenous relatives who lived on a houseboat near Smithland:

> I'll tell you a kind of a story about my grandfather and his cousin. They
> were young, and he was living near Smithland then. They still used a
> skiff for transportation from Smithland to Paducah, even way back then.
> And they'd been down to Smithland to get a supply of groceries, two
> young fellows, and they got thirsty.
>
> Well, a farmhouse was sitting up on top of a hill, and they went up
> there to get them a drink of water out of the pump, where it's cool. Well,
> they got up there and hollered, "Hello!" and couldn't raise nobody. They
> were gonna tell them they were gonna get a drink of water from the
> pump, and they kept looking and knocking and couldn't see nobody,
> and they went around the back and the back door's wide open and there's
> one of those number six box cook stoves sitting there with a dinner kettle
> full of beans cooking for a dinner and they happened to look out across
> the field and there was a lady way out there picking stuff to bring up for
> dinner. Well, they got their drink of water and they started off, and my
> grandfather's cousin, he was always a fellow that was pretty mischie-
> vous, said, "Ain't you getting hungry, Joe?"
>
> He said, "Yeah."
>
> He says, "Well, you pick up the beans," he said, "I'll take the stove.
> We'll set it in the boat and finish cooking it on the way up. We'll have
> beans on up the river."
>
> So they did. He reached and got some gunnysacks, and laid it up on
> his shoulder, and my grandfather helped him get that stove up here now
> with the fire in it, put it on his back, and he got the pot of beans, and

they went on down and set it in the boat and pulled on up the river, and
my grandfather often said he wondered how that lady felt when she come
back and her stove and beans were gone.

Despite this and similar stories, it is unfair to stigmatize today's
river folk as thieves, especially considering that they are so often
themselves victims of theft by outsiders. Many fishermen have actually left the trade because of problems with boat, gear, and motor
theft.

Negative stereotypes of fishing and fishermen are not confined
to the American Midwest. Fisheries scientist Andres von Brandt of
the U.N. Food and Agricultural Organization notes, "The lowlier
plight of the `poor' fisherman is practically universal, at least in
Western culture." In many places in the world, fishermen are reputed to have a high rate of alcoholism. Some Ohio Valley fishermen are abstainers, especially those who attend evangelical
churches, and several area counties are dry. Many fishermen are
moderate drinkers, and beer and whiskey seem to be important social lubricants among people in the area. There are, of course, also
some drunken fishermen in the Ohio Valley, but most of them seem
to be part-timers and those who can no longer make a living on the
river. The hard-drinking stereotype persists, perhaps because of the
association of hard drinking with riverbank squatters, some of
whom attempt to subsist on fishing.

Handling fish slime and stale-cheese bait will, at least temporarily,
make the river fisherman unfit company for land-dwellers and contributes to the negative stereotype. As an apprentice fisherman ad-
justs to the bad odor, he or she confirms a separate identity from
those who are offended by the smells of the trade.

Practices such as fishing blind and avoiding attention from
sportsfishers, part-timers, and conservation authorities have led to
a necessary deceptiveness on the part of Ohio Valley commercial
fishermen. This is also the case in many of the world's other fishing
grounds, and it contributes to the negative stereotype.

There may be a universal conflict between sportsfishers and
people who fish for commerce. It is based on the unjustified belief
that commercial fishermen are hauling in, with their nets, all the
fish for which sportsfishers are angling. In Harold Weaver's words:
"The sportsfishermen have made it awful hard on us, telling false-
hoods about commercial fishermen having and catching a lot of
game fish."

Commercial fishermen see sportsfishers as wasters of valuable food. Stanley Murphy explains: "They'd rather throw them away than clean them or dress them, and a commercial fisherman, if they'd let him catch crappie, he'd sell them. They wouldn't go to waste."

Most commercial fishermen in the Ohio Valley bemoan the pro-liferation of "kneebooters" or "weekenders"—sportsfishers who buy commercial licenses for leisure use. Although some of these are va-cationers from the city, most are local people who fish for recreation but who work other blue-collar jobs in the area, such as in mining, construction, factories, or transportation. Those who sell their catch undersell the prices of commercial fishermen, and they do not know the customs regarding territoriality and noninterference with oth-ers' gear. Theft and vandalism of commercial fishermen's gear and boats are attributed to vacationers and kneebooters, who "think they own the river because they rent a cabin out there."

Stanley Murphy often contends with this problem when he fishes the Ohio off Roper's Landing, Illinois, site of many weekend cab-ins: "I started there in 1960, wasn't nobody around, very few people. But then they got to coming in there and, boy, there's lots of them. You know there's fifty, sixty people there every weekend, and they think they own the river. They want you to just get away and let them have it, and you've been a-fishing there for years trying to make a living at it. They put their stuff out right on top of you. They expect you to move."

The vicissitudes of fish availability and marketability keep most fishermen from realizing any substantial profits. Roy Lee Walls ex-plains: "I've been around this Ohio River fishing all my life and I've never seen a millionaire come out of it yet. Now, if certain times of a year, if you could do like that all the year through, and get rid of the amount of fish that you caught, why, you could probably be-come a millionaire, but fishing don't work that way." Walls believes that one's success or failure as a fisherman is determined by the will of God:

> It's just something there that some way the good Lord repairs things to make a way for the fisherman. Now I've had people out here on the river, before, fishing along beside of me and if they didn't catch some fish, why they'd just stomp, cuss, and carry on. Well, I think if the good Lord wants you to catch them fish, he'll give you the knowledge where to put that net, and if he don't, well, you're not gonna catch them. On the other hand, if he had you catch a load of fish every day, you'd get to be a rich man. You'd get to where you didn't appreciate nothing.

Serious fishermen agree that regulation and conservation are necessary for their livelihoods, but they consider many of the laws needlessly arbitrary. Conservation officers or game wardens have been in the lower Ohio Valley since the 1880s. In the early days, game wardens were political appointees who were paid a portion of the fines they levied. Since the 1950s they have been professionalized according to Civil Service standards. In the early days, enforcement was lax and arbitrary. Consequently, instances of enforcement were highly resented and the officers' motivations distrusted. Fishermen in the Cave-in-Rock vicinity recall that at least one overly zealous officer was murdered by a resentful area fisherman. Fishermen are still quick to criticize those conservation officers whom they consider unfair or overly zealous.

The difficulty of enforcing all the detailed regulations makes it possible for fishermen to violate some laws without expecting to be apprehended. Some officers have reputations for relative permissiveness. Although they would never ignore gross violations, such as dynamiting, fishing without licenses and tags, or taking and marketing game species, such minor infractions as incorrect spacing of stages on a jumperline or continuing to haul on a drifted gill net after sunset are often overlooked. In some localities, minimum size limits for fiddlers are not strictly enforced among commercial fishermen, provided violations are not too blatant. During the time in the 1970s when small-mesh fiddler nets were prohibited on the Ohio River, some officers simply neglected to measure mesh-sizes on the gear of those licensed fishermen whom they knew fished for a living. Information about strictness or laxity of law enforcement circulates informally by word of mouth. As one fisherman said, "All those years, you were just a little on the shady side of the law, or you didn't make a living."

In some instances, tacit agreements exist between fishermen and conservation officers. An officer levies a fifty- or one-hundred-dollar fine against a fisherman once or twice a year and then ignores most of his activities for the rest of the time. The fisherman, in turn, knows how far he can go in violating regulations and avoids any serious breaches that the officer could not overlook.

Certain fishermen are noted for their ability to outwit conservation officers by such gambits as constantly changing the times and places where they fish. It is also difficult to surprise a fisherman on the broad expanse of the Ohio between Smithland and Cairo. One fisherman explains:

Different times, different places. Wouldn't put my boat in at the same place. A creature of habit's really easy to catch. If he has a set pattern, it's easy to catch him, but a broken pattern, it's hard to figure it out. They watch me today, they sit there and watch, and you're somewhere else, that's all. I just lucked out and kept one jump ahead. Well that's a big river, and it's hard for you to get down here with a pair of binoculars and look down there and watch a guy and see him raise a net. It's hard for you to go down there and raise that net if he hasn't got a buoy on it, and I used real short tail line there. I knew right where it was at.

He also believes that once a fisherman has a reputation for being easy to catch or for readily confessing when confronted, the officers will concentrate on him and leave the others alone.

Fishermen have considered a few individual officers unfair or corrupt. One occasional complaint is against officers who levy a cash fine on the spot instead of a summons. The money goes into the warden's pocket, so this practice is, in effect, a form of extortion with which the fishermen complies only because it costs less than a real fine plus lost work time. In general, fishermen take a philosophical attitude toward the fining system. Laurel Millis says: "They do some unreasonable things, but then I know lot of times I did something illegal, like that jerking law. I never got caught at it. But then I've paid fines when I shouldn't've had to done it."

The tension between fishermen and authorities leads to a whole genre of "game warden stories." These are by no means exclusive to the Ohio River, and they have been collected in fisheries all over those parts of the world where game laws are enforced. In most of these stories, the fisherman bests the officer. The ultimate game warden story on the lower Ohio may be the one, cited previously, of Bill Cox's victorious suit against two wardens in the Illinois State Supreme Court.

In Illinois, it is illegal for a commercial fisherman to buy fish from another fisherman for resale, unless he has an expensive wholesaler's license. This is a difficult regulation to enforce, but when it is, it hurts the fisherman who happens to receive an order for fish on a day when he has a bad catch. The regulation is often ignored. One Wabash River fisherman recalls a time when he made a large purchase of live buffalo and carp from another fisherman, only to be reported by a disgruntled neighbor:

Well, I went to a guy one time that lived out of Crossville. I'd come back, I'd just filled my box full. I had at least six hundred pound of carp and buffalo out there, and I'd buy them and then skin them. I'd get them from him for ten cents a pound and sell them for a quarter. I made more than he did. I might've made some more, but I skinned them, wrapped them up, and if any died I had to take that loss. I just got them in there [in the livebox] good and up come the game warden. And the fish, after it's been out of water, if it's cold weather in the spring, why they'll stay alive, they hibernate, you know. They're all in there getting their breath back on top of the water, and you'd know the conservation officer'd notice anything, he'd had to get out there and see that. He said, "You're not buying any fish, are you?" This guy up here had told him about it. I said, "I don't need to buy any fish." I never did say I hadn't bought any. And I just walked over to my box, I had a box about four feet square I could open up, and I just opened it up. They was just laying in there, just plumb cold and trying for to get going again. I opened up the box and if he'd've known, why he could've looked at them and seen I just had them in there five minutes. "Naw," he said, "you don't need to buy any fish." I never did tell him I was buying.

Orval Loven tells a story of a poverty-stricken subsistence fisherman near Mt. Carmel, Illinois who intimidated local conservation officers to make them leave him alone:

I knew a bunch of game wardens back then. They went up here about seventeen, eighteen miles. There's an old boy up there who was as poor as he could possibly be. He got out and hoed corn, got a little money to buy him some twine. Well, he made him four or five nets. Set there and worked real hard to make them, all right. He didn't have no money to go down and buy a bunch of tags. Actually, at that time, he was hoeing corn for probably fifty cents a day. He got the twine, got them built, till a bunch of game wardens come along, and he didn't have no tags on them. That was the law. They'd go down and take nets and burn them, that used to be the law. Just pile them up on a brush pile, pour gas on them and burn them if there wasn't a tag on them or a license.

They gathered his nets up, piled them on a brush pile, poured kerosene on them, and was about to burn them. He come up with an old shotgun worth about fifty cents. A man in that condition, I've been that way, he don't care much for nothing and so he said, "Well, now, boys, that is the law for you to burn my nets up. You fellows can burn my nets. But I've worked hard to get that and I'm feeding my children. I'll tell you what to do. You set that brush fire and burn my nets, and I'll burn all three of you right on top of the same brushpile."

And one of them said to the others, "Well, we don't just have to burn his nets up, do we?"

Other one said, "No, I don't believe we do. You go ahead. Take these nets back to those fish."

It was a matter of that was the law, and that was their duty, but a

Orval Loven on the Wabash River near Grayville, Illinois, 1978.

man in such conditions can take a little bit into consideration. I would if I was game warden.

Territoriality in the lower Ohio Valley has always been informal and loosely enforced. This contrasts with other North American inland fishing areas, such as the middle Mississippi and the White River of Arkansas, where whole stretches were reserved by individual fishermen who sometimes patrolled their territory with a shotgun. There are a few exceptions, such as Matthew Vaughn, who guarded a fishing spot at Cairo Point at the exact confluence of the Ohio and the Mississippi. Usually respect for territoriality is simply a matter of refraining from placing one's gear across someone else's. In the days when fishermen cleared specific areas of riverbottom for seine-hauling, these places were considered to belong to the fishermen who had done the work. Territoriality is a more significant problem for mussellers, who must work the limited locations where there are mussel beds.

Years ago, commercial fishermen's fishing grounds were avoided by other users of the river. Stanley Murphy remembers: "It ought to be back like it was when I was a kid. You stayed away from commercial fishermen's fishing grounds. Everybody did. He had a certain spot he'd fish and everybody stayed from. It was just natural." Many people fishing today do not know the courtesies regarding gear placement that have developed as traditions among long time fishermen. Roy Lee Walls explains: "And somebody hasn't been a fisherman, up until he learns what the ropes are, well, he thinks wherever he puts his rigging out, that ought to be his ground, a hundred percent, but it doesn't work that way. A fellow accidentally gets in on top of you, you don't destroy his rigging. Now if he's messing with your rigging, yeah, then you start thinking about straightening him out." But some part-timers will deliberately place their rigging on top of a full-timer's gear in hopes that it will be a good fishing spot.

Fishermen have to use their own means to discourage theft and vandalism of boats, motors, and gear and the theft of fish from gear. They attribute such deeds to outsiders. Fishermen are convinced that their colleagues leave their equipment alone. There have, of course, always been a few dishonest fishermen who did not "play by the rules" and who stole gear or ran others' gear to poach their fish. Fishermen suspected of "messing with" others' gear have had theirs destroyed in turn. This is not a practical solution today because the culprits usually do not depend on fishing to make a living, whereas a full-time fisherman cannot afford to have his gear harmed in turn.

There are also stories of net and boat thieves shot by their victims. Some fishermen advocate resumption of vigilante justice as the only solution to widespread theft and vandalism. Bob Cox remembers the dispensing of frontier justice on the Ohio River near Golconda in the 1940s: "Certain people were always known for having a lot of fish and not too much equipment. They were the ones who'd raise other people's nets and steal the fish. A guy caught stealing nets got put in his hoop net and rolled overboard and drowned. One fellow actually got out of this, but his hands were all scarred up from where he tore at the nets to try and get out."

As with many occupational groups, fishermen sometimes play jokes on each other. Sometimes these are part of initiation into the group, but since few traditional Ohio Valley fishermen train outsiders to fish, such instances are relatively rare. The grunt or ripping sound of white perch is a source of amusement to river people. Tommy

Sherer reports a practical joke he played on a novice fisherman. He took the new man out to a place where he knew white perch were shoaling. Then he cut the motor and told the other fisherman to listen for the grunting of "catfish" down below. Subsequent attempts to catch catfish in areas of much grunting produced plenty of unmarketable white perch and few desirable cats.

Sherer also tells stories of how years ago, when fishermen used to concentrate fish in one end of an overflow lake with a seine for later retrieval, other fishermen would sneak down to the lake at night, put out a trammel net next to the seine and beat the water, and then take out most of the fish.

Harold Weaver describes a prank he and another man once played at Saline Landing:

> Old man John Lambert had a boatpad down there and there was a crosstie drifted in there, and me and Greasy John, while the old man wasn't there, we scooted that tie away in under the boat and put a nail through the bottom of the boat into the tie so it stayed under there. He pulled that around there for a week, and finally he said, "Weaver, I wish you and Greasy'd help me pull this boat out."
>
> We pulled it out and turned it up and there was that tie on there, and he said, "You know, I wouldn't have to go too far to spit on the two guys had done that." He knew we did it.

Although the sheltered waters of the Ohio Valley are safer than the open expanses of the ocean and the Great Lakes, they are not without danger, and fishermen often speak of drownings and close calls. As with many outdoor occupations, fishermen share narratives of danger, "close call stories." Donald "Dutch" Moore told of a drowning he witnessed at Lock and Dam 50 on the Ohio River by Golconda.

Lack of mobility caused by heavy loads of shells and equipment carried while musselling can be a problem when a storm comes up suddenly. Curtis Lang recounted one such incident:

> I mean I've been awful scared out there, awful scared! I was musselling. I'd have my boat loaded. I'd see a storm. You could always see it. I'd be a-musselling over here by this bridge. Benjie's, that's the name of the landing over here. I'd see a storm coming up. I'd say, "Well, I'll go." My boat'd be loaded, usually be late in the afternoon. I'd start across the river and it'd hit me. I was loaded so heavy I couldn't run through it. So I'd just throw my brails off to lighten my load and anchor with them. Sit there and ride it out until the storm got through and the river calmed

down. I'd just ride it out and when the storm got over, I'd be there maybe thirty minutes, then I'd take my brails up and come on in.

Several area fishermen have lost their lives to lightning while on the river. Others have drowned when their boats capsized or swamped during a storm or when they fell in and became tangled in their gear while raising or lowering it. In the winter, death by exposure is inevitable after only a few minutes in the water. Today, most fishermen wear life preservers while on the water, but only recently have they become a regular part of the fisherman's equipment.

One often hears fishermen discuss water quality and its effect upon fish and mussel resources. Most agree that the worst pollution years were the 1940s through the 1960s, but it was not until the 1970s, after the adoption of environmental protection laws targeting the discharge of pollution from factories, sewage disposal, and shipping, that a noticeable improvement took place. From the late 1980s through the 1990s, deterioration of the fish resource again increased. Environmental experts believe that this may be owing to the cumulative effects of nonpoint pollution sources, such as acid rain, automobile exhaust, and runoff of chemicals from agriculture and petroleum products from highways and river transportation. The new high-lift dams, which do not aerate the water flowing through them as did the old wicket dams, have created large stagnant impoundments that are low in oxygen and retain pollutants. "I don't call the Ohio River a river anymore," says Tommy Sherer. "I'd call it a row of many bathtubs."

Complaints about pollution problems and their effects on the fish are not new on the river. Author Ben Lucien Burman and sociologist Ernest Theodore Hiller reported such charges from houseboat folk in the 1920s and 1930s and Reuben Thwaites heard them in the 1890s.

Sherer recalls a conversation in the 1950s with an old houseboater named Hardy:

We were sitting there talking about the river and the conditions of it. He said, "Well, I'll tell you, young fellow. I have been up and down the Ohio River from Pittsburgh, Pennsylvania to Cairo, Illinois, and I know the approximate population of every city between Pittsburgh and Cairo." And he started with Pittsburgh and he gave the population, and he went through Portsmouth and smaller places, right on down the river. When he got done, he said, "Now just think," he said, "just think. All that sewage going in raw. If every man, woman, and child took one leak a day, the whole damn river must be piss."

I said, "Well, I guess you got it figured out pretty well, all right."

Fishermen are very much aware of the role that environmental regulations have had in improving water quality and the quantity of fish caught. Despite a traditional cynicism toward government and law, they are pleased with efforts by government agencies to improve the water. In 1978, Bill Nichols of Horseshoe Lake near East St. Louis wrote a five-page report to the Illinois Department of Conservation, later reproduced and distributed, detailing the ups and downs of water quality in the lake, before it became part of the state park system. Nichols concluded, "I hope to have conveyed to you my deep feeling for the old river oxbow called Horseshoe Lake, and hope you treat it with as much respect in the future as I have in the past years. In so doing, I am sure that it will reward you as it has me.

It is the affective bond with the river to which river people refer when they say, "The river gets in your blood." Fishermen respond emotionally to the changes of the seasons on the inland waters and their environs. In Bill Williams's words, "That fishing is just something! It just never ceases to be something new comes up. It gets you, kind of. There's always a challenge there every day. It gets in your blood. It's hard to get away from."

One often hears about the way the river looked at a particular time. Some river people photograph unusual occurrences, such as floods, freezes, or drought, or unusually large fish or great hauls of fish. Houseboater Maggie Lee Sayre's lifetime work chronicling river life with her camera is the finest example of this tradition, which may partly stem from the many itinerant photographers who were once part of the nomadic population. Many fishing families are avid curators of family albums with pictures of their boats, markets, and unusually large fish they have caught.

Donald "Dutch" Moore continued to fish even after he could no longer make a living at it: "It's been wonderful. Nobody liked the river as much as I did. I fished not for the money, just because I liked to do it. Course I had to go get a job. I had a family, and after so long a time around this here fishing, I had to go somewhere and work too."

Some fishermen express the aesthetic aspects of their culture in subtle ways. Preparing and building gear and boats take considerable expertise, and although fisherfolk are usually proud of their ability to knit a good net or build a good boat or repair a motor, they rarely acknowledge consciously the artistic facets of these skills. Instead, qualities such as efficiency and longevity are what they say they admire in a net, a boat, or a musselling outfit. But the beauty of the river and its banks at sunset or in its seasonal changes, the thrill of seeing area wildlife and catching the fish, and especially the splendor of the pearl mussels and their rare gems, are aesthetic features often communicated by fishermen. There are examples of conscious artistic work derived from the skills of the river. Bill Cox's scrollworked johnboat would be one. Another would be the brightly colored nylon macramé made by netmaker and retired fisherman and bridge-toll collector Lee Anderson of New Harmony.

Fishermen often express pride in their occupation, despite its low prestige. Ira Gene Bushey, who is one of the younger fishermen on the lower Ohio River, speaks of how proud he is to be one of the very few fishermen who can fish full-time, year-round, and who does not even operate a retail market in order to survive. Tommy Sherer has fished full-time for most of his life despite the fact that it has rarely given him more than a marginal income. In his own words, "I don't make a lot of money, but I have a lot of fun."

Competence on the river and mastery of the river's resources are the foremost nonmonetary sources of satisfaction among river folk. Those who can make a living playing by the informal rules and only marginally skirting the law earn the respect and admiration of their peers. Knowledge of the river, the fish, and the ways to work them are the sources of river folk identity and self-respect. Pride in independence, particularly in being able to live off the river, "like the pioneers," to quote Ira Gene Bushey, may be the strongest incentive of all.

Conclusion

A young person learning to fish is enculturated with the fisherfolk identity as he or she learns how to hang a net, prepare a jumperline, fish blind, or locate a spawn run. This is "river knowledge" not shared by others who may happen to be on the river but not of it. It is also during the apprenticeship that one learns the subtle rules of territoriality, gear-placement, and fair marketing, again not shared by outsiders who happen to be on the river. This knowledge, together with the distinctive verbal culture, is part of a complex of traditional activities that establish and sustain one's identity as a river fisherman. The river folks' separate identity is recognized by many land people as well, especially those who are longtime residents of river communities where fishermen and their families live and work.

Farmers or townspeople occasionally express admiration for those who are able to live by fishing the river. "They're real 'folk!'" was the way local civic leader Corliss Miller described the river fishermen of the Metropolis-Brookport area. She saw the expression of the fisherfolks' differential identity in their distinctive material culture, such as hoop nets hanging from riverbank trees, outfitted boats at nearby landings, and small fisherman-owned retail markets. Even when people in the area express the more typical negative attitudes toward fisherfolk, they are implicitly recognizing the river way of life as something special and separate from life in town or on the farm.

Most river fishermen are honest, industrious people who strive to live as independently as possible. Many are poor. Some have a middle-class income, especially if they market and ship fish retail and wholesale. Almost all readily express a deep love of the river, of fishing, and of the skills of gear preparation and maintenance. Many also express a deep identification with what they characterize as a "pioneer" way of life.

River folks' verbal culture takes its form in first- and third-person narratives about the river, fish, and fishing. The idea of a "golden age" of life on the river plays a prominent role in that culture. Although the majority of fishermen in the early twentieth century were not nomadic, retrospective and nostalgic attention is directed at those who were because it was they who were *the* river people, in greatest contrast to land-dwellers.

In many places in the world, the forces of increasing regulation, sportsfisher hostility, and popular stereotyping reinforce insularity among commercial fishermen. Timothy C. Lloyd and Patrick B. Mullen have noted this on Lake Erie, as has Janet Crofton Gilmore in various places on the Great Lakes and the Oregon coast, and Steve J. Langdon in southeast Alaska. In the latter case, the Alaska fishermen are Haida and Tlingit Indians whose Native-American identity distinguishes them even more from mainstream society than would their occupation alone. To some extent an older traditional identity, apart from fishing itself, also separates Ohio Valley fisherfolk from their more conventional neighbors, despite the fact that river folk and land-dwellers have the same ethnic background. This identity may be derived, at least in part, from a sense of identification with the houseboat subculture, even among those fishermen not directly descended from the nomadic life.

As the number of people able to make a living by fishing the rivers has dwindled, their visibility and sense of identity have fluctuated. Their social status in their respective localities has been consistently low. During the early nineteenth century, midwestern river fishing was a marginal activity, a way of extracting a resource that was not particularly desired but was often necessary as supplemental sustenance. Fishing was marginal in relation to the central tasks of settlement—land-clearing, farming, transportation, and commerce. As demography changed, with African Americans coming north and central European immigrants settling midwestern cities, river fishing became more economically important yet was still linked to low-status population groups and their base foods. Sedentary fishing businesses prospered despite the unwillingness of the mainstream American midwesterner to utilize their product. At the same time, more economically marginal nomadic fishing families achieved a greater visibility with their widely scattered houseboats and their appearance at landings with fish to sell. The "river rat" stigma became associated with economic activity based on the river's resources. As the days of river-fisherman prosperity dwindled by the middle of the twentieth century, river fishing became even more isolated from mainstream life.

The custom of fish eating among poorer people persists in the lower Ohio Valley because of the availability of the resource from commercial fishermen. Thus there is a larger culture of fish-knowledge, fish-preparation, and fish-eating that overlaps the culture of the fisherfolk. Fisherfolk culture exists within a larger culture that both disdains and desires river fish. The separateness, based on work, custom, memory, and verbal lore, that so many river fisherfolk cultivate is their way of both affirming the distinctiveness of the river way of life and asserting its legitimacy within the larger culture.

Fishing in the lower Ohio Valley mediates between man and nature, for sportsfishers as well as commercial fishermen. This is despite the fact that human impact weighs heavily on the rivers of this industrialized region. The hours spent alone on the river in close proximity to the water give a fisherman time to think and reflect about the river, its resources and dangers, its beauty and its vitality. Some see their way of life as an idealized pioneer existence. Others see the hand of God in their ability to make a living from nature's resources.

Commercial Fish and Aquatic Life Species in the Lower Ohio Valley

Both minor and important species of fish and aquatic life caught commercially in the lower Ohio Valley are listed in alphabetical order by local folk name. Official common names and scientific names appear in parentheses.

blackhorse (white sucker, *Catostomus commersoni*)

black, blue, or gourdseed sucker (black or blue sucker, *Cycleps elongatus*)

blue cat (blue cat, *Ictalurus furcatus*)

buffalo and many variant names including black, blackhorse, blue, common, gourdhead, horse, jewelmouth, lake, mongrel, mule, niggerlipped, quillbacked, razorback, redmouth, roachback, rooter, round, sheep, thicklipped, and whiteline (bigmouth buffalo, *Megastomatabus cyprinellus*; black buffalo, *Ictiobus niger*; smallmouth buffalo, *Ictiobus bubalus*)

bullhead (black bullhead, *Ictalurus melas*; brown bullhead, *Ictalurus nebulosus*; yellow bullhead, *Ictalurus natalis*)

carp, yellow carp, German carp (carp, *Cyprinus carpio*)

eel, freshwater eel (American eel, *Anguilla rostrata*)

fiddler, channel cat (channel cat, *Ictalurus punctatus*)

flathead, yellow cat, mudcat, cushawn (flathead cat, *Pylodictis olivaris*)

gar (longnose gar, *Lepisosteus osseus*)

grinnel, dogfish, mudtrout, cypress trout (bowfin, *Amia calva*)

hackleback (shovelnose sturgeon, *Scaphirhynchus platyrhynchus*)

highfin, quillback (carpsucker, *Carpiodes carpio, C. cyprinus, C. velifer*)

niggerlipper, coalbolter (variant of channel cat, formerly eel cat or willow cat, *Ictalurus punctatus* var. [formerly *I. anguilla*])

redhorse (redhorse, *Moxostoma* spp.)

shad (Ohio shad, *Alosa alabamae*, formerly *A. ohiensis*)

snapper, snapping turtle (common snapper, *Chelydra serpentina*)

spoonbill, spooney, shovelbill (paddlefish, *Polyodon spathula*)

white carp, amur carp, grass carp (grass carp, *Ctenopharyngodon idellus*)

white perch, perch, sheepshead, gaspergou, croaker, grunter (freshwater drum, *Aplodinotus grunniens*)

Mother-of-Pearl Mussel Species in the Lower Ohio Valley

*black sand shell, pink sand shell, stock sand shell, or nigger dick (*Ligumia recta*)

bullhead (*Plethobasus cyphyus*)

butterfly (*Ellipsaria lineolata*)

buzzard head or three-horned wartyback (*Obliquaria reflexa*)

*eggshell or hickory nut (*Obovaria olivaria*)

*fat mucket (*Lampsilis radiata siliquoidea*)

fat pocketbook (*Potamilis capax*)

heel-splitter (*Lasmigona complanata*)

ladyfinger or spike (*Elliptio dilatatus*)

*maple leaf (*Quadrula quadrula*)

*monkey face (*Quadrula metranevra*)

*mucket (*Actinonaias carinata*)

mule ear or elephant ear (*Elliptio crassidens*)

*niggerhead, ebony, or black (*Fusconaia ebena*)

*pigtoe (*Pleurobema cordatus*)

*pimpleback or wartyback (*Quadrula pustulosa*)

pink heelsplitter (*Potamilis alatus*)

*pistolgrip or buckhorn (*Tritogonia verrucosa*)

pocketbook (*Lampsilis ovata ventricosa*)

purple wartyback (*Cyclonaias tuberculata*)

rabbit's foot (*Quadrula cylindrica cylindrica*)

rock pocketbook (*Arcidens confragosus*)

spectacle case (*Cumberlandia monodonta*)

*three-ridge or three-finger (*Amblema plicata*)

*Wabash pigtoe (*Fusconaia ondata*)

wartyback (*Quadrula nodulata*)

*washboard (*Megalonaias nervosa*)

yellow sand shell or yellow buckhorn (*Lampsilis teres*)

Harmful exotic mussels in the lower Ohio Valley

Asiatic clam (*Corbicula manilensis*)

European zebra mussel (*Dreissena polymorpha*)

* Denotes species most often bought by shell traders

Glossary

all-purpose net: a large hoop net with a relatively tight mesh, suitable for use baited or unbaited. Used for catching catfish and scale fish.

anchor line: a piece of rope connecting an anchor to a boat or to a piece of fishing gear, such as a net or trap.

antique: an attractive freshwater pearl with a slightly irregular surface.

bait net: a hoop net set with bait, often waste cheese or soybean meal, typically used to catch catfish.

bank pole: a simple fishing pole consisting of a length of wood or bamboo with a hook and line attached. The pole is attached to the bank and left to catch fish.

baroque: an irregular-shaped but attractive freshwater pearl.

birdsnest: a jumperline prepared for use by rolling it in a circular loop.

birdwing: a large, attractive, asymmetrical, somewhat wing-shaped freshwater pearl.

blockline: fishing gear made up of a floating block of wood suspending a hooked baited line and set adrift by a fisherman for later retrieval.

boneless cat: the white outer meat of the spoonbill or paddlefish (*Polyodon spathula*), sold as fillet or as fish sandwiches.

box trap: a rectangular fish trap made of wooden slats and fitted with one or more throats, often set baited.

brail: 1. (*or* mussel brail) a device for harvesting freshwater mussels, consisting of a length of pipe suspended from a rope tied to the boat and dragged just above the bottom of a river. Rows of hooks are suspended from it by short lines. The hooks snag mollusks lying on the bottom. 2. a stick attached to the end of a small seine to keep it from collapsing on itself.

brush dragnet: a piece of brush dragged through the water to snag fish.

bulkhead: an upright watertight partition.

bushline *or* brushline: a dropline attached to an overhanging tree branch or to a riverside or underwater root.

bycatch: fish of another species caught incidentally along with those of the species for which one is fishing.

cathead: a projecting piece of timber on which a line is attached or wound.

cheese net bait: waste cheese rind from cheese factories, bought in bulk and used for baiting nets for catfish.

coalbolter: niggerlipper.

cork: a float of cork, styrofoam, or other buoyant material attached to a corkline to make it float.

corkline: a floating line, originally a line fitted with pieces of cork, used to float the edge of a net.

crowfoot dredge: mussel-harvesting gear consisting of a brail fitted with crowfoot hooks attached to a line and operated by a musseller.crowfoot hook: a homemade hook of stiff wire, the bottom of which has four upward-curving points, like a small grappling hook, used to snag mollusks.

cutoff: a new channel cutting through the narrow neck of an oxbow.

differential identity: a sense of belonging to a specific group of people who are identifiably different from other groups of people because of occupation, ethnicity, class, or other distinction.

dip net: a simple net consisting of a handle attached to a wire hoop that suspends a bag of netting. Used to help land a fish caught on a line.

drift: to fish with a vertically suspended gill or trammel net, either by letting it drift in the current or by dragging it under power until it entangles a shoal of fish.

dropline: a single line suspended in water ending in a baited hook, attached ashore or to a boat or held by a fisherman.

exotic: a species not native to an area that has become established there.

fiddler: an immature channel catfish (*Ictalurus punctatus*), usually one under ten inches in length.

fiddler net: a small hoop net with relatively fine mesh, usually set baited to catch small catfish (fiddlers).

fish blind: to leave fishing gear in the river unmarked and find it by "marking the bank."

fish box: an enclosure that keeps fish alive in the water without letting them escape.

fisher: a person who catches fish for sport or commercially.

fisherfolk: members of a subculture with a differential identity based on making a living directly from fishing. It includes fishers themselves as well as their nonfishing immediate family members, such as spouses and children.

fisherman: a fisher. In the Ohio Valley and other places, refers to any person who fishes, regardless of gender. Used in this book to refer to any Ohio Valley commercial fisher, regardless of gender.

flatboat: a flat-bottomed boat. In the Ohio Valley, a historical means of transportation consisting of a flat-bottomed boat with a superstructure that encloses its cargo. Also used as a synonym for a johnboat, especially an older wooden one used for transporting fish.

flathead: 1. a species of catfish (*Pylodictis olivaris*), also known as a mudcat or yellow cat. 2. a nineteenth-century derogatory name for a poor, ignorant white river-bottomland settler (usually a squatter). 3. [usually capitalized] a member of any of several gangs of southern Illinois riverbank bandits in the early and mid-nineteenth century.

folklife: people's traditional customs, way of life, and expressions, especially those passed down through generations.

full-fisher: a type of skiff with a narrow bottom and sharply raked sides.

fuzzy tug: a tuft of unraveled nylon twine at the hook on the end of a jumperline stage, used as a lure in lieu of bait.

fyke net: hoop net.

gaff: a bent steel rod or tool used for hauling a fish into a boat or a turtle out of a pond or mud.

game fish: 1. fish caught primarily for sport, such as largemouth bass. 2. a legal designation that reserves a species of fish for sportsfishing and restricts numbers caught, gear used, season, etc.

gig: a spear or other pointed tool used for spearing fish.

gill net: a vertically deployed net consisting of a single slack-meshed wall of webbing that entangles fish swimming into it by their gill-covers and pectoral fins.

gill webbing: light-gauge slack webbing that forms the middle of three layers in a trammel net and forms the pocket that entangles a fish.

grappling hook: a small anchor with four upward-curving points, used to snag underwater gear and drag it to the surface

half-fisher: a type of skiff with moderately raked sides.

heart and lead net: a fish trap combination consisting of a hoop net with a vertical, heart-shaped netting enclosure that directs the fish into the mouth of the hoop net, and a long, vertical wall of netting that leads fish into the heart.

heart net: a fish trap combination consisting of a hoop net with a vertical, heart-shaped netting enclosure that directs the fish into the mouth of the hoop net.

high-lift dam: a modern type of nonnavigable dam on inland river systems that produces a deep channel and is operated by lifting huge, movable gates that rest on a permanent sill on the river bottom. As the gates are lifted water flows beneath them; as they are lowered they impound the water behind the dam. Watercraft must pass around a high-lift dam in a lock.

hoop net *or* **fyke net:** a type of fish trap consisting of a row of hoops with netting stretched over them, closed at one end, open at the other, and containing one or more tapered netting throats to lead fish into the trap.

-horse: a suffix used in the name of several species of sucker, such as blackhorse and redhorse. The term "sucker" is usually not used for a species when it is eaten.

houseboat: a boat used as a dwelling by nomadic river folk. Traditional design consists of a roofed superstructure supported on a flat-bottomed barge. *See also* "shantyboat."

jig: to snag fish by dragging naked hooks through shoals of fish.

johnboat: a traditional small, open boat used on inland waters, having a flat bottom, a rectangular raked bow, and a square stern; its sides can be either vertical or tapered.

jugline: fishing gear made up of a floating sealed jug or can suspending a hooked, baited line and set adrift by a fisherman for later retrieval.

jumpbox: a rectangular box with shallow sides that have rows of notches, each of which suspends one hook from a jumperline; used to keep a jumperline in order when not in use.

jumperline: a type of trotline that can be moved easily, usually by keeping it in a jumpbox when not in use.

knobby hook: a modification of a crowfoot hook for use on rocky bottoms, made with thinner and more flexible wire and with the four points pointed downward; each point ends in a little sphere made by melting the wire with a welding torch.

lead [pronounced LEED]: a wall of netting suspended vertically in the water that acts as a barrier to encourage fish to enter a net or trap.

lead [pronounced LED]: a lead sinker attached to a leadline to make it sink.

lead [pronounced LEED] **net:** a hoop net set with one or more leads that direct fish to its mouth.

leadline [pronounced LED-line]: a weighted line, originally a line fitted with pieces of lead, used to sink the edge of a net.

line: 1. a connecting piece of rope or twine. 2. a piece of twine used for fishing by suspending a hook or hooks. 3. a number of nets, lines, or traps that are visited in succession during a run.

mainline: the main line of a trotline or jumperline.

mark the bank: to line up onshore landmarks visually to find the approximate place in the river where one has set one's gear.

material culture: the material goods that are part of a culture, such as its distinctive tools, furniture, clothing, food, architecture, etc.

mesh: the size, usually measured in inches, of the spaces knit into webbing.

mule: 1. a homemade device consisting of a sheet of thin plywood or canvas suspended from a stick frame. It catches the current and draws a boat and its suspended brail across a mussel bed. 2. a washtub suspended from the end of a drifted gill or trammel net that keeps the far end of the net out in the current.

mussel: in fresh water, one of several dozen species of clam, family *Unionidae*, some of which are harvested for their valuable pearls and mother-of-pearl.

musselling: commercial harvesting of freshwater mussels.

nacre *or* **mother-of-pearl:** a layered structure of tiny calcium carbonate crystals producing an iridescent sheen and found in the shells of some mollusks.

Netcoat (trademark): a petroleum-based net-preservative made by Texaco.

net sinker: a peanut-shaped stone found in some inland rivers in North

America, believed to have been used by indigenous people to weigh down a net during fishing.

New Yorked: of spoonbill or paddlefish, prepared with the head, skin, and dark inner meat removed, for shipment to urban areas, where it may be sold as sturgeon.

nigger fish: used by racially prejudiced whites to denote those fish that local whites disdain because they are associated with the traditional African-American diet: usually buffalo, carp, white perch, and several species of sucker.

niggerlipper *or* **coalbolter:** the local name for a late-run variety of channel catfish (*Ictalurus punctatus*) with distinguishing physical characteristics.

oxbow: a crescent-shaped lake or pond in an old riverbed, caused when a river changes course.

panfish: fish caught by anglers primarily for eating rather than for sport, such as fiddlers and crappie.

rake: in the dimensions of a boat, inclination or diviation from the perpendicular.

rig: a complete set of fishing gear used by a fisherman.

river folk: individuals who are part of a traditional culture that identifies its home, life, and work with the river.

river rat: 1. a derogatory term for dissolute people who live on or near the river, especially if they attempt to make a living from the river's resources 2. a derogatory term used by land-dwellers for nomadic river folk. 3. a derogatory term for *all* river folk, used by people who make their living on land. As with many derogatory terms, "river rat" is sometimes used affectionately or proudly by the folk themselves.

rosebud: a relatively round and symmetrical freshwater pearl with an attractive but irregular surface.

rough fish: scale fish.

run: 1. to visit a net, line, or trap or a line of nets, lines, or traps to retrieve caught fish. 2. a seasonal voyage, usually inland or upriver, made by certain species of fishes for mating and/or spawning.

scale fish: certain species of river fish, notably buffalo, carp, suckers, and white perch, considered lower in quality than gamefish, catfish, spoonbill, or sturgeon. All scale fish have scales.

score: to make closely separated rows of cuts on bony-fleshed fish, such as buffalo, carp, or highfin, so that the bones will be rendered edible.

scow: a square-ended, flat-bottomed boat, of which a johnboat is one type.

scow-ended: of a boat, having square ends, especially at the bow.

sealine: a line that is let out into the water.

seine: a wall of netting dragged through water to concentrate and encircle fish.

seining barge: a type of small flatboat or large johnboat with a deck mounted on its bow, used for shooting a seine.

set net: any type of net that is fished by being left in place for a while.

shantyboat: a houseboat used by nomadic river folk; considered derogatory by river folk and used primarily by land-dwellers.

shoot: to let out the forward end of a seine, or of a drifted gill or trammel net, in the direction of fish that one is attempting to catch.

skiff: a small open boat with a pointed bow and raked sides.

slat trap: a rectangular or cylindrical-shaped fish trap made of wooden slats and fitted with one or more throats, often set baited.

slug: a small freshwater pearl of poor quality but good enough to be ground into pearl dust used in cosmetics or special finishes.

snagline: one of several types of lines consisting of a mainline suspending a row of shorter lines bearing sharp hooks. Set or dragged in the water unbaited, it snags fish by hooking into their flesh.

sow: a female catfish, especially when mating or spawning.

spawn run: a seasonal voyage, usually inland or upriver, made by certain species of fishes for spawning.

spike: a cone-shaped, pointed-ended freshwater pearl.

spoonbill *or* **spooney:** the local name for paddlefish (*Polyodon spathula*).

stage *or* **tug:** a short line with a hook at each end, attached to a mainline on a jumperline, snagline, or trotline.

sucker: a member of a large family of freshwater fish (*Catostomidae*) common in North America whose mouths are specially adapted for bottom-feeding.

swivel: a small metal device that connects two lengths of line and can turn in any direction, thus making it difficult for a caught fish to pull off a hook; used on trotlines and jumperlines and on angling gear.

throat: a funnel-shaped structure made of netting on a hoop net or wooden slats on a slat trap. Fish easily enter its wide opening and then squeeze through the narrow end and are unable to turn back.

trammel net: a three-layer net consisting of two outer layers (walling) around a middle layer (gill webbing). A fish swimming into a vertically suspended trammel net makes a pocket of gill netting, thus entangling itself.

trotline: a long line to which shorter lines, called stages, are attached, each stage ending in a hook. A trotline is set baited in the water and occasionally visited to retrieve the fish. In the lower Ohio Valley, usually refers to a line that is repeatedly fished in the same location. A trotline moved around is usually called a jumperline.

walling: the two outer layers of a trammel net, with a much larger mesh than the gill webbing.

waste cheese: stale rinds trimmed from large cheeses in cheese factories and sold in bulk to be used for bait.

webbing *or* **netting:** twine knit into fabric for fish nets before it has been made into usable net.

weir: a rigid, more or less permanent barrier of wood or stone used by fishermen to concentrate or trap fish.

white perch: a local name, especially among whites, for freshwater drum or sheepshead (*Aplodinotus grunniens*).

wicket dam: an older type of navigable dam consisting of a row of separate wooden barriers, called wickets, each attached by a hinge to a sill on the river bottom. Wickets can be lowered to allow water and watercraft to pass over, or raised to impound water behind the dam.

yawl: on inland North American rivers, a type of skiff with relatively vertical sides and a box-shaped stern.

Bibliographical Essay

Abbreviations

AFST   American Fisheries Society. *Transactions.*
NAWCT   North American Wildlife Conference. *Transactions.*
USCFFB   U.S. Commission of Fish and Fisheries. *Bulletin.*
USCFFRC   U.S. Commission of Fish and Fisheries. *Report of the*
             Commissioner.
USCFRC   U.S. Commission of Fisheries. *Report of the*
             Commissioner.

Constantine Samuel Rafinesque's descriptions of Ohio Valley fish and fisheries occur in *Ichthyologia Ohiensis, or Natural History of the Fishes Inhabiting the River Ohio and Its Tributary Streams*, rev. ed., ed. Richard Ellsworth (1820; Cleveland: Burrows, 1899). John James Audubon's account is "Fishing in the Ohio" in his anthology *Delineations of American Scenery and Character*, rev. ed. (New York: G.A. Baker, 1926).

Travel writers describing fishermen and fishing include Nathaniel Bishop, *Four Months in a Sneak Box: A Boat Voyage of 2600 Miles Down the Ohio and Mississippi Rivers* (Boston: Lee and Shepard, and New York: C.T. Dillingham, 1879); Thomas Hulmes, *Hulmes' Journal of a Tour in the Western Countries of America*, vol. 10 of *Early Western Travels, 1748–1846*, ed. Reuben Gold Thwaites (Cleveland: A.H. Clark, 1904); François André Michaux, *Travels to the West of the Allegheny Mountains* (London: D.N. Shury and B. Crosby, 1805); Reuben Gold Thwaites, *Afloat on the Ohio* (Chicago: Way and Williams, 1897); and Reuben Gold Thwaites, *On the Storied Ohio: An Historical Pilgrimage of a Thousand Miles in a Skiff from Redstone to Cairo* (Chicago: A.C. McClurg, 1903); and John Woods, *Two Years' Residence on the English Prairie of Illinois*, ed. Paul Angle (Chicago: Lakeside Press, 1968).

Physical descriptions of the Ohio River and its tributaries occur in a number of sources. See, for example, *Ohio River Basin Energy Study (ORBES): Preliminary Technology Assessment Report, Phase I*, prepared by Indiana University, Ohio State University, and Purdue University (Washington, D.C.: U.S. Department of the Interior, Office of Energy, Minerals, and Industry, Office of Research and Development, and Environmental Protection Agency, 1977), vol. 2A, part 1; and U.S. Army Corps of Engineers, Ohio River Division, *Ohio River Navigation: Past—Present—Future* (Cincinnati: Corps of Engineers, 1979). For a historical perspective on the Ohio River, see Walter

Havighurst, *River to the West: Three Centuries of the Ohio* (New York: G.P. Putnam, 1970).

The definitive source for information on fishing methods and gear, worldwide, is Andres von Brandt, *Fish Catching Methods of the World*, rev. ed. (Farnham, England: Fishing News, 1984). A useful article on the history and use of nets in the nineteenth- century United States is C.H. Augur, "Fish Nets: Some Account of Their Construction and the Application of the Various Forms in American Fisheries," *USCFFB* 13, for 1893 (1894): 381–88.

The fishing of both Mound Builders and later Native Americans is described in Erhard B. Rostlund, *Freshwater Fish and Fishing in Native North America*, University of California Publications in Geography, no. 9 (Berkeley: Univ. of California Press, 1952).

The ultimate guides to the travel literature of the Ohio Valley are John A. Jakle, *Images of the Ohio Valley: A Historical Geography of Travel, 1740 to 1860* (New York: Oxford Univ. Press, 1977); Ralph Leslie Rusk, *The Literature of the Middle Western Frontier* (New York: Columbia Univ. Press, 1925); and Robert R. Hubach, *Early Midwestern Travel Narratives: An Annotated Bibliography, 1634–1850* (Detroit: Wayne State Univ. Press, 1961).

Guides to the literature of fishing on the American frontier include Daniel F. Jackson, "Historical Notes on Fish Fauna," in *Aquatic Life Resources of the Ohio River* (Cincinnati: Ohio River Valley Sanitation Committee, 1962), 1–19; and *The Fish and Fisheries of Colonial North America*, part 7, *The Inland States*, ed. John C. Pearson (Springfield, Va.: U.S. Dept. of Commerce, National Technical Information Service, 1972).

Subsistence fishing by military personnel, explorers, and earliest settlers appears in many early Ohio Valley travel accounts, such as Morris Birkbeck, *Notes on a Journey in America from the Coast of Virginia to the Territory of Illinois* (London: James Ridgway, Piccadilly, 1818); Daniel Bradley, *Journal of Capt. Daniel Bradley*, ed. Frazier E. Wilson (Greenville, Oh.: F.H. Jobes, 1935); Nicholas Creswell, *The Journals of Nicholas Creswell, 1774–1777* (New York: Dial Press, 1924); St. John De Crèvecoeur, "The Discovery, Settlement, and Present State of Kentucky," in G. Imlay, *A Topographical Description of the Western Territory of North America* (New York: Samuel Campbell, 1793), 2:26; LePage DuPratz, *The History of Louisiana* (London: Privately printed, 1774); Thomas Hutchins, *A Topographical Description of Virginia, Pennsylvania, and North Carolina*, ed. Frederick Hicks (Cleveland: Arthur H. Clark, 1904); John May, *Journals and Letters of Col. John May of Boston* (Cincinnati: Robert H. Clark and the Philosophical Society of Ohio, 1873); and "Journal of Col. John May Relative to a Journey to the Ohio Country, 1789," *Pennsylvania Magazine of History and Biography* 45 (1921): 115–27; "The Moravian Records," *Ohio Archaeological and Historical Quarterly* 21 (1912): 38–46; William Oliver, *Eight Months in Illinois, With Information to Immigrants* (Chicago: Walter M. Hill, 1924); William Priest, *Travels in the United States of America* (London: J. Johnson, 1802); Johann D. Schöpf, *Travels in the Confederation, 1783–1784*, edited and translated by Alfred J. Morrison (Philadelphia: William J. Campbell, 1852); and George Washington, invoice in *The Writings of George Washington*, ed. John C. Fitzpatrick (Washington, D,C.: U.S. Govt. Printing Office, 1931): 62.

The most important of the guidebooks of the early nineteenth century were Zadok Cramer's series *The Navigator: Containing Directions for Navigating the Monongahela, Allegheny, Ohio, and Mississippi Rivers* (Pittsburgh: Press of Zadok Cramer, 1801—1808; Pittsburgh: Cramer and Spear, 1814–1824).

Naturalists describing the aquatic life resources of the early Ohio Valley include John James Audubon, "Fishing in the Ohio" (cited above); Jared P. Kirtland, "Descriptions of the Fishes of Lake Erie and the Ohio River and Their Tributaries," *Boston Journal of Natural History* 3–5 (1840–1847); and Jared P. Kirtland, "Fishes of Ohio," *Family Visitor* 1–2 (March 7, 1850–March 27, 1851); and Constantine Samuel Rafinesque, *Ichthyologia Ohiensis* (cited above).

Accounts of early and middle nineteenth-century Ohio Valley commercial fisheries and fish-marketing appear in Zadok Cramer, *The Navigator* (1805, 1811, and 1814); Jared P. Kirtland, "Descriptions of the Fishes of Lake Erie and the Ohio River and Their Tributaries"; Jared P. Kirtland, "Fishes of the Ohio"; Constantine Samuel Rafinesque, *Ichthyologia Ohiensis;* and Thomas Hulmes, *Hulmes' Journal of a Tour in the Western Countries of America* (all cited above); Mary Verhoeff, *The Kentucky River Navigation*, Filson Club Publications, no. 28 (Louisville: John P. Morton, 1917); and John Woods, *Two Years' Residence on the English Prairie of Illinois* (cited above).

From the middle of the nineteenth century into the first few decades of the twentieth, two different kinds of literature give accounts of the area's commercial fisheries. First of these are the travel, geographical-descriptive, and outdoor accounts. They include H. Bennett Abdy, *On the Ohio* (New York: Dodd, Meade, 1919); Ward Dorrance, *Where the Rivers Meet* (New York: Charles Scribner, 1939); Raymond S. Spears, "Commercial Fishing," *Hunter—Trader—Trapper* 44 (July 1922): 64–65; Reuben Gold Thwaites, *Afloat on the Ohio;* and Reuben Gold Thwaites, *On the Storied Ohio* (last two cited above).

Important works by biologists and fisheries statisticians, most of them government-employed, include Barton W. Evermann, "Descriptions of a New Species of Shad (*Alosa Ohiensis*)," *USCFFRC* for 1901 (1902), Appendix 10, pp. 275–88; Barton W. Evermann and William C. Kendall, "Descriptions of New or Little-known Genera and Species of Fishes from the United States," *USCFFB* 17 for 1897 (1898): 125–33; R.H. Fiedler, "Fishery Industries of the U.S., 1932 [actually 1931]," *USCFRC* for 1933 (1934), Appendix 3, pp. 149–419; Stephen Alfred Forbes, *The Fishes of Illinois* (Danville, Ill.: Natural History Survey of Illinois, State Laboratory of Natural History, 1908; rev. ed., Springfield: Illinois State Journal, 1920); David Starr Jordan, "The Catfish Family," in *The Fisheries and Fishery Industries of the United States*, ed. G. Brown Goode, in 27 Cong., 1st Sess., 1881–1882, *Senate Miscellaneous*

Documents, no. 6, serial no. 1998 (1884), 1:627–29; David Starr Jordan, "Report on the Fishes of Ohio," State of Ohio, Geological Survey, *Report* 4 (1882): 735–1002; David Starr Jordan, "Review of Rafinesque's Memoirs on North American Fishes," *U.S. National Museum Bulletin* 9 (1877): 5–8; Oscar E. Sette, "Fishing Industries of the United States, 1923 [actually 1922]," *USCFRC* for 1924 (1925): Appendix 4, pp. 141–359; Hugh M. Smith, "Statistics of the Fisheries of the Interior Waters of the United States [1894]," *USCFFRC* for 1896, part 22 (1898): Appendix 11, pp. 489–574; C.H. Townsend, "Statistics of the Fisheries of Mississippi River and Its Tributaries [1899]," *USCFFRC* for 1901, part 27 (1902): 659–740; and U.S. Bureau of the Census, *Fisheries of the United States, 1908: Special Report* (Washington, D.C.: U.S. Dept. of Commerce and Labor, 1911).

Middle and late twentieth-century accounts of commercial fishing and fish-marketing in the Ohio Valley include Paul Bryan, "Spoonbill Fishing New Valley Industry," *Alabama Conservation* 14 (September 1942): 7, 15; Paul Bryan and Clarence M. Tarzwell, "A Preliminary Report on the Census of Commercial Fishing in T.V.A. Impoundments," *NAWCT* 6 (1941): 265–72; James R. Charles, "Commercial Fishing Activities in the Kentucky Waters of the Ohio River," in *Aquatic Life Resources of the Ohio River* (Cincinnati: Ohio River Valley Sanitation Committee, 1962): 103–19; William C. Starrett and Sam A. Parr, *Commercial Fisheries of Illinois Rivers: A Statistical Report for 1950*, State of Illinois, Natural History Survey Division, Technical Notes, no. 25 (Urbana: State of Illinois, Department of Registration and Education, 1951); Clarence M. Tarzwell, "The Possibilities of a Commercial Fishery in the T.V.A. Impoundments and Its Value in Solving the Sport and Rough Fish Problems," *AFST* 73 (1943): 137–57; Clarence M. Tarzwell and Paul Bryan, "Changes in the Commercial Fishery of the Tennessee River," *Journal of the Tennessee Academy of Science* 20 (1945): 49–54.

In the decades since World War II, reports of fisheries for the entire Mississippi Basin, including the Ohio Valley, can be found in U.S. Dept. of Commerce, Bureau of Commercial Fisheries' Current Fisheries Statistics series, titled *Mississippi River Fisheries*; National Oceanic and Atmospheric Administration, National Marine Fisheries Service's Current Fisheries Statistics series, titled *Mississippi River Fisheries: Annual Summary*; National Oceanic and Atmospheric Administration, National Marine Fisheries Service, National Fishery Statistics Program's Statistical Digests series, titled *Fishery Statistics of the United States*; and U.S. Dept. of Commerce, Bureau of the Census's *Statistical Abstract of the United States: National Data Books and Guides to Sources* (1988).

Harlan Hubbard's travel journal is *Shantyboat: A River Way of Life*, rev. ed. (1953; reprint, Lexington: Univ. Press of Kentucky, 1977). Fictional accounts of river folk include Lois Lenski, *Houseboat Girl* (Philadelphia: J.B. Lippincott, 1957); and Cormac McCarthy, *Suttree* (New York: Random House, 1979).

Twentieth-century houseboat and riverbank life are described in Carl R.

Bogardus, *Shantyboat* (Austin, Ind.: Muscatatuck Press, 1959); Clifton Johnson, *Highways and Byways of the Mississippi Valley* (New York: Macmillan, 1906); Clifton Johnson, "Houseboat Life on the Mississippi," *Outing Magazine* 46 (Apr. 1905): 81–91; Dexter Marshall, "The River People," *Scribner's Magazine* 28 (July 1900): 101–11; Tom Rankin, "River Life," in *The Encyclopedia of Southern Culture*, ed. Charles Reagan Wilson and Bill Ferris (University, Miss.: Center for the Study of Southern Culture; Chapel Hill: Univ. of North Carolina Press, 1989): 357–58; Raymond S. Spears, "Commercial Fishing," *Hunter—Trader—Trapper* 44 (July 1922): 64–65; Raymond S. Spears, "Vagabond Specialists of the Open Country," *Saturday Evening Post* 204 (Nov. 14, 1931): 28, 86, 89–90; John Leisk Tait, "Shanty-boat Folks," *The World Today* 12 (May 1907): 473–78; Mary and Lewis Theiss, "Homes Without Rent," *Good Housekeeping Magazine* 50 (June 1910): 699–701; and Malcolm Walker, *The River-people of Clayton: Poor Whites in a Community in Southern Illinois*, Southern Illinois Studies, no. 6 (Carbondale: Southern Illinois Univ. Museum, 1971).

The life and work of houseboat photographer Maggie Lee Sayre is described by Tom Rankin in "The Photographs of Maggie Lee Sayre: A Personal Vision of Houseboat Life," *Folklife Annual 90* (Washington, D.C.: Library of Congress, American Folklife Center, 1991): 100–131, and Maggie Lee Sayre, *"Deaf Maggie Lee Sayre": Photographs of a River Life*, ed. Tom Rankin (University, Miss.: Center for Southern Culture and the Univ. Press of Mississippi, 1995). Her photographs were toured by the Southern Arts Federation in the exhibition "Maggie Lee Sayre: A Pictorial Narrative of River Life," which is now permanently located at the Pilot Knob Folklife Center at Nathan Bedford Forrest State Park in Eva, Tennessee. They were also shown at the Smithsonian's Festival of American Folklife.

Ben Lucien Burman's nonfiction works about river folk are *Big River to Cross: Mississippi Life Today* (New York: John Day, 1938); *Children of Noah: Glimpses of an Unknown America* (New York: Julian Meissner, 1952); *Look Down That Winding River: An Informal Profile of the Mississippi* (New York: Taplinger, 1973); and "Shanty Boat Coming Down," *Saturday Evening Post* 210 (Oct. 15, 1938): 8–9. He has also written five novels about river folklife: *Blow for a Landing* (New York: John Day, 1938); *Everywhere I Roam* (Garden City, N.Y.: Doubleday, 1949); *The Four Lives of Mundy Tolliver* (New York: Julian Meissner, 1951); *Mississippi* (New York: Farrar and Rinehart, 1929); and *Steamboat 'Round the Bend* (New York: Grosset and Dunlap, 1933).

Sociologist Ernest Theodore Hiller's study is *Houseboat and River Bottoms People: A Study of 683 Households in Sample Locations Adjacent to the Ohio and Mississippi Rivers*, Illinois Studies in the Social Sciences 24:1 (Urbana: Univ. of Illinois, 1939).

There are many useful guides to fish species in the Ohio Valley and elsewhere, some historical and some contemporary. Among those consulted for this work are American Fisheries Society, Committee on Common and Scientific Names of Fishes, *A List of the Common and Scientific Names of the Bet-ter Known Fishes of the United States and Canada* (Washington, D.C.: American Fisheries Society, 1970); "Species Characteristics, Importance, Management Implication," in *UMRCC Fisheries Compendium: A Compendium of Fisheries Information on the Upper Mississippi River, March 1967*, compiled by Robert C. Nord (Rock Island, Ill.: Upper Mississippi River Conservation Commission, 1967), 56–68; A.J. McClane, *McClane's Field Guide to Freshwater Fishes of North America* (New York: Holt, Rinehart, and Winston, 1978); Joseph R. Tomelleri and Merle E. Eberle, *Fishes of the Central United States* (Lawrence: Univ. Press of Kansas, 1990); and Milton B. Trautman, *The Fishes of Ohio* (1957; Columbus: Ohio State Univ. Press, 1981).

For a catfish overview, see John Madson, "To Catch This Fish, Put Hand in Mouth, Hang On—and Pull," *Smithsonian* 15, 6 (Sept. 1984): 54–63. A detailed historical description of the catfish family is given in David Starr Jordan, "The Catfish Family" (cited above). Giant catfish stories occur in Bonnie J. Krause and Kay Carter, *Tall Tales, Ghosts and Omens of the Illinois Ozarks* (Ullin, Ill.: Shawnee Hills Craft Program and Illinois Ozarks Craft Guild, 1978), 8–9; and Warren Stanley Walker, "Dan'l Stamps: Tall Tale Hero of the River Country," *Midwest Folklore* 4 (1954): 156–67. Giant catfish and other enormous and unusual midwestern river creatures are the subject of Dick Kaukas, "What Really Lives in the Ohio? `Sure We Have Monsters Down There,'" *Louisville Times, Saturday Scene* (Sept. 6, 1980), 3–4, 22; and Virginia S. Eifert, *River World: Wildlife of the Mississippi* (New York: Dodd, Mead, 1959). For the place of catfish in southern culture, see Dianne Young, "Catfish," in *The Encyclopedia of Southern Culture* (cited above), 378–79.

For information on carp, see S.P. Bartlett's articles "Carp, as Seen by a Friend," *AFST* 34 (1905): 207-16; "Discussion on Carp," *AFST* 30 (1901): 114-32; "The Future of the Carp," *AFST* 39 (1909): 151-54; and "The Value of the Carp as a Food Product of Illinois Waters," *AFST* 29 (1900): 80-87. See also Leon J. Cole, "The German Carp in the United States," *USCFFRC* for 1904 (1905), 523–641; and Rudolph Hessel, "The Carp and Its Culture in Rivers and Lakes; and Introduction into America," *USCFFRC* for 1875–76 (1878), 865–900. Carp's place in the historical American diet is revealed in H.F. Taylor, *The Carp: A Valuable Food Resource, with Twenty-three Recipes*, Bureau of Fisheries, Economic Circular no. 1 (Washington, D.C.: U.S. Department of Commerce, Bureau of Fisheries, 1917). A recent work on the subject is *Carp in North America*, ed. E.L. Cooper (Bethesda, Md.: American Fisheries Society, 1987).

For information on white perch (freshwater drum) when it was still an important food fish in the Ohio Valley, see David Starr Jordan, "The Freshwater Drum—Haploidonotus Grunniens," in *The Fisheries and Fishery Industries of the United States*, ed. G. Brown Goode (cited above), 1:370–84.

For snapping turtle information, see Simon J. Bronner, "The Paradox of Pride and Loathing," *Western Folklore* 40 (1981): 115–24; Simon J. Bronner,

"Turtle and All the Trappings," *Center for Southern Folklore Magazine* (Fall 1980), 11; Karl F. Lagler, "Economic Relations and Utilization of Turtles," *Investigations of Indiana Lakes and Streams* 2 (1945): 139–65; and Robert J. Schoffman, "Turtling for the Market at Reelfoot Lake," *Journal of the Tennessee Academy of Sciences* 24 (1949): 143–45.

The variety of homemade boats on inland rivers during the early nineteenth century was noted by Timothy F. Flint in *Recollections of the Past Two Years Passed in Occasional Residencies and Journeyings in the Valley of the Mississippi from Pittsburg* (Boston: Cummings, Hilliard, 1826); and Timothy F. Flint, *The History and Geography of the Mississippi Valley* (Cincinnati: E.H. Flint and Carter, Hendee, 1833).

Malcolm L. Comeaux, "Origins and Evolution of Mississippi River Fishing Craft," *Pioneer America* 10, 1 (June 1978): 72–97, is full of information about skiffs, johnboats, houseboats, and fish boxes as used by fisherfolk on inland rivers. The D. Lyon Skiff Works is the subject of Clifford Robinson, "Last of Skiff-makers in Family Watches 106-Year-Old Trade Dwindle," *Louisville Courier-Journal*, magazine section, Aug. 30, 1936, 3.

Johnboats and similar craft are covered in Larry Dablemont, *The Authentic American Johnboat: How to Build It, How to Use It* (New York: David McKay, 1978); and Dana Everts-Boehm, *The Ozark Johnboat: Its History, Form, and Functions*, The Masters and Their Traditional Arts series, ed. Ray Brassieur and Howard Wight Marshall (Columbia: Univ. of Missouri, Cultural Heritage Center, Traditional Arts Apprenticeship Program, 1991).

Traditional houseboats are the subject of Walter S. Chansler, "Water-craft of the Lower Wabash," *Fur News and Outdoor World* 34 (Sept. 1921): 10–11, 15; Jens Lund, "Nomadic Architecture: The River Houseboat in the Ohio Valley," in *The Old Traditional Way of Life: Essays in Honor of Warren E. Roberts*, ed. Robert E. Walls and George H. Schoemaker (Bloomington: Indiana Univ. Folklore Institute Trickster Press, 1989): 241–57; and Raymond S. Spears, *The Cabin Boat Primer* (Columbus, Oh.: A.R. Harding, 1913).

The evolution of the inland river houseboat from a nomadic home to a recreational craft is chronicled in Fritz Parkins, Richard Nugent, and Charlotte Knaster, "Houseboating Heritage," *Heartland Boating* 2, 3 (June 1990): 20–23; 2, 6 (Oct. 1990): 24–27; and 3, 1 (Mar./Apr. 1991): 26–29.

The theory of Medieval Balto-Scandinavian origins of the hoop net (*ryssja*, in Swedish), based largely on linguistic evidence, is explained in Ivar Modéer, "Den Nordiska Ryssjans Ursprung och Ålder," *Uppsalas Universitets Årsskrift* 10, part 2 (1939): 162–78.

An otherwise excellent description of hoop net types and their use in U.S. waters, which unfortunately and inexplicably excludes inland river fisheries, is Hugh M. Smith, "The Fyke Nets and Fyke-net Fisheries of the United States," *USCFFB* 12, for 1892 (1894): 299–56 and Plates LXIII–XCI. Smith's article advances the theory that the device was introduced to the East Coast by the Dutch and to the Great Lakes by Canadians, having been brought to the Saint Lawrence River first by the French.

An article by Malcolm L. Comeaux summarizes inland river use of the hoop net from the nineteenth century to the present: "Use of Hoop Nets in the Mississippi River Basin," *Journal of Cultural Geography* 10 (1989): 75–87.

The types of hook-and-line fishing in use in the greater Mississippi River basin are described in Malcolm L. Comeaux, "Hook-and-Line Fishing in the Mississippi River System," *Pioneer America* 21, 1 (1989): 23–49. Several photos and descriptions in both of his articles are from the lower Ohio River.

Commercial use of jumperlines in the upper Mississippi is the subject of John T. Greenbank, "Comparative Sizes of Hooks (for Trotlines): Prepared March 11, 1949," in *Upper Mississippi River Conservation Commission Investigational Reports*, ed. Kent D. Keenlyne (Rock Island, Ill.: Upper Mississippi Conservation Committee, 1974). The subject is also covered in William C. Starrett and Paul G. Barnickol, "Efficiency and Selectivity of Commercial Fishing Devices Used on the Mississippi River," *State of Illinois, Natural History Survey Bulletin* 26 (1955): 324–66.

Descriptions of *woven* fish traps and their use in inland rivers include Jim Brown, "Alabama Folkways: The Great Fish Trap," *Alabama Folkways: Occasional Papers of the Alabama State Council on the Arts and Humanities* (May 18, 1978), 1–Ad2; and Theodore M. Rosengarten, *All God's Dangers: The Life of Nate Shaw* (New York: Random House and Alfred A. Knopf, 1964). A stationary rigid trap appears in Clyde Reed, "A Night on the New River at the Reed Fish Trap," *Tennessee Anthropological Association Newsletter* 4 (Jan.–Feb. 1979): 1–9.

Nineteenth-century seining in the Ohio Valley is described in Zadok Cramer, *The Navigator* (1814), 27–28; and in Constantine Samuel Rafinesque, *Ichthyologia Ohiensis*, 47 (previous two cited above). The great midwestern seine-hauls of carp are described by S.P. Bartlett in "The Value of Carp as a Food Product in Illinois Waters," *AFST* 29 (1900): 80–87. Dynamiting is described and deplored in J.F. Boepple, "Notes on the Fish on the Cumberland River," *AFST* 41 (1911): 181–82.

Hugh M. Smith's article "Statistics of the Fisheries of the Interior Waters of the United States [1894]," *USCFFRC* for 1896, part 22 (1898), Appendix 11, pp. 489–574, relates the spearing of buffalo and other suckers in Illinois during spring spawn runs and the connection between that practice and the state's traditional nickname.

The literature of the freshwater musselling and pearling industry in the Midwest is extensive. The most complete source is Cheryl Claassen's monograph "Washboards, Pigtoes, and Muckets: History of Musselling in the Mississippi Watershed," *Historical Archaeology* 28, 2 (1994). Some of the sources dealing with the Wabash River pearl rush are "The Pearl Industry" *Vincennes* [Ind. Daily] *Commercial* (Sept. 8, 1905), 6; Sisley Barnes, "The Great Indiana Pearl Rush," *Ford Times* (Nov. 1975), 52–57; Richard Day, *Vincennes: A Pictorial History* (St. Louis: G. Bradley, 1987); and Diantha DeGraw, "The Great Wabash River Pearl Strike," *Indiana Bell News* (Jul.–Aug. 1962), 400–401.

Sources on the Wabash River "Queen Pearl" legend include those cited in the previous paragraph and Lelah Allison, "Stories from the Illinois Wabash," *Illinois Folklore* 1 (1947): 15–16; "'Jumbo' Adams Gets Parole," *Vincennes* [Ind. Weekly] *Commercial,* Oct. 23, 1912; and "Queen May [*sic*] Asks for Pardon," *Vincennes* [Ind. Weekly] *Commercial,* Oct. 4, 1912.

Articles about musselling in the Wabash and nearby rivers in recent years include the following: Nis Kildegaard, "'Granny' Reaps Harvest from the Wabash: Palmer, Pearls, Horseshoes," *New Harmony* [Ind.] *Times,* Oct. 13, 1977, 1; Al C. Lopinot, "The Illinois Mussel," *Outdoor Illinois* 6 (May 1967): 12–13; and George McCormack, "Reviving Pearl City," *Indianapolis Star Magazine* (Oct. 16, 1960), 18, 52–53.

Other articles on pearl rushes and musselling on inland rivers include the special pearling issue of the Batesville, Ark., historical journal *Independence County Chronicle* 9, 4 (July 1968); Robert W. Ingersoll, "Part IV-W: Mollusks: in General," in *The Fisheries and Fishery Industries of the United States,* ed. G. Brown Goode (cited above), 1:700–740; George Frederick Kunz, "The Freshwater Pearls and Pearl Fisheries of the United States," *USCFFB* 27, for 1897 (1898): 375–425; George Frederick Kunz, *Gems and Precious Stones of North America* (Philadelphia: J.B. Lippincott, 1913); George Frederick Kunz, "On Pearls and the Utilization of the Shells in Which They are Found," *USCFFB* 23 for 1893 (1894): 439–57; and Herbert H. Vertrees, *Pearls and Pearling* (New York: Fur News, 1913).

Two wall-posters provide local and scientific names for freshwater mussel species: U.S. Department of the Interior, Fish and Wildlife Service and U.S. Army Corps of Engineers, *Fresh-water Mussels of the Upper Mississippi River,* parts 1 and 2, I19.76:80-447, and *Fresh Water Shells of Indiana* (Terre Haute, Ind.: M.D. Cohen Co. [1980s]). See also Donna Turgeon *et al., Common and Scientific Names of Aquatic Invertebrates from the United States and Canada: Mollusks,* Special Publication no. 16 (Bethesda, Md.: American Fisheries Society, 1988).

The manufacture of button blanks from Ohio River mussel shell is the subject of Nancy G. Hart, "The Pearl Button Company: The Working Process of Button Manufacturing," *Indiana History Bulletin* 58 (July 1981): 121–25.

The status of various fish as food in the Ohio Valley is described in George W. Miles, "A Defense of the Humble Dogfish," *AFST* 42 (1912): 51–59; and in the works of John W. Bennett, notably "Food and Social Status in a Rural Society," *American Sociological Review* 8 (1943): 396–408, and "Subsistence Economy and Foodways in a Rural Community: A Study of Socio-economic and Cultural Change" (Ph.D. diss., Univ. of Chicago, 1946). The concept of status-hierarchy and food is explored in Gunther Wiegelmann, "Innovation in Food and Meals," *Folk Life* 12 (1974): 20–30. For a perspective on catfish's changing social status, see Dianne Young, "Catfish: Netting a New Image," *Southern Living* 19, 7 (July 1984): 134–41. Catfish and the negative southern stereotype appear in Jack Temple Kirby, *Media-Made Dixie* (Baton Rouge: Louisiana State Univ. Press, 1978): 79.

The relationship of catfish and buffalo with the traditional southern African-American diet is explored in Sam Bowers Hilliard, *Hog Meat and Hoecake: Food Supply in the Old South, 1840–1860* (Carbondale: Southern Illinois Univ. Press, 1972), 85–86. Catfish's place in traditional southern cooking, together with recipes, appear in Marshall Fishwick, "Southern Cooking," *American Heritage Cookbook* (New York: Simon and Schuster, 1964), 65, 126–27. Catfish as a delicacy on the Kentucky frontier is discussed in Harriette Simpson Arnow, *Seedtime on the Cumberland* (New York: Macmillan, 1960), 57, 237. Fiddlers as traditional regional food in the Paducah area are noted in Jane Stern and Michael Stern, *Roadfood* (New York: Random House/ David Obst, 1978), 147–48. Gladys and Louis DeFew's fish breading business is the subject of Caroline Rothe, "Meal Mix Is `D-Lit' to Those Who Eat It & Those Who Make It," [Benton, Ky.] *Tribune Courier, Leisure Scene Edition '78*, May 28, 1978, 32–33, 36. Two lower Ohio Valley cookbooks with recipes for local river fish are Dick and Erma Beisel, *The Old House Cook Book* (Louisville: House of Donahue, 1962); and *The McCracken County Homemakers Cookbook* (Paducah: WPAD, 1964).

Buffalo's superior nutritional value and its rejection by consumers is the subject of M.C. Kik, "The Nutritive Value of Buffalo Fish and Other Arkansas Pond-Reared Fish," in *Fish and Nutrition*, ed. Eirik Heen and Rudolf Kreuzer (London: Fishing News and U.N. Food and Agricultural Organization, 1962), 257–58. African-American preference for buffalo is noted in Marsha A. Walters, *Wholesale Demand for Buffalofish*, Industrial Research and Extension Center Publication E-24 (Little Rock: Univ. of Arkansas, Coll. of Business Administration, 1961); and L.T. Hopkinson, *Trade in Fresh and Frozen Fishery Products and Related Marketing Considerations in Louisville, Kentucky*, Economic Circular 50 (Washington, D.C.: Dept. of Commerce, Bureau of Fisheries, 1921).

The influence on midwestern fisheries by the mid- to late nineteenth-century settlement of cities by immigrants and African Americans is discussed in Harriet Bell Carlander, *History of Fish and Fishing in the Upper Mississippi River* (Davenport, Ia.: Upper Mississippi River Conservation Committee, 1954); and John Kevin Sullivan, "The Development and Status of the Upper Mississippi River Commercial Fishery" (Ph.D. diss., Univ. of Michigan, 1971). A taste for turtle and gar among African-American migrants from the Deep South to southern Illinois is noted in Ruby Berkeley Goodwin, *It's Good to be Black* (Garden City, N.Y.: Doubleday, 1953), 68.

The folklore of river folk is discussed in the works of Benjamin A. Botkin, *A Treasury of Mississippi River Folklore* (New York: Crown, 1955); Ben Lucien Burman, *Big River to Cross, Children of Noah, Look Down That Winding River*, and "Shanty Boat Coming Down"; Ernest Theodore Hiller, *Houseboat and River Bottom People*; Richard M. Dorson, *Man and Beast in American Comic*

Legend; Dick Kaukas, "What Really Lives in the Ohio? `Sure We Have Monsters Down There'"; and Warren Stanley Walker, "Dan'l Stamps: Tall Tale Hero of the River Country" (last eight cited above). River folk are described as tale-tellers in Ward Dorrance, *Where the Rivers Meet;* and Reuben Gold Thwaites, *On the Storied Ohio* (both cited above).

River folk are revealed as singers of traditional songs and performers of traditional music in Ben Lucien Burman, *Look Down That Winding River;* George Frederick Kunz, "The Freshwater Pearls and Pearl Fisheries of the United States"; Ernest Theodore Hiller, *Houseboat and River Bottoms People;* Harlan Hubbard, *Shantyboat: A River Way of Life* (all four cited above); and in Archer Butler Hulbert, *Waterways of Westward Expansion: The Ohio River and Its Tributaries,* Historic Highways of America Series, vol. 9 (Cleveland: Arthur H. Clark, 1903).

Many of the tales and songs mentioned in chapter 9 are variants of traditional material or popular material that has gone into tradition. For Harold Weaver's dog story, see Motif X1215.8(ab) from Ernest W. Baughman, *Type and Motif Index of the Folktales of England and North America,* Indiana University Folklore Series no. 20 (The Hague: Mouton, 1966). "The minnow and the moonshine" is Motif X1314*(a); "the underwater lantern" is Tale Type 1920H*, and it contains Motif X1154(c). "`X' marks the fishing spot" is Tale Type [1278A and it contains Motif J1922.1. "Snotty Nose and Shitty Britches" appears in Gershon Legman, *Rationale of the Dirty Joke: An Analysis of Sexual Humor* (New York: Grove Press, 1968), 66.

Regarding songs, "Freckle-faced Consumption Sarah Jane" is a variant of a minstrel song better known as "All-go-hungry Hash House." "The Juice of the Forbidden Fruit" is Song Number 403 in Vance Randolph, *Ozark Folksongs,* vol. 3 (Columbia: State Historical Society of Missouri, 1949). It is related to "Jesse James, I," which is Laws E1 in G. Malcolm Laws, *Native American Balladry,* rev. ed., Publications of the American Folklore Society, Bibliographical Series, vol. 1 (Philadelphia: American Folklore Society, 1964). "The Oxford Girl" is Laws P35, "The Wexford Girl." "I Was Born about Four Thousand Years Ago" is Song Number 410 in Randolph. "The State of Arkansas" is Laws H1, "An Arkansas Traveler," and Song Number 347, "State of Arkansas," in Randolph. "Travellin' Man from Tennessee" is Song Number XI:5, "The Travelling Coon," in Newman Ivey White, *American Negro Folk-Songs* (Cambridge: Harvard Univ. Press, 1928). "Blue-eyed Soldier Boy" was originally "My Sweetheart Went Down with the Maine," updated to World War I.

Hollering is discussed by Ray B. Browne in "Some Notes on the Southern `Holler,'" *Journal of American Folklore* 67 (1954): 73–77; and Peter Bartis, "A Preliminary Classification System for `Hollers' in the United States" (M.A. thesis, Univ. of North Carolina—Chapel Hill, 1974). Red "Buck" Estes's Green River holler appears on *"I'm On My Journey Home": Vocal Styles and Resources in Folk Music,* recorded by Charles Wolfe, New World Records

LP-record NW223 (New York, 1978). Estes and hollering are discussed in Charles Wolfe's notes to that recording.

The traditional stereotypes (both "in group" and "out group") of fisherfolk are the subject of Janet Gilmore, "Fishermen Stereotypes: Sources and Symbols," *Canadian Folklore* 12:2 (1990): 17–38.

Theodore Weatherford's poem "The River Rat" is in his book *Country and Sentimental Poems* (Mount Vernon, Ind.: Privately Printed, 1970).

In *Lake Erie Fishermen: Work, Tradition, and Identity.* (Urbana: Univ. of Illinois Press, 1990), Timothy C. Lloyd and Patrick B. Mullen maintain that the "game warden story" (or "authority story") and the "close call story" are common and characteristic genres among fisherfolk. They note that Lake Erie is also the scene of both complementary negative stereotypes and conflict regarding access to the fish resource between sports- and commercial fishers. These stories are also noted in Timothy S. Cochrane, "The Folklife Expressions of Three Isle Royale Fishermen: A Sense of Place Study" (M.A. thesis, Western Kentucky Univ., 1982).

The case that established the right of Illinois fishermen to fish the Ohio on a Kentucky license alone was Illinois State Supreme Court 46-632: *W.A. Cox v. Ray Cox and Albert Sailer* (1949).

The aesthetic aspect of love of place is defined by Yi-fu Tuan in *Topophilia: A Study of Environmental Perception, Attitudes and Values* (Englewood Cliffs, N.J.: Prentice-Hall, 1974); and Yi-fu Tuan, *Space and Place: The Perspective of Experience* (Minneapolis: Univ. of Minnesota Press, 1977). Its history is outlined in Paul Shepard, *Man in the Landscape: A Historic View of the Esthetics of Nature* (New York: Alfred A. Knopf, 1967). Its application to local traditional culture is discussed in Edmunds V. Bunkše, "Commoner Attitudes Towards Landscape and Nature," *Annals of the Association of American Geographers* 68 (1978): 551–66; and D.W. Meinig, "Environmental Appreciation: Localities as Humane Art," *Western Humanities Review* 25 (1970): 1–11.

The concept of culture mediating between man and nature originates in the works of Claude Lévi-Strauss, notably *The Raw and the Cooked* (New York: Harper and Row, 1969). For folklife's mediating function, see Henry Glassie, "Review Article: Structure and Function, Folklore and the Artifact," *Semiotica* 7 (1973): 313–51.

Index